FAILURE

AN INDICTMENT OF THE CHRISTIAN CHURCH

A Guide for the successful Christian

G. Vaughn Smith

Thirsty Turtle Press

All rights reserved. No part of this book may be reproduced or transmitted in any form or by any means, electronic or mechanical, including photocopying, recording or by any information storage and retrieval system, without written permission from the author, except for the inclusion of brief quotations in a review, which may be used with proper citation.

First Printing 2005
Copyright ©2005 G. Vaughn Smith

Thirsty Turtle Press
PO Box 402
Maggie Valley, NC 28751

Email: info@thirstyturtlepress.com
www.thirstyturtlepress.com

Cover Design by Amy Howell
Edited by Beverly Knight

ISBN 0-9729038-1-X
Library of Congress Control Number: 2005901724

DEDICATION

To my Lord and my God who brought me out of the depths of despair, depression, poverty, and sickness, to a life of peace and prosperity, and seemingly endless love.

STATEMENT OF PURPOSE

This book is intended as a primer and a blueprint for any person or family that is experiencing anything other than a truly blessed life. If you desire to truly serve the one true God, and you want a life full of peace, health, and happiness, then take the time to read this book and follow it.

My prayer is that your life will become as blessed as God has made my own.

BIOGRAPHY

Born in Barberton, Ohio in 1939, his family moved to the Rio Grande Valley of Texas, where he learned the work ethic of a poor farm family. Returning to Ohio where he finished High School, he worked as a merchant seaman, then joined the Army where he was stationed in Germany during the building of the Berlin Wall in 1962.

After discharge, he attended Kent State University, where he both worked full time and attended school full time, graduating in 1968.

Vaughn reached the pinnacle of his profession in 1985, as Director of Quality for a division of a major corporation but in 1990, after losing everything, he decided to find out for certain whether God really existed

Broke, depressed to the point of suicide, physically ill, and jobless with absolutely no hope of recovery, Vaughn began reading and rereading the New Testament from cover to cover to see whether he could determine what God was all about and whether He even existed.

Today, as the head of two businesses, successful, healthy, and with a peace and fulfillment which very few people achieve, he shares what he has learned and his own personal path to success with a loving, caring, and very personal God.

Contents

INTRODUCTION	IX
THE BEGINNINGS OF FAILURE	1
FINANCE AND THE MODERN CHRISTIAN	26
CALVINISM	43
WHO *REALLY* KILLED JESUS?	72
THE GREATEST OF ALL COMMANDMENTS!	80
FIXING THE CHURCH	108
FIXING THE CHURCH PART II	140
PREPARING TO WORK FOR GOD	171
WORKING FOR GOD	204
A MESSAGE FOR SINGLES	228
ARE YOU WILLING	236
SO YOU WANT TO BE A CHRISTIAN?	273

INTRODUCTION

First of all, I think that it would be appropriate for me to warn you, the reader, that the book that you have just opened is among other things "way over the top" within the context of the world of Christianity today. The purpose of this book is not to injure or turn people against the church, because the church was established and endorsed by Christ Himself when He told the Apostle Peter, "You are the rock upon which I will build my church." The purpose of this book is to facilitate a reformation within the church which hopefully will bring it to the next level of service to our God, just as happened when Martin Luther nailed his ninety-five theses to the church door.

As in Martin Luther's time, the church has reached a plateau whereby the leaders of the church are allowing God's work to stagnate through actions and policies which subvert the teachings and intentions of our Lord, because the leaders of the church have placed the politics of the day and the construction of ever larger and ever more magnificent buildings before the care of God's people.

This book began fourteen years ago when, at age fifty-one, I accepted Jesus Christ as my Lord and Savior, and I began attending a local Baptist Church. I was invited to join a Sunday school class and for the first time in my life, I began to read the Bible. Since I was going through a very rough period in my life where I had no job and no family, I was able to sit down and read the Bible every day, which is something that I learned later, very few Christians do.

After only my first year of attending an organized church, I began to feel that the same lessons and the same sermons were being taught repeatedly, resulting in what I felt was Christianity at a "kindergarten" level, where the participants never progressed beyond the very first level of pre-Christianity, resulting in what I began to call kinderChristians who had never been exposed to, and had no concept of, the application of Christianity in everyday life.

Over the years, I changed churches, and even denominations frequently, in a search for the next higher level of worship and service to a God who, through my repeated reading of the Bible from cover-to-cover, had become very familiar to me, and who had begun to affect my life in a very real and very meaningful way.

As I made the understanding and the knowledge of God my first priority, God began to change my life from one of sickness, poverty and desperation to a life that seemed to be blessed beyond imagination. As I looked back to Christians who had seemingly put God into their lives years before me, I saw lives that were not as blessed as my own, and I had those same Christians tell me that they had prayed continuously for relief of sickness and problems within their own lives with no result. I began to wonder why God had chosen me to be blessed when others who also professed the knowledge of God seemed to be mired in failure.

Over the period of the next ten years, God continually brought lessons into my life that illustrated the failure of Christian churches of every denomination to understand the purpose and the teaching of the very one whom they acknowledged as their leader and founder. As I searched for a church home, I met pastors who had never read and didn't understand the Bible and who could only spout the dogma of the particular denomination for which they had studied. I found churches whose only reason for existence seemed to be to build ever larger buildings (clubhouses for the faithful) while thousands of local people lived below the poverty line.

As I finished reading the Bible from cover-to-cover for the fifth time, God began to prick me, even as He had pricked Saul on the road to Damascus, and I knew that I was being ordered to serve Him through the writing of this book in the hope of achieving a new Reformation similar to the work of Martin Luther almost five hundred years ago.

While the primary thrust of this work would seem to be negative and oriented toward criticism of the church itself as an organization, in reality the purpose of this work is to provide a simple and easily implementable program whereby every person who recognizes the existence of God can achieve a meaningful and highly successful relationship with that same loving God, thereby providing the workers to bring others to the knowledge and love of God instead of turning them away.

G. Vaughn Smith

THERE IS ONLY ONE WAY TO **PLEASE** GOD

and

THERE IS ONLY ONE WAY TO **SERVE** GOD

1
THE BEGINNINGS OF FAILURE

THE CHRISTIAN CHURCH HAS FAILED. It failed in the Dark Ages during the first Crusades when Christians who happened to live in Jerusalem were slaughtered along with the thousands of Moslems who were defending their homes and families. And for what, a chunk of real estate? Which is more important, a few relics and some real estate, or the loss *forever* of the chance to win the entire nation of Islam to the love of Jesus Christ?

As if it were not enough to slaughter innocent non-Christians who were just trying to live out their lives, even Christians were murdered in a rampage that filled the very streets with blood. The Christian church continued its policy of murder and mayhem on its own people through what is known as the Inquisition and even into what was supposedly the Renaissance during the time of Martin Luther and John Calvin. Right here in the United States, the pilgrims, a supposedly deeply religious people, murdered anyone even suspected of being a witch.

If you are thinking all that was in the distant past and we are much more civilized now, remember the draggings, drownings and lynchings that took place in the 1960s during the Civil Rights struggle. Remember also that not one white Southern Baptist Church stood up for equality with their black brothers. As a point of fact, most, if not all, Southern churches endorsed slavery, and the Southern Baptist Church was formed for the sole reason of enforcing and allowing slave ownership. As I write this in the new millennium, the Catholic Church is suffering through the stigma of child molestation by its own leaders, and a man in Los Angeles, just because he has a different opinion on whether or not God exists, has received over one hundred death threats and over one thousand obscene and hate-filled phone calls from *CHRISTIANS*.

It is totally beyond my comprehension why the very people who call themselves "Christians" are usually the ones at the forefront of activities that can only be described as hateful. When "Christians" do not agree with the beliefs or practices of someone else, they (no thankfully not all of them) feel that it is their God-given right to take whatever action(s) necessary to bring about change. The fact is that those self-justified actions, which sometimes include murder and bombing, subvert the Bible and even the very life of Jesus Christ. Keep in mind the fact that Eric Rudolph, the man convicted of the Atlanta Olympic bombing and the bombing of an abortion clinic in Birmingham, Alabama, was raised a "Christian," and the men and women responsible for the torture and murder of 14-year-old Emmit Till, who was killed for allegedly whistling at a white woman, called themselves "Christian."

It is time for Christians to start acting like Christians, and that is the point of this book. My question to you is this: "Why have Christians, in the name of Jesus Christ, performed these terrible acts of violence in the past, and why have they allowed them to continue today.

If you don't believe that they are happening today, then I suggest that you go to Northern Ireland, one of the Croatian republics, Israel or right here in the United States where bigotry is alive and well and includes the bombing of abortion clinics and the murder of doctors *in God's name*. The answer is this: the Christian church and its leaders, from the Pope down to the pastor of the smallest church, have failed their flock because they are more interested in the happenings of this world than they are in God and His Word.

A recent news story identified the Pope as being against the entry of Poland into the European Union. Personally, I am of the opinion that God would be better served if the Pope were to let God run the world, and he (the Pope) were to take care of the children that are being raped by the priests of the Catholic Church. What even I failed to realize is the fact that child sexual abuse has been practiced within the Catholic Church for the last 400 years. Karen Liebreich, in her brilliantly researched book, *Fallen Order*, brings to light a scandal of child abuse from the time of Galileo and Caravaggio that implicates no less than Pope Innocent X, who knowingly appointed a prolific child abuser to a position of authority within the system of Catholic schools of the time.

Ms. Liebreich's words are so poignant when she states, "The contemporary Catholic Church's practice of moving a suspected pedophile away from the original scene of the crime for fear of the ensuing scandal and the backlash clearly has long antecedents."

Before you form the opinion that I am bashing the Catholic church (only), let me tell you that there have been several convictions for child abuse that have been prosecuted this year, right here in what is known as the buckle of the Bible Belt. The Baptist and other Protestant churches are no less guilty. They campaign against State Lotteries and for State laws, appoint practicing homosexuals to positions of authority within the church hierarchy and preach "separation" from anyone who believes even slightly differently than they. Churches today have forgotten their command to reach all people and have become nothing more than exclusive clubs for "believers" engaged in the building of ever larger "clubhouses" and continuing the fight to control the lives of everyone else.

Everyone who purports to believe in God seems to forget that God (remember Him – the One who originally created all of this) really IS alive and well and, I promise you, is still running the world. Do our Church leaders really think that God needs their help, whether in appointing a president or making laws?

I recognize the fact that I have made a very strong and very controversial statement when I say that the church has failed in its mission. It would be totally correct for you to say to me at this point, "Whoa there, big boy. You are making a way-out radical statement, and before you proceed any further, I want to see some proof." O.K., you got it. My statement was that the church has failed in its mission, so let's investigate and try to determine just what the church's mission is supposed to be.

Jesus Christ spent 33 years here on this earth, and while He was with us He accomplished a lot. As a matter of fact, Jesus did things that no man has ever duplicated. He gave sight to a man who had been blind from birth. He raised a man from the dead who had been in the grave for four days. He healed the servant of a Roman soldier without even seeing or going near the man. Jesus did all of these things and more, but in one of His last teachings, He gave His disciples, and therefore us, one job. Only one job. Of course, you know what job I am talking about; we call it the "Great Commission." And that one job is, in a nutshell, the mission of the church. That mission is the same now as it was two thousand years ago, to reach and teach the love of Jesus Christ to all nations. Now that we have established the mission of the Christian Church, let's investigate and see whether that mission is being accomplished, and in order to do that, I want to ask you a question. That question is this: What is the fastest growing religion in the world today? Do you know the answer? Just in case you don't, the fastest growing religion in the world today is – ISLAM!

There is your proof, and you may not like it, but that is the fact – the Christian Church has failed to follow Christ's own orders, but that's not all. I have another question for you. What is the normal reaction that you get when you try to witness to people who either do not believe in God or do not know Jesus Christ as their personal Savior? Yes, I'm talking to you. When was the last time that you witnessed to someone? If you are like most Christians, you gave that up long ago. And why? Because the reaction of the person to whom you were witnessing ranged from resentment to disbelief to downright anger. Why? Here is the key to my second reason why I contend that the church has failed. The church does not teach Christians *how to be Christians*. How can we "witness" when we don't know how to be Christians ourselves. I have a friend who, in all seriousness, thinks that no one can be a true Christian until he votes the straight Republican ticket. I guess he thinks Jesus was a Republican.

The modern Christian Church today has just one goal— getting people to accept Jesus Christ as their Savior—BUT THEN THEY STOP RIGHT THERE! If you join the Baptist Church, they send you off to some Sunday school, where 95% of the time the teachers have never even read the Bible. Yet that person (the new member) is expected to learn to become a Christian by listening to teachers who don't know the Bible themselves. Listen to me closely: accepting Jesus does not make anyone a Christian. Accepting Jesus on face value is just the first step, and let me emphasize that it is just a "baby" step. From that point, the real work begins, and I will address this process in more detail later, but I want to open another area in which the Church has failed.

I want to talk about the Bible, God's Word, and I am going to ask you, the reader, a question that I am going to ask over and over again in this book. Have you read God's Word, the Bible? No, I'm not talking about reading through a few verses once a month or maybe even every night. I am asking you whether you have sat down and read the Bible from cover to cover. If you haven't, you aren't alone. In a small, very informal and very unscientific survey of the members of what used to be my church, I found that less than 5% of practicing Christians had read the Bible from cover to cover. If we extrapolate this survey of active Christians to the entire universe of people who would describe themselves as "Christian," I estimate that less than one one-hundredth of one percent of all the Christians in the world have read the entire Bible, and therein lies the reason that

Christianity has failed. The main premise of Martin Luther, almost five hundred years ago, was the fact that the church of the time was not following the Gospel and that premise continues today, and is the reason for this book.

Let me repeat myself. The Christian church has failed because its members and, yes, even its leaders, have not read the Bible. In what used to be my church, we had four pastors, each in different areas, and not one of them had read the Bible from cover to cover. How can we, as Christians, expect to succeed in God's work if we don't even care enough to read the instruction book? I am going to make a statement here that will probably make a lot of people angry. Anyone who calls themselves a Christian but has not read the Bible *is just pretending*. Notice that I didn't say that if you don't attend church you are just pretending. I said that if you have not read the Bible you are just pretending. Why?

A phone conversation that I had just this morning with a good friend comes to mind as a means to describe what the Bible is to a Christian. We were discussing the Bible and the fact that so many Christians just don't even bother to read it, and my friend, Charles, said, "The Bible is life's GPS." I said, "What?" (Sometimes, I'm about twenty cards short of a full deck). "You know, GPS. The Bible is the global positioning system for our lives." "Wow," I said, "I never thought of it that way, but you are so right. The Bible guides us to the correct path and the correct destination every time, if we will just let it."

Let me go back in my own life and explain. For the first 51 years of my life, I have to admit that I didn't know whether God really existed or not, and I was raised in the church. I was a choir boy until my voice changed, and I can still recite the service almost word for word, but I just wasn't sure that God existed, and if He did, did He even know or care about me? Sound familiar to you? I can still remember that I justified the fact that God seemed to totally ignore my existence because He was just too busy running the entire universe. I have since learned that nothing could be further from the truth, but I can still remember that my adolescent view of God was of Him sitting in front of some very sophisticated control panel (picture Captain Kirk) keeping the planets in their orbit.

In the aftermath of 911, literally billions of people are asking those same questions? Does God exist? If He exists, how can He let something like 911, sickness, the death of a loved one or _____ (fill in your own problem) happen? And do you know what? The church isn't answering the question, because the church leaders don't know the answers, since they haven't read the Bible either.

When was the last time that your church initiated a formal program wherein the objective was to get every member to read the New Testament? Never? Again, you are not alone and I am going to tell you why. It is entirely a matter of control. One of the most often-quoted verses of the Bible states that the truth shall set you free, and I think that is one of the greatest fears of our clergy, that their congregation will, in fact, read, at least the New Testament, and begin to confront some of the distorted views that are being put forth from pulpits today.

The question that most often occurs to me regarding our clergy is this: How can a person who professes to have been called into God's service, ignore the only book that contains specific directions for becoming and being a Christian? I don't profess to know the answer, but most of the blame has to lie squarely on the heads of those who profess to have been "called" into the ministry by God himself. It seems rather strange to me that someone would be "called" to the ministry without being "called" to read God's instruction book in its entirety.

I have a solution to the problem though; every church selection committee should begin "uncalling" any pastors who cannot prove that they have read the Bible from cover to cover. Of course, this brings up another problem. How can the selection committee judge correctly, since none of them have read the

Bible either. Do you see my point? The modern Christian Church has become the parable of the blind leading the blind, and as Christ pointed out, they have both fallen into a hole.

The blame for the fact that most of our Christian leaders have not read the Bible must also rest squarely on our seminaries and divinity schools. They are so hungry for students (read: money) that they will accept anyone who can pay the tuition, and our churches are paying the price right now as they hire pastors who don't even know who the Holy Spirit is, and many of our churches have become havens for homosexuals and sexual perverts. Not one pastor that I have talked with knows how many commandments have been given to us by God. By the way, I am willing to bet that if you are a normal practicing Christian, you don't know how many commandments there are either. What do you say? Wanna bet?

Let me clarify just what I am talking about when I use the word "commandment." I am asking how many formal, specific instructions that have been called "commandments" have been given by a member of what we call the Trinity. I will give you a hint. In the Old Testament, God gave Moses Ten Commandments written on stone tablets. Now, my question to you is this: Did Jesus Christ, whom most of us recognize as the Son of God, and therefore God, also give us any commandments? The answer is a resounding YES, but the church fails to recognize anything more than the original ten. In the Gospel of John, Jesus Himself gave us a new commandment to follow.

Let me create a worldly parable for you, because, if you remember, Jesus was fond of doing that, although I certainly am not placing myself in His category. Let's suppose that your boss has invited his (or her) entire staff for dinner and you are included. As all of you arrive at the appointed time, he begins acting very strangely, and as you enter the dining room, he insists that you sit down so that he can remove your shoes and wash your feet. You think that this is kind of weird and you protest but he insists, and you just go along, because, after all, he is the boss.

During the dinner, your boss now stands, and after getting everyone's attention he makes the following statement: "I am now giving all of you a new and very specific order." Remember now. This is your boss talking and he seems to be serious, so you might want to pay attention (if you want to keep your job). Even more strange, after he tells you the new "order," your boss does something that he has never done before. He tells you what turns out to be the very important reason why he has given that specific order.

Wow, that was a strange dinner that you attended last night. Your boss gave everyone new and specific marching orders, which you don't really like or even agree with, yet he seemed really serious, especially with all the other information that he shared. Perhaps the most confounding statement that he made last night was the one where he said that if you followed and obeyed his new order, you would forever be identified as one of the people that worked for him. Is that strange or what?

So what do you do? You (read we, meaning all of us Christians) have been given an order and the reason for that order. Do you ignore your boss? That is exactly what the leaders of the church have done. They have ignored the most specific order (commandment) given by the "boss" and founder of the church, Jesus Christ, because they didn't understand it and it flew in the face of their own self interests. I am going to discuss this "commandment" in detail in a later chapter, but for now I want the reader to be aware of the fact that during His three years of ministry, Jesus referred to only one specific sentence as a commandment, and the church has ignored that order for two thousand years.

If you will remember earlier, I cited the fact that we Christians have been given only one job, that which we call the Great Commission, in which Jesus told us to go out and teach the world. What the church and we Christians fail to recognize is that in giving us what I define as the Eleventh Commandment, Jesus told us exactly how to accomplish that mission. Not one of us can bring someone into the knowledge and love of God with only our mouths, and Jesus recognized this. We can open a person's heart only through our own love and servanthood as we emulate within our own lives the life and actions of the one that we call our Savior. Is it any wonder that our verbal witness is ignored?

FAILURE!

I want to add one note here; for hundreds of years Bible translators and Bible editions have recognized Jesus' specific word, "commandment," to describe the instruction that He was giving. Every edition of the Bible from the original *King James*, to the *New King James*, to the *New American Standard Bible (NASB)* and others, have translated the word "commandment" in the sentence: "A new *commandment* I give to you...." I find it strange that only the newest translation, known as the *New International Version* changes the word "commandment" to the word "command." Please understand that I am not normally a conspiracy theorist; however, I see a combined attempt at duplicity, since the church refuses to recognize Christ's specific words as a commandment, and now the newest Bible translation attempts to follow that same distorted path. Why will the church not recognize, not only Christ's words, but His intent to initiate a new commandment? I confess that I do not have the answer, but I pray that every Christian reading this book will bring this question before their church leaders.

Tell me fellow Christian, when was the last time that you "hated," or even used the word "hate," to describe your feelings for someone or something. I will tell you this; anyone who even uses the word "hate" cannot be a disciple of Christ. Jesus Christ never hated anyone and neither should we. A man that I work with frequently purports to be a Christian and is a member of one of our Baptist "mega" churches, but to talk with him one would never guess it, because hate and vilification continually spew from his mouth to the point that the only subjects that he can find to talk about are the things that he dislikes. We may not like or we may disagree with actions that people or organizations do, but we are not to "hate" anyone or anything, and it is time that the church started teaching this concept, because we (all of us) are compromising and already have compromised our witness.

Speaking of witness and witnessing, why does the church feel that anyone who has become a Christian within the last ten minutes is now qualified to "go forth and bear fruit" through witnessing to the "lost." Again, this is a major failure of the organized church. As an example, let's say that John Doe, who was a thief, tax cheater, wife beater and drunk, suddenly becomes "reborn" and immediately goes out into the same community that knew him before and tries to witness for Christ. How effective do you think that his testimony will be? On a scale of one to ten, his witness will rate a zero. As a matter of fact, his witness will create a negative image for the church. Has John really changed his ways? That is not for you and me to judge. The point that I am trying to make is this; the best witness that John Doe can have is his new lifestyle while he LEARNS what is expected of a Christian and turns his life around.

Remember Paul, formerly named Saul when he eagerly killed Christians? Paul was an intelligent and very educated man, yet even he had to spend three years of study in the desert before he even attempted to witness. What makes us feel that we can effectively witness before we have even read the Bible, or begun to change our lives? So, to solve this problem, some churches offer a "canned" witness program, in which everyone memorizes a stock reply to any question that might be asked.

This is pure baloney. Again the church is looking for the easy way out, and, in effect, is turning us all into used car salesmen with a pat but phony answer for everything. When was the last time that you talked to someone who had all the answers? That's right; you became immediately suspicious of that person, and especially of what they were espousing. The bottom line is this. You, me or anyone else can only witness through our lifestyle. Our lives, and the believability of Jesus Christ, can only be reflected through how we live. Our personal ethics, our language, our business practices, our interaction with others, our courtesy, our driving habits, our anger, our negativity, our relationship with our family, our happiness, our lies, _____ (add your own here); THESE ARE OUR WITNESS. These are what people see, and these are what people believe about you. I should add, possibly the most important aspect of anyone's own personal development, is to read the Bible. It is without a doubt the most interesting book ever written. Start with the New Testament, and as you do, God will begin to talk to you on a one-to-one basis.

There is a Christian song entitled *"YOU'RE THE ONLY JESUS THAT SOME WILL EVER SEE."* Think about that for a second, because it is so important that it is the total key to the Great Commission. Any person who wants to witness cannot be unloving, angry, greedy, self-centered, uncaring, sinful, negative, selfish or discourteous, because the person to whom you are witnessing can only see the actions and the lifestyle of the person in front of them. People cannot see Jesus; they can only see you. If the association with Jesus Christ has not changed you, how can it change them, or they may be saying to themselves, "I sure don't want to become like them!"

I've got to tell a story on myself, because I'm not perfect either but I am trying. My neighbor and I went for lunch at a typical fast-food restaurant several months ago. It was a hot day, I had been working outside and I got a burger and water. After we ate and started to leave, I went to fill up my water, and I put a little lemonade on top of the water. When I climbed into my truck and set my glass in the cup holder, my neighbor looked into the cup and said, "You stole some lemonade." Wow, I wanted to crawl into a hole. I was so embarrassed that I couldn't even reply, because I knew that he was right, and even if I had taken only one drop of lemonade, IT WAS STEALING. Listen closely. Once you compromise your witness, trust can never be regained, and you had better believe that. What I did is this; I didn't tell anyone about it but I went back to that store and bought lemonade and got water. God has forgiven me because I made retribution, but my neighbor will never forget.

Let me return to my main thesis concerning the failure of the church. As I have tried to point out, this "failure" can be traced to what I consider to be lazy interpretations of Scripture. Almost everyone is familiar with what are commonly known as the "Beatitudes," given at the Sermon on the Mount and found in the Gospel of Matthew. It is at the end of this "sermon" that Jesus talks about the man who built his house upon a rock, versus the foolish man who built his house upon sand. From these verses, we sing about Jesus being the solid rock upon which we stand, and we think about Jesus himself being our "rock" and our foundation. I do not have a problem with thinking of Jesus Christ as the "rock" of my faith in a figurative sense or even in a very real sense.

The problem is that Jesus did not want to be known as our "rock." He wanted *HIS WORDS* to become our rock. Jesus stated very specifically that *"... everyone who hears these words of mine, and acts upon them may be compared to a wise man, who built his house upon the rock."* Did you get it? Jesus did not want to be known as the rock, He wanted His words to be our rock; the rock of our faith. How important are the words in this sermon? In my opinion, the 110 verses which comprise the Sermon on the Mount could be our entire Bible. These 110 verses give total and complete instructions for living the Christian life; yet except for infrequent excerpts found in modern sermons, this most important discourse is almost totally ignored by pastors today. I have to ask why? Is the reason that Jesus' guidance is difficult to follow? The answer is no, but most Christians don't want to give up their ways of the world, and most Christians don't want to give up control *of anything,* much less their own lives.

Christ came to serve, and not just by giving His life, but as an example to us. He served everyone who asked and even those who could not ask. I want to make a specific point here to every Christian reading this. As you read the New Testament, note who the people were whom Christ served. Ninety-nine percent of the people that Jesus helped in some way were sinners and "bad" people as defined by the Church. I can think of only two instances where Jesus helped his friends, or "so-called" good people. The first was the mother of one of the disciples, and the second was Lazarus whom He raised from the dead. Shouldn't we Christians, who are supposedly following Christ's example, also be helping sinners, not just our fellow Christians? After all, we know and trust that God will take care of us, because we are His people. Remember what Christ said: I did not lose one of my sheep. Are you willing to be one of Jesus' lambs? It may be work that you are not willing to do, but I promise you that the rewards are great.

I recognize the fact that it is not easy to befriend someone who does not live a lifestyle of which you wholly approve; however, remember back to the days before you began to put God in charge of your life. Were you then living a lifestyle of which you would approve today? Of course not, and I didn't either. You know, I don't envy those people who came to Christ as children. I did not put God into my life until I was 51 years old, and I believe that fact made it so much easier for me to take God seriously, simply because I had a prior history of doing things in my own way – and falling on my face. I will get to my own story later, but I had failed at everything, and those prior failures made it so much easier to recognize what was happening when God began to interact in my life.

Allow me to identify one of the greatest farces in the Christian church today. The church calls it "outreach," but, in fact, it should be called "inreach." When a Christian or a Christian family moves to a new city, they begin visiting the local churches in an attempt to find one that they like. Whenever anyone visits a Christian Church, they are encouraged to fill out a "visitors" form which is then put into the collection plate. This form lands in the inbasket of the "outreach" committee, who then calls and/or visits the family that filled out the form in an attempt to get them to join the church. Do you see why I call it "inreach"? All these efforts are being made toward people who are already Christian, or who have made the effort to come to the church. My question is this, where is the reaching OUT? Outside the church that is?

Oh, yes, I have to admit, albeit reluctantly, that most churches do practice a form of "outreach," but I would call it "wayoutreach," and again it is a farce and totally impractical. It works like this. A youth group, or a group of strong young people, hops into the church van and travels 500 miles from their hometown to the hills of wherever and builds houses or makes repairs, or some other constructive endeavor for a weekend, or a week, or maybe longer. Sound like a great idea? Sure! But let's just think about it for a minute. I will be the first to admit that more efforts just like this are sorely needed, and this is what Christianity is all about, helping our fellow man. Here is the problem. Efforts like this become just a shot in the dark. The group pulls up, builds like crazy and then disappears forever. No personal *lasting* relationships have been given a chance. There is no opportunity for continuing personal help and interaction, because everyone is again 500 miles away.

WHY DON'T THE CHURCHES OF ANYTOWN, USA, HELP THE PEOPLE OF ANYTOWN, USA? My former church is in Greenville, South Carolina. Last year the youth of that church traveled to Kentucky and to Europe on so-called "mission" trips. They did not even once travel to the poor section of their own city to help their own neighbors. Why? I think that I know the two answers, and you are not going to like either one of them. First, traveling is one big vacation. Work is only purported to be the reason for the trip; the real reason is a fun vacation. The second reason is more serious and more telling about the superficiality of modern Christianity. If we helped someone right here in our own city, it might lead to a continuing relationship of personal growth and challenge, because we wouldn't be insulated by that 500 miles of distance. No right minded pastor could allow that. No self serving Christian Deacon could allow the members of his church to become involved with saving "local" souls. MY GOD, they might want to join our church. I grow faint at the thought.

If you remember, I told about my church's youth group traveling to Kentucky to build homes for the poor last year. That same summer, I was staying at a motel in Alabama, while on an engineering assignment, and I met another group of youth workers that had come to Alabama to repair homes for the poor. Can you guess where they were from? That's right; they were from Kentucky. No, I didn't make any comments, because I didn't want to burst their bubble, but as I look back now as I am writing this book, I can see how God works in my life. He brings all of these strange happenings right before my eyes and allows me to think and ponder upon them until He is ready for me to use them for His work. I promise you that if you wait and watch and prepare yourself, God will do the same with you – no matter who you are.

I want to ask (just one more time) any pastor or youth pastor reading this, "Why isn't your church helping the people of your town?" Do you really think that there is no one who needs help in your town or are you afraid of initiating lasting relationships among God's people? Oh, yeah, you want to "witness," but the type of witness that you are performing would be just as effective if you stood on the back of a pickup truck with a bullhorn while driving down the Interstate.

Search beneath the façade of 98% of practicing Christians and you will find a person who, deep down, does not like people. Scratch that pious surface by getting to know a practicing Christian and you will see inside a person who is no more than a gunslinger carving notches on his Bible. The church of today is in a race to collect the most names for their rolls. By the way, once a name is "collected," not even God Himself could remove it from the roll. How do I know? I have been given names of people to call who joined another church two years ago, and my own name is still carried on the rolls of churches that I haven't attended in years.

The primary interest of most denominations today is not bringing the unsaved to Christ; their primary interest is in bringing new members to their own exclusive club, whereby only they can recognize the "true" way. This was brought home to me in a very real way one afternoon when I was pumping gas into my beat-up old pickup truck. A car pulled up in the next lane, a man got out, walked over and asked me whether I knew God. Even when I replied in my most sincere voice that God was the center of my life and that Jesus Christ was my Savior, the man proceeded to tell me that my interpretation of the Bible was incorrect and implied that I should join their church. You see, he wasn't interested in my salvation; he was interested in adding me as a notch on his gun and a member of his congregation. Is it any wonder that people become immediately suspicious the moment that God is brought up in a conversation? Do Christians always have to proselytize? Why can't they just talk about the wondrous changes that have taken place in their lives since they have dedicated themselves to God? Believe me, if I see great things happening in someone else's life, I'm going to want some of that action.

Why is it that a lot of Christians just don't have anything good to relate about what God has done in their life? Very simple. It's because God isn't working in their lives. Why? Here is the answer, they aren't working in God's life. Am I playing word games with you? No, I just want to uncover another area in which the church has failed to teach its members. Most Christians today are what I call "welfare Christians." That is, they don't want to *work* at being a Christian. They just want to have everything handed to them. This was brought home to me about five years ago, when one Sunday morning while on my way to Church, I stopped to get gas. I filled my tank and walked into the convenience store to pay, and as I reached for my wallet, I asked the clerk, "Is God blessing you today?" Her look spoke volumes, and even though she didn't give many details, it was obvious that in her mind, God was not helping her at all. After listening to her story, I asked her a bottom line question that God gave me right out of the blue. I asked her, "What have *you* done for God lately?"

Her eyes got wide and she looked like she had received a life-changing revelation (because she had). You see, God had just given me, and I had passed on to her, the true secret of enjoying God's favor. It's not about prayer. I've had Christians who have been in distress tell me that they have prayed continually, and nothing had changed. I just wish that I had known then what I am going to tell you in this book. As I said, the church has again failed to teach the Bible, and what they have failed to teach is that while God has made us many promises, God's promises are conditional. While there are a few of God's promises that aren't conditional, almost every one that I have noted has a condition attached. The Bible verse that I have taken as my personal verse is John 14:7, and it is also a conditional promise. Take a moment to look it up, and you will see what I mean. Even the promise that God made to the Israelites as they entered the Promised Land after wandering 40 years in the desert was conditional, and that is the reason that the Jews lost Israel.

God promised the Israelites that wonderful land and His continuing protection if and only if they made Him their God. Think about this for a moment. Why are the Jews in Israel today having so much trouble and having to continually defend their territory? The answer is this: first they have repeatedly abandoned God as their leader and begun to depend upon their politicians, and second the Jews reserve the act of revenge for themselves, which leads to a continuance of revenge killings. Is this the same mistake that America is making today? As I write these words, a national election is only two weeks away, and I ask you, "Who is your God? Is he some politician on whom you are depending to change the world, or are you ignoring politics and depending upon the one true God, who I promise you will appoint the politician that He wants."

The United States of America is over two hundred years old and we have had politicians in charge of this country for every one of those two hundred years. Since life here doesn't seem to be getting any better, isn't it time that we asked ourselves the question, "Are our politicians really the answer, or do we trust the wrong entity to run our lives and our country." For the life of me, I just cannot understand how someone can say that he has dedicated his life to serving God and then worry or even concern himself with politics. But then again, this paradigm is the result of another failure of the church, because the church endorses political activism in the false hope that the world can be made into a better place, or that suddenly everyone will accept Jesus.

Let me make it abundantly clear; the world cannot be made into a better place. I will say it again; nothing that we can do will make the world better. Does this mean that everything is hopeless? Shall we dig a hole and bury our heads in the sand? Shall we give up? If you think that I am giving you all bad news, then pay attention, because the good news is coming; but first I want to illuminate the basic reasons why the church has failed.

The Church has been overthrown! A revolution took place over a thousand years ago in the Catholic Church. That revolution is taking place right now in the Protestant Church, *and nobody is paying attention.* Nobody is noticing, and the reason is that this "revolution" took place quietly and surreptitiously, *and in the name of God.* The other reason for the fact that this revolution goes totally unnoticed is that the people perpetrating the revolution are the very people who are the leaders of the church. The very people who are supposed to be acting within God's Will, in fact, are pursuing the goals of their own will. What goals am I talking about? For starters, how about those very personal goals of paying less or no taxes? Or what about those goals of forcing the government to pay for us to send our children to a private school so the little dears won't have to mix with _____ (fill in your own ethnic hatred here). What about the goal of eliminating the welfare system? Now that is real progress in the name of Christ. We can just let those "scum" starve. The world will be so much better off, and the only ones left will be us "Christians."

    Just when did the Christian Church become so confused that they forgot the word "give" and instead substituted the word "take" (for themselves) into the theology of Jesus Christ? Jesus Christ never took anything. He gave, and then He gave some more. Jesus gave so much of Himself that from time to time He had to be alone to recoup. We modern Christians give a lot also. We give all of our time and money to make sure the "right" politician is elected so that we won't have to pay taxes. Take a note here, friend. The same people who worry about paying taxes are the people who refuse to give their tithe as God required. I'm going to talk about tithing later on and you will be surprised by my own experiences with money as it relates to a meaningful relationship with God.

    While I am on the subject of money, what do you think that the Christian church of today is doing with its money? Good question and here is the answer: the Christian church is spending ten times more money building ever larger clubhouses than on missionary work. My own church spent $538,471.03 on paying down the mortgage for their new addition, while they only gave $25,405 to the Annie Armstrong and Lottie Moon missionary funds in the year 2001. In my opinion, this is a gross misappropriation of funds given to the church in the name of God. Where does it say in the Bible that God's people are to build ever larger monuments to their own greed? Modern Christianity is personified by a selfishness that is almost surreal, a selfishness that is so pervasive that it cannot be recognized by even its own practitioners.

I attended a meeting in one of our local mega-churches several months ago, and the appointments of the meeting room rivaled the conference rooms of some of the finest Las Vegas hotels. I have to admit that I truly felt ashamed as I sat in that elegant room and thought of the thousands of homeless people who were sleeping under bridges that very night. Is this what Christianity has degenerated to, the use of money given in God's name to build ever finer and ever larger churches and private schools for our own use, while people are homeless, while children are abused, while workers are laid off, while the banks repossess property that will later be sold at a profit?

In view of the fact that Christian churches today have become "for-profit" entities, i.e. money taken in is used for "their" own growth, I am of the opinion that Congress should change the law to remove non-profit or charitable status from any organization that does not give away to charity, at least sixty percent of their gross income.

I alluded earlier to what I call "Welfare Christians," i.e. those church members who take all they can get but give back very little. Oh, yeah, I have heard all of your excuses, from your lack of time to the price of gasoline, and none of them, no not one, is valid. Tell me, have you ever been to a Christian Church that had more than enough volunteers to work with children? I haven't. Well, I am ashamed to admit that I was once like that myself, until God called me to teach a class of seventh and eight graders. Have you ever heard someone talking about a "call"? I have to confess that I doubted that a "call" could even exist. I just figured that everyone was using that expression to identify the fact that they had decided (on their own) to go into the ministry or some other area of service; but I had a "call" from God Himself one Sunday morning and it was the most awesome experience of my entire life.

Let me tell you the story by starting with a conversation that I had several weeks earlier. The church I attended at that time was, like all churches, needing volunteers to teach youth. I remember confiding to a friend, "I've raised my children, and I'm not, under any circumstances, going to work with kids again." (One thing that we had better understand is that it is very dangerous to tell God that you are refusing to do something).

At that time I had been leading an adult Sunday school, and as I was driving to church one Sunday morning several weeks after making that rash statement, a song came on the Christian radio station. I listened to it, and the words just seemed to be directed right at me. I had heard that particular song dozens of times before, but that morning God was using the song to call me to His service. As I listened to the radio, tears began flowing for absolutely no reason, and I knew immediately that something special was taking place.

As I continued to drive, I began crying so hard that I could not even see, and I immediately asked God what He was trying to tell me. The message came through loud and clear that I was to teach kids. Did I want to? No! Could I refuse? Yes! One of the great things about God is that He gives us the right to make all decisions, but what a loss it is (to us) when we resist His will. Through my tears, I continued on to church, walked into my class and told them that I had been called elsewhere and this would be my last Sunday with them. Monday morning, I walked unannounced into the office of the youth pastor and told him that I had been called and did he need me anywhere? His answer floored me, although it shouldn't have. He said, "Vaughn, I have been praying for someone to help out. You will be teaching the Young Pioneers, and you start Wednesday evening. The most awesome part of the story is this; teaching those kids was one of the most rewarding times of my life and I wouldn't have missed it for the world. If you are one of the typical "welfare" Christians, think what you may be missing.

If you think that the church has not failed, and therefore that my premise is incorrect, then why are Christians and the church pictured as idiots or worse in even television situation comedies such as *Everybody Loves Raymond*. Perhaps you would want to ask why even Oprah Winfrey features the three daughters of a church pastor who repeatedly raped them. The next time that you stay at a large hotel that caters to church pastor's conferences, ask the manager if there is a particular time during which they experience a larger than normal demand for "adult" movies. You will (won't) be surprised.

In this opening chapter, I have talked about the failure of the church. I have talked about the failure of the leaders of the church, but now the time has come when I want to identify the *primary* cause for the church's failure, the people who sit so comfortably and complacently in the pews each Sunday morning. The nursery rhyme taught to me by my mother comes to mind:

Here is the church,
Here is the steeple,
Open the door,
And look at the people.

A church IS people! A church isn't a building. If a church has failed, it is because the people that make up that church have failed to own up to their responsibility. Do you remember that I stated that approximately 95% of Christians have never read or taken the time to read the Bible? That is the primary reason that the Christian church has failed in modern times. The Christians of the Middle Ages had an excuse; they didn't have a Bible because the printing press didn't yet exist.

Today, the modern Christian has no excuse except laziness when church leaders misinterpret God's word for their own self interest or for some other worldly agenda. Remember Jim Jones who advocated the suicide of hundreds of adults and their children? That is only one example of the members of an organization such as a church following a "personality" rather than the authentic leader of the Christian church, Jesus Christ.

If I may use the Baptist Church as an example, each church is controlled by the elected deacons of that church. This group of deacons has the power to hire and to fire and to reprimand any person working for the church, including the pastor. I have personally witnessed at least one example of the misuse of power of a group of deacons who did not agree with a pastor's sermon. I do not want to go into the subject matter of the sermon for now because that will be covered in a later chapter, but when this group of deacons disagreed with a particular sermon, the pastor was reprimanded, and even the audio tape of the service was destroyed. I do not understand how a group of men who probably have not even read the Bible presume to dictate what God's word means to their own pastor.

This is but one example of a group of people gaining control of an organization in order to further their own agenda, but the real fault lies with the ordinary people who allow it to happen. In the instance that I just described, the blame must also rest at the foot of one other person – the pastor. He did not have the moral fortitude or the strength of belief in God's Word to fight for what he knew to be right. That pastor should have taken the time to teach and convince those deacons or given them his resignation on the spot. Was he afraid that God could not find him another church? Personally, because this man is the pastor of the area's largest mega-church, I think that he sold out to his own bank account. What he doesn't realize is that he will have to pay a heavy price when he faces God at the final judgment.

In this one small example can be found three specific examples of failure at every level of the church. The first failure was allowed by the ordinary members of the church when they allowed deacons to be elected who had never even read the Bible and who were more interested in the world than in the teachings of God. To state it more simply, most people running for the office of deacon have an agenda, and it is not the agenda of God.

The second failure was perpetrated by the deacons themselves when they allowed what is nothing more than an untrue belief to challenge what the Bible clearly states, in the words of Jesus Himself. The third failure, as I stated earlier, belonged to the pastor, when he allowed the challenge to his sermon to go unanswered. Jesus Christ did not knuckle under to the challenges of His day, or the Temple leaders of His time, and neither should we.

As I conclude this opening chapter, citing the failure of the Christian Church, I recognize that many causes could be identified and many people and/or organizations could be blamed. There is, however, only one cause that is so pervasive that it must be identified as the initial failure. That cause is nothing more than the complete complacency of almost every Christian warming a pew today, a complacency that allows the people who call themselves "Christian" to ignore the most important book ever written, the New Testament of the Bible. No man, no woman, no church, no preacher, no teacher can teach you or me the meaning of the most complex book ever put together. Only the Holy Spirit of God can teach the Bible. Will you sit down, ask the Holy Spirit to guide you and begin reading today? Only then can "free" Christians enable the church to succeed.

2

FINANCE AND THE MODERN CHRISTIAN

Let your character be free from the love of money, being content with what you have...

For the love of money is a root of all sorts of evil, and some by longing for it have wandered away from the faith, and pierced themselves with many a pang.

We Christians concern ourselves with the silliest things. Almost every Christian that I talk to, sooner or later brings up the subject of money. This subject seems to dominate Christian thought, whether it's in the form of taxes (I list this first because it seems to be number one on the sliding scale of concern), wages, prices, social security, the stock market or the fact that we just never seem to have enough. Of course, no one ever has enough money to fit the lifestyle to which they would *like to* become accustomed. Although I have never personally verified this fact, I can remember several sermons that stated that Jesus talked about money in one form or another, more than any other subject. I guess He knows us pretty well, huh?

We Christians have a love/hate relationship with money. We would like to have plenty of it, but then we would feel guilty about having it. There is absolutely no reason to feel guilty about being wealthy. I'm going to start this chapter by telling you my personal story about finances and how God has made me a wealthy man. First of all, notice exactly what I said. I didn't say that I *became wealthy*; I said very specifically and clearly that God made me wealthy. I had to find out the hard way, that I, no matter how hard that I tried, could not even take care of myself, much less become wealthy. Did you catch that? I had to learn, by some very difficult circumstances, that I wasn't smart enough to even feed myself.

I have to tell you that it is a very difficult and humbling lesson to learn that you can't even support yourself, and I want to make the point that this is the first lesson that you must learn. Oh, yeah, there are lots of people who have brilliant ideas and make millions of dollars. Ted Turner and Bill Gates come to mind, but when you learn the secret, you are going to feel sorry for them rather than envy them. I used the word "secret" purposefully, because the church won't tell you what I am about to share, and it's almost as though they don't want you to know so that they can stay in control. You may be aware that one of the primary methods of controlling people is to keep them subservient with nothing but hope. The Catholic Church did this to the serfs, the servants (really the slaves) of the rich landowners, throughout the dark ages, and it worked for hundreds of years. The modern church, in my opinion, continues this tradition today, and the reason is almost the same, CONTROL.

My story starts on a small farm in Southern Texas in an area known as the "valley." My grandfather had died and our small plot was surrounded by the ranches of the well-to-do farmers of the area. Our farm was too small to support itself, and so we leased our land to the big operators, while we tried to just feed ourselves by raising chickens and tilling a garden. Our only monetary income came from my aunt, who was a teacher in a public school, and it wasn't much, but I was never hungry.

I would have never known that we were poor except for my treatment by my classmates in school. There was very little overt discrimination, but there were no offers of friendship and, of course, no invitations to birthday parties or other functions. It had never crossed my mind until I started writing this, but these other kids mostly came from Christian families, and I was being "ostracized" by "Christians." Let's make a note here: this is happening today, at all levels. Do you know of anyone being discriminated against? Are you part of the problem? Even if you are not the problem, or even part of the problem, if you are aware of discrimination's presence, what are you (yes, you) going to do about it?

To go back to my story, this discrimination did two things. First, it gave me a resolve to work hard so that I would not be poor all my life, and, second, it taught me how it feels to be an "underdog." Because of that experience, I have been a champion of the downtrodden all of my life, and this was reinforced when I became a Christian. My family moved back to Ohio, where I was born, and I finished high school, although I didn't graduate. In 1959, I joined the Army, and this experience became a turning point in my life, because I decided that if I wanted to be able to accomplish my goals, I would have to go to college, which I did in 1964.

To make a long story short, I worked long and hard and by 1985, I had reached the top of my profession as the director of quality for a jet engine manufacturer. What was most surprising about this story was that when I reached my long sought after goals of money, power and prestige, I wasn't happy. Here I was, making all the money that I had ever dreamed of. I had sixty people working for me, a multi-million dollar budget, a company car and a company airplane to take me wherever I wanted to go, but **I wasn't happy**! What a letdown. I just couldn't figure it out. Have you figured it out?

Yes, sometimes God gives us everything that we want, just to show us that if it doesn't involve Him, we won't be happy. God was also showing me that wealth, power, and prestige can and will never make anyone happy. One of the best examples of this theory is Ross Perot. He has mega-millions, but he is so insecure that he has to control everything, including his own employees. Did you know that Ross makes everyone on his staff wear dark blue suits? I guess that he wants a staff of clones.

Anyway, I'm not the brightest light in the tree, and I still didn't get it, so God just let me go my merry way until 1991. By October of 1991, I didn't have a job, had been through a divorce, was dead broke and was ready to try suicide. You see, I felt that I had failed at everything (that's true), and that I, at age 52, had no hope left (that's not true). God in His infinite wisdom sometimes has to let those of us who are supremely hard headed, hit the absolute bottom of the barrel before we are able to recognize we can't do anything by ourselves.

What is the moral of the story? That money won't bring happiness, and neither will anything else that is of this world, but now let me continue my story, because here again is where the church fails to teach us how to have a successful relationship with God.

In October of 1991, I took Jesus Christ as my savior and began reading the Bible and attending church. Here is what seems to be a strange part of the story, because eight months later, my life still had not changed, and I began to ask God why. As a matter of fact, I can remember sitting at my kitchen table in June of 1992 and calculating the money I had going out every month in the form of mortgage payments (my payments at that time were about $1,300.00 per month), bills, including electric, phone and food, versus my average monthly income, which wasn't much. The bottom line to the calculations came down to the fact that by December of that year I would be broke.

I knew that God wanted something more from me, but I didn't know what it was. You see, when I took God into my heart, I had no doubts about His power, and I had no doubts that He loved me and would take care of me. I knew in my heart that all I had to do was follow His lead and do what He wanted, and the reason that my circumstances had not changed was that there was something more that I had to learn. I remember asking God to show me what He wanted and continuing to ask that same question throughout the following weeks.

Before I continue my story, I want to ask every reader of this book to spend a moment in prayer. I want you to take this story to heart, because every word is true, and I would like you to individually ask God to show you anything that He wants you to know. If you just did that, I want to caution you not to expect an angel to suddenly appear. I promise that God will, if you ask Him, communicate with you in a very real way, but God's communication channels take place in the *real and normal, day-to-day world.* What I mean by this is that God will communicate with us through our normal, real world contacts and friends. If you can accept that premise, let us continue with my story.

To summarize for just a second, I am dead broke, I have taken Jesus Christ for my Savior, and I am doing my best to change my life, but in nine months nothing has changed. I have now asked God to show me exactly what He wants, so let's see what is going to happen.

I used to be the kind of person that has to go to church every Sunday. If I miss church, it's like I just missed a meal, and being a big man, I hate to miss a meal. It is now three weeks later (did you catch that – three weeks), and I am sitting in church listening to a sermon on tithing. TITHING – I can't even feed myself and I am listening to a sermon on tithing? I cannot begin to describe to you the sadness and hopelessness that I felt listening to that sermon. Remember now. At this time, I am dead broke, and as I left the church that morning, I was actually in tears. You see, the sermon had hit home with me, because God had pricked my heart, but I did not see a way that I could please God in this area because of my desperate financial situation. I remember asking myself how I could possibly give ten percent of my income when, for all practical purposes, I had no income. (Remember, my calculations had determined that I would be broke by December.)

For the next three weeks, I could not forget that sermon. I would be working on the farm and the Holy Spirit would bring it into my mind. I would be lying in bed and it would come into my mind. That sermon (read Holy Spirit) just would not leave me alone. It was driving me crazy, and when something is driving you crazy, you had better believe that God wants you to make a decision. Keep in mind that I had asked God to tell me what He wanted. This was not the answer that I had in mind or that I even wanted to hear and I have to tell you right now, that this is usually the case in ALL of our lives. We ask God a question, and then when He tells us the answer, it's not what we want to hear, but if you plan on working for God, I have some advice. GET USED TO IT!

As I said, that sermon drove me crazy for three weeks. I finally came to the point where I just couldn't take it any more and I had to make a decision. The options that I had were these: I could decide that God was wrong because there was no way that I could give God ten percent of my income. Remember, ten percent of nothing is still nothing. Or I could decide that God was trying to see what was most important in my life – money or serving Him. I'm not going to lie to you, making this decision was the most difficult of my life, and I was able to make the right decision only because of my total desperation. Remember, the question facing me was this, do I trust God, or do I plan for my own suicide in six months? Here is what I decided.

By the end of the third week, there was no doubt in my mind that it was God, through the Holy Spirit, who was talking to me about my finances. There was also no doubt that I had to make a decision, and I had to make it now. There is one more thing that I want to make sure that everyone is aware of, and that is the fact that God would allow me to make the wrong decision. You see, even though God was calling me to trust Him, He would allow me to make the wrong decision, and that is where most of us Christians fail, because we either put off a seemingly unpleasant decision, or we make the wrong decision, *and God will allow it.*

Why in the world would God allow us to make the wrong decision? Because He is a God of freedom. God does not want slaves or robots that can do nothing else but His bidding. I guess God just isn't like Ross Perot. God wants free people who are allowed the choice to make a wrong decision. At first glance, this might seem strange, but consider two things. First, if God will not allow us to make the decision that we *feel* is correct, we will always resent being forced to follow the decision of another. Fellow Christians, please consider that last statement closely and carefully, because that is one of the prime reasons for the failure of Christianity, we don't want to allow others to make the wrong decision; therefore, we force other people to conform to our rules by electing officials who will make laws that we want enforced.

The second reason that God allows us to have total autonomy over our own decisions is because we (most of us) learn from our mistakes. Learning from a mistake can be a valuable lesson, because we will have learned that we aren't so smart after all, but perhaps the most important lesson of all, that when we resist what God wants us to do, we will *always* be unhappy. Why is that? It's very simple really, God created us, and just like any loving father, He wants His children to be happy. Think about it, dads and moms, don't you want your children to be happy? Of course you do.

Back to my story, I was at my wit's end, I couldn't get that sermon out of my mind, and so I finally said to God, "O.K., I give up! If you want me to tithe, then I will tithe. I am going to make this promise to you God, if I get a dollar, you get ten cents. I'm not going to deduct taxes, I'm not going to deduct expenses and I'm not going to deduct **anything**. God, You need to understand one thing. I'm doing this because I am broke and I need your help." Well, you have to give me credit for being brutally honest. I didn't tell God I was going to tithe because I loved Him or some other crap that would have been a bald faced lie. I admitted to God that I needed help and I admitted to myself that I couldn't go it alone anymore. In effect, although I didn't realize it at the time, I was humbling myself before God and saying, "Take over."

To be totally honest, I really don't know why all the time intervals in this story are each three weeks, but sure enough, three weeks after I made the promise to tithe, I received a phone call on a Friday evening. It was from a man at a company where I had been trying to get a consulting job for the past two years. They had needed a quality program initiated for a long time, but whenever I had called, there was always some obstacle. I just couldn't get in the door, and whenever I called, the answer was "NO."

After I made the decision to follow God's direction, God made sure that I knew that He was involved in my life, and I started work around the first of September, and here is the great part of the story. Do you remember that I would have been broke by December? I will never forget New Year's Eve of 1993. I sat down at my kitchen table that night and I wrote checks totaling over $5,000.00, and I **had money left over**! There are a lot of lessons to be learned here, and I couldn't cover all of them in ten books, but I would like to take the time to point out some important facts that may help you understand how to establish a relationship with God.

Very few people understand what tithing is all about, again, because the church won't tell us. Some people tithe because they think that God needs the money. What a laughable idea that is. After all, God created all of the money and He owns it all anyway, along with all of the gold, silver and precious gems in the world. God doesn't need anything, but there is something that He wants. God wants to know just how important He is within the context of your life. Is money so important to you (as it was to me) that you are unwilling to share a measly ten percent with Him? When we are willing to share our blessings with God, that act, by itself, tells Him that we are willing to demonstrate our care and our love.

Another thing that people do not understand is that tithing to God does not necessarily mean that we must give to the church, although the church *certainly doesn't tell us that*, and in order to prove that I am going to tell you another true story. In 1995, I sold seventy acres of timber for $38,000. After receiving the check from the timber company, I paid off the mortgage on my land and prepared to write a check to my church for ten percent of my sale income, but something told me not to. This was the strangest feeling that I ever had, and I was really torn over what to do. After all, I had made a promise to God. Was this hesitation the devil telling me to renege? I really felt that it was the Holy Spirit talking to me, but why was He telling me not to tithe to the church? I decided to delay writing the check to see whether God would further enlighten me.

Two weeks later, I visited a church that I had attended about three years ago, and there sat a lady who had been an acquaintance. She began to tell me about the fact that she felt that God wanted her to become a doctor, and she had just been accepted to medical school. At age thirty-five, she was the oldest woman ever accepted into medical school, and she had absolutely no money to pay for her schooling but she was going to attend on the faith that God would provide.

As she was telling me her story, The Holy Spirit pierced my heart, and I immediately knew that sitting right next to me was the person to whom my tithe was to go. After the service, I told her the story of the timber sale and the hesitation to write the check, and I then told her that God was leading me to start a scholarship fund for her education. The story ends like this. Four years later she graduated with honors and she is now a doctor practicing in North Carolina, but I haven't told you the most astounding part of the story. If you remember, she had absolutely no money to attend medical school (about $100,000 then), but when she graduated, she did not owe one penny. Is God indeed an awesome God? I certainly believe it. No, I did not pay for her schooling. My continuing contributions were less than one-tenth of her needs. God provided the rest through other resources.

From everything that I have written up to this point, there may be someone reading this and thinking, "Gee, all I have to do is start tithing, and God will make me rich because He will be so grateful." As I stated earlier, God doesn't need the money, so don't count on His gratitude. As a matter of fact, for those people who desire to "serve" God, do not under any circumstance, think of your tithe as service to God. Your tithe may be of service to your church, but it definitely is not "service" to God, because as I said before, **God doesn't need the money**.

Tithing is something that we do out of loyalty to our God because He demands it. That's right. He demands nothing less and He demands nothing more. I have been to several churches where the members were asked to give more than their tithe to fulfill some project (usually to build a bigger church), and I do not believe that is what God wants.

Let me give you another story from my own experience. As I continued working for God, He continued to reward me in a mighty way. I came to a point in my life where I felt that I had more than enough money to live my very simple lifestyle, and I wanted, as a way of showing my gratitude, to give more than my tithe. As a matter of fact, I wanted to give it all away, and just keep enough to live. The answer I got from God was surprising to say the least. He shut off the tap. My income stopped. I didn't get it right away, because I was wrapped up in contemplating all the good things that my money could do, but when it came time to write checks, there wasn't any well from which to draw. I was at a total loss for an explanation as I watched my income go to zero and my bank accounts start into serious decline.

My usual practice, when something bad happens to me, is to go to God in prayer and ask Him what it is that He wants me to learn. His response was immediate. He seemed to be saying, "I want your tithe but nothing more." To this day, I am not sure that I really understand why, but that is the way that it is and I don't intend to question Him further. Even though I didn't understand why, I chose to acquiesce to His wishes, and sure enough, He again opened the financial tap, and He has chosen to keep it open since then.

Allow me to digress from strictly the subject of finances and into a general discussion of our relationship with God, because the above story makes a point that I believe is extremely important and I want to share it with you. I don't know how your relationship with God works, but I know without a doubt that anytime that I am having problems; it is because God wants to teach me something.

Am I saying that all my problems are caused by God? No, but when problems happen that He has not caused, I seem to have a peace about them, i.e. I know that He will enable me to handle them. It is when problems occur that seem to come out of nowhere, that seem to have no solution and that trouble me inordinately, that I know that God is acting and wants some specific action on my part. When this happens, I know it almost immediately, and I just ask God to teach me what it is that He wants me to know.

Having a relationship with God is so powerful, and so wonderful, because even when I screw up, God, through the Holy Spirit, gently and lovingly guides me back to the right path, without anger or recrimination. Have you developed a working relationship with our loving God? I promise you that He wants one, but you have to take the first steps to establish it. He is standing right in front of you with His arms outstretched, but it is up to you to step forward.

Let us return to the subject of finances, tithing and the church. When most Christians tithe they give to their church, but how many of those Christians take the time to analyze where that money, supposedly given to God's work, is put to use? It was just this year that I left my church, First Baptist, Mauldin, S.C., for that very reason. Two years ago, the church built a 25 million-dollar addition which included a new kitchen, dining rooms and lots of new Sunday school classrooms. Sounds great doesn't it? Frankly, this addition was needed, but the financing plan has become a "millstone" around the Church's neck. What I mean by that is that in their haste to pay off a huge debt, the church has almost totally ignored their reason for existence. As documented in the 2001 Analysis of Revenues and Expenses report on file in the treasurer's office, this church spent $538,471.03 on Capital Development (read: paying for the new addition) but this same church spent ONLY $46,455.00 on missions.

This is without a doubt a travesty beyond all sanity, and it is happening in Christian Churches throughout the world. It is almost as though Christians everywhere are obsessed with building useless monuments to their own selfishness. I have a question for you. Where does it say in the Bible that we are to forget about Christ's Great Commission and build massive buildings? Did anyone take a calculator to the above figures? If you did, you will find that this one church spent less than ten percent of the amount that they spent on buildings on missions! What a shame. What a travesty of God's word. What is worse is that it is happening all over the United States. Catholics just spent $60 million on a recently opened cathedral in Los Angeles. Is it any wonder that Islam is the fastest growing religion in the world? We, dear Christians, have no one to blame but ourselves. While we build "clubhouses" for ourselves, the Moslems are building converts. Listen closely, the figures must be reversed – ninety percent of our money, our time and our talents, must be spent on missions, and only ten percent on clubhouses for the privileged few.

Let me be brutally clear right here. I use the word "clubhouse" because the Christian Church today has become a "social club" where a select few go to be entertained within the confines of a beautiful building with plush seating. A clubhouse is a place where people go to interact with others at their own societal level, or the societal level to which they are trying to climb, or with their friends, and it's also a great place to network. How many so-called Christians use the church to promote their businesses? Stockbrokers, financial advisors and real estate agents are the prevalent scum involved in this practice, but it doesn't stop there.

In beginning the research for this book, I attended several CHURCH SPONSORED seminars on so-called Christian financial practices. Each one of these seminars was a thinly disguised sales pitch for the speaker's business, with the sole goal of the attendees being the accumulation of wealth. Is that why you are a Christian, in order to have a leg up toward being wealthy? If that is the case, then I suggest that you pay attention to Jesus when He said, "*It will be easier for a camel to pass through the eye of a needle than for a rich man to go to heaven.*" Which is it that you want? Monetary wealth here on earth or the riches of eternal life? Do you want to be wealthy like Madonna (about $100 million) or how about Donald Trump (mega-billions), or myself when I was the director of quality? Well, you can be, and you can be just as unhappy as they are, and just as unhappy and dissatisfied as I was.

I want to make what is commonly called a disclaimer here. I am not acquainted with either Madonna or Donald Trump, and I want you to understand that they are probably pretty nice people. As a matter of fact, they are just like you and me except that they are both probably a lot smarter than we are, and I would give anything to spend seventy-two hours with either one of them, just so I could show them that true happiness really does exist. Let's just pretend that I really did have the opportunity to spend seventy-two hours with them or anyone else that possesses everything in the world but happiness, peace and contentment. What would I tell them?

Would I tell them to give away all of their money in order to find true peace and happiness? Absolutely not! Let me introduce you to another concept that the Christian Church does not teach. There is nothing wrong with being wealthy; however, what is important is **how** you spend your money. I have found that most Christian denominations have a very subtle message that says, in effect, *It is more acceptable to God for you to be poor* (and continuing with the logic of their reasoning). *Therefore, give all of your money to the church* (presumably so that they can build a bigger clubhouse, because they certainly aren't going to give it to the needy).

While I am on the subject of clubhouses, let me return to my old church, First Baptist Mauldin. Can you guess the theme which they use in order to entice their congregation to contribute over one-half million dollars each year for three years to help pay for the new addition (meanwhile forgetting about missions)? I warn you, you are really going to have to stretch to guess this one. Their theme is: *FREEDOM TO LIVE GOD'S DREAM.* Does anyone really, for one nanosecond, believe that God dreams about having a larger church building when there are thousands of people living on the streets and sleeping under bridges who don't know Jesus Christ?

How about the 540,000 children up for adoption, just in the United States, who will never have a mother or a father, when only one-tenth of one percent of Christian families adopt children from their own country? Oh, yeah, I forgot. It's more exciting and more glamorous to adopt a foreign child, something akin to keeping an exotic pet, while tens of thousands of black and white and Hispanic children will never know the love of real parents. While I am on this subject, God has brought to my attention the fact that some black Christians have objected to the adoption of black orphans by parents of another ethnicity. HOW ARROGANT. This action personifies the absolute height of race hatred. How mean, how nasty, to deny a child (of any color) a loving home. When I said "race hatred", I meant hatred of their own race. Because which is more important, for a child to know love or to just know "black"? It is my humble opinion that there would be a lot less strife and hatred in this world if EVERYONE totally forgot about their own ethnicity and instead concentrated on being a member of the Christian "race."

The subject is finances, and the bottom line is why all these so-called Christians don't believe what the Bible clearly states: we don't have to worry about finances because God takes care of His people in all ways and all times. Are we concerned about making money and about paying too much in taxes because we don't believe God, or because we are just too darn greedy for our own good? Yes, there are financially troubled Christians in this world, but it doesn't have to be that way. I challenge any financially troubled Christian reading this book to:

1. Read the New Testament
2. Ask God what it is that He wants you to learn or do.
3. Begin giving ten percent of your money to charity. (not necessarily the church)
4. For a change, ignore the things of this world.
5. Begin working for God in whatever way that He wants. (this is important)
6. Watch your life start to change.

Let's take a moment and review one of the most often quoted (inside the church) verses of the Bible pertaining to money. If you remember, earlier I talked about the fact that very few of God's promises were *not* conditional, and here is one that is a flat-out promise without any conditions attached, yet Christians (through their actions) refuse to believe it.

And my God shall supply all your needs according to His riches in glory in Christ Jesus.

Oh, yes, I have heard entire congregations mouth that verse ad infinitum; yet they still refuse to believe it. It is as though Jesus is still talking to the Jews and saying, "*...your hearts have been hardened.*" Why do Christians have such a difficult time believing the Bible when God made it so easy?

Take a moment and reread my own personal story about finances which I told earlier in the chapter. Since I have put serving God first in my life, I haven't had to give the first thought to supporting myself financially. As a matter of fact, I don't even consider myself smart enough to support myself – God does it all.

If the verse above states that God shall support all my needs, shouldn't that take into consideration "financial needs" also? Well, I would think so since that verse is quoted most often by the church within the context of finances; yet Christians seem to be the people who are most often concerned about money, taxes, etc.

I have thousands of people who come out to my business every year, and the only people who seem concerned about cost are (you guessed it) Christians. The church has again failed by seeming to teach through default that "fiscal conservatism" is a Biblical term. Want to know my definition of fiscal conservative? Here it is: A fiscal conservative is a greedy person whose entire goal in life is to gather the most money possible for their own use and benefit and to keep as much of the money that they have already accumulated from falling into someone else's hands (especially someone who might need it).

FAILURE!

The real reason that a lot of well meaning Christians are failing financially is simply because they are concerned about money, and because of that fear or concern, they aren't tithing. My own story is a good example of a person whose concern and worries about money became a block in my relationship with God, and until I was able to overcome that obstacle, I couldn't grow in His service. Ask yourself whether you worry about or are concerned about money or taxes or any financial aspect whatever, because if you are, you will never be successful.

The second reason for the financial failure of any Christian is due to the fact that they are working for the wrong person. What I mean by that is the fact that while we have a worldly job, either operating our own business or working for some large or small corporation, our personal goal should be to serve (work for) God. When we follow His example and teaching and listen to His instruction, we won't have to worry about success in our worldly job.

Working for God does not mean that we have to become a pastor or even a missionary. Working for God simply means putting His agenda first in your heart and following His orders and direction. I do have one caveat about what working for God is **NOT,** and that is the fact that working for God is not walking around mouthing the name of Jesus without changing your own life; neither is it telling everyone else how to live their own lives.

Since I have an entire chapter dedicated to the subject of working for God, let's return to finances for a moment. No person will ever have enough money to be satisfied, not Donald Trump, not Ted Turner, certainly not Bill Gates and not you – until you give control of your finances to God (only), and this one simple fact is the single easiest way to judge whether you are truly a Christian.

One of the primary problems with this money thing is that the church wants you to feel guilty if you do have money. I suppose that is their way of trying to get into your pocket, but nothing could be further from the truth because riches by themselves are not sinful. What is sinful is not using the money that God gave you to serve Him by using it to help others.

I want to close this chapter with one simple thought, and that is the fact that what a person or a family does with their money is what determines their attitude toward God and, conversely, determines God's attitude toward them.

Want to be successful? Find a charity that you believe in, such as the Salvation Army, local children's home, meals on wheels, etc. Give them ten percent of your income and your time and watch God start to work in your life.

3
CALVINISM

It is impossible for those who have once been enlightened, who have tasted the heavenly gift, who have shared in the Holy Spirit, who have tasted the goodness of the Word of God and the powers of the coming age, if they fall away, to be brought back to repentance, because to their loss they are crucifying the Son of God all over again and subjecting Him to public disgrace.

When a person makes the decision to "follow Jesus Christ," i.e. become a Christian, it is usually because they have recognized the transitory nature of life here on this planet we call earth and recognized that they need help from a "higher power." They may also have come to the realization that this earthly existence will not last forever and that they are going to someday "die." I am going to address "help from a higher power" in a later chapter, but for now I want to discuss "eternal life" or "salvation," what most more fundamentalist denominations call "being saved," and whether the state of "being saved" is permanent or whether salvation itself can be lost through our own continuance of an ungodly lifestyle, but *not* due to the existence of a whimsical and possibly cruel God.

Over the two thousand years of its existence, the Christian religion has undergone many modifications, most of them conflicting with our Lord's original teachings in an attempt to oversimplify Jesus' Gospel for the lowest common denominator, i.e. those converts who were (are) too lazy or unwilling to read the words of Jesus for themselves. Through the years God produced "prophets" such as Martin Luther, whose 95 theses forever removed the abomination of "purchasing" the forgiveness of sins. However, some of these modifications, while well intentioned, have caused divisiveness and have misinterpreted the words of Jesus Himself.

One of these "modifications of the Gospel" which in my estimation is a gross misinterpretation of Jesus' teachings is the premise that most fundamentalist Christian's think of as *"once saved, always saved,"* also known as "Calvinism." This premise is not just a dogma of the fundamentalists and regardless of whether it is accepted by a particular denomination or not, most Christians feel the need to believe that there is no way that they can lose their salvation or the promise of eternal life (in heaven) by "falling out of favor with God."

Some of the most quoted and remembered words of Jesus are contained in the phrase in which He said, "Believe in Me and you shall be saved." Let me make myself totally clear. In no way and in no sense am I questioning that statement; however, one cannot *add* meaning to Jesus' words without inadvertently changing their entire intent. In other words, Jesus told us that when we believed in the fact that He was the Son of God, and when we believed in the fact that He had been sent by God, then we became His, and through our faith, we would obtain eternal life with Him in God's heaven.

What is implicit in Jesus' statement but goes unrecognized by most Christians and most Christian churches is the fact that through our newfound belief, our lives and everything related to them *must* of necessity be *changed*. What does this mean? Suppose that a person who has committed murder finds themselves converted to a belief in Christ as the Son of God. That person now asks for and receives forgiveness for their sins. Does that person now have eternal life? The answer is a resounding *YES,* without question and without qualification. But let's suppose that this same person again commits murder. Can they still count on continuing to have salvation? The answer this time is sadly NO, and this is where the church has again failed in its mission, because the church has made the belief in, and recognition of, Jesus Christ as Savior, the final goal, *not the first step* on a long road leading toward the ultimate goal of becoming like Christ.

"Calvinism" supposedly originated with a man named John Calvin, but the doctrine of "Calvinism" as we know it today came into being long after John Calvin's death. This scheme of doctrine and the five points which comprise modern Calvinism was developed as a counter to the doctrines of one Jacobus Arminius, during the council of Dort in 1618. In order to understand the fallacy of "Calvinism" one must understand the doctrine of Calvinism and how it contradicts the teachings of the words of Jesus Christ and the entire Bible. The scheme of the doctrine of Calvinism is traditionally recalled through the acronym TULIP and rests upon five points which I would like to discuss and refute from both a Biblical standpoint and from the intentions of a very loving and forgiving God.

The letter "T" in the acronym TULIP stands for the fact that Calvinist doctrine theorizes the *TOTAL DEPRAVITY* of man. If there were no other reason to refute this doctrine as a total abomination, this portion of Calvinism would stand alone as an untruth which not only contradicts the very first page of the Bible, but contradicts the very intent of our God the Father when, in the greatest act of love in history, He created man with His own hands.

To believe in the total depravity of all men (and women) is to believe in the total depravity and the total evil of God's entire creation, because man and woman were the crowning achievement of God's wisdom and abilities. Think about this for a second. If we decide to believe that God's crowning creation, the human race, is totally depraved and without any redeeming virtue, then we must by association believe that God Himself is totally depraved and, again, without any redeeming value because the Bible states that we were created in His (God's) likeness. As the Apostle Paul said, "May it never be!"

Now, the first thing that someone is going to say to me is, "Look at the newspaper, the TV, listen to the radio. Look at wars, hatred, murders, rape and robbery. How can you say that the human race isn't totally depraved?" To those critics I say, look at all the good people of the world. Look at Albert Schweitzer, look at Mother Teresa, look at the men and women who climbed 80 stories up a burning building, look at the people who risk their lives every day to protect you and me. Are they totally depraved also? Am I going to tell the angel of mercy who is giving me oxygen after I have had a heart attack, or the medic who has crawled through a firefight to stop my bleeding, or the policeman who is exchanging bullets with a killer to "get away from me because you are totally depraved."? I think not, and neither would you.

Because 99% of all Christians think of themselves as totally perfect, they expect and demand that everyone else be perfect. What they fail to realize is the fact that none of us is perfect (including themselves). Stop reading for just one minute and ask yourself a question. "Am I a totally depraved person without any redeeming value?" Personally speaking, I have met some preachers, deacons, and elders, who might be described as totally depraved, but I have no doubt that not one person who asks themselves that question in all sincerity and with some soul searching will answer in the affirmative. Why not? Because every person on this earth has done some good or has tried to do good at some time in their life. Sadly, most of us have made incorrect choices, or we have been abused by a Mother or Father, or our brains have become miswired, or we have chosen to follow the wrong leader or we have been tempted by worldly things. I would go so far as to say that even the most self righteous, hypocritical, pontificating, hypercritical Christian has *some* redeeming feature. At least I hope so.

Let's go back to that defining document upon which all of our faith is based, the Bible. In the last verse of the very first chapter of the very first Book of the Bible, Genesis, God looks back at all He has created, including the first human, and this is what is written: (Genesis 1:31) *"...and God saw every thing that He had made, and behold, it was very good."* Let me ask you two questions. If God made it, "Is it good?" I think that we would have to say "Yes." The second question is this, "If God thought it was good, was it truly good, or was He mistaken?" Again, we have to answer, "Yes, it was good." If God Himself considers His own handiwork as "very good," then how can we even begin to question the wisdom of God, because that is what we are doing when we consider ourselves, as the Calvinists, and most modern Christian denominations would have us believe, "totally depraved."

At this point, it would be appropriate to ask ourselves how this theory of "total depravity" came into being and, further, how it could be accepted by otherwise intelligent thinking human beings. Have you ever met someone who was raised in an abusive situation? Of course you have, although you may not have recognized the situation as such. Any person who was raised by an abusive family will never feel that they are worthy of anything, much less the love and acceptance of God. The children of abusive parents, whether that abuse evidenced itself physically or not, continue through their entire lives in a trauma of anger, fear and frustration stemming from a feeling of negativity and self-loathing.

Those same feelings of worthlessness are then reinforced and justified when that same person joins the church and is taught (wrongly) that they are totally depraved. The church in its misguided dogma has finally completed the full circle in supposedly identifying exactly why that person has felt worthless all of their life. I would be willing to give odds (if I were a betting man) that whoever developed this misguided theory of "total depravity" was in fact abused as a child, and this theory was developed as a means to justify their own feelings. What I cannot understand is how such a theory could be accepted by an organization that purports to teach the love and the perfection of the entity that we call "God." If our God were in fact both loving and perfect, would He take pleasure in creating something that was totally depraved? I don't think so, and I'll bet you don't either.

One of the most often misunderstood passages of the Bible is Romans 3:23 which states, ***"For all have sinned, and fallen short of the glory of God."*** This passage is used to supposedly prove that man is inherently evil, but my answer is this: Of course man has fallen short of the Glory of God. How could anyone or anything match the glory of God? It is impossible! Does that mean that we are totally worthless as we have been led to believe? The simple answer is NO. We were created by God and therefore we are "good," because that is exactly what God said that we are. What we have to remember is that we are not perfect, nor were we intended to be perfect when we were created. I think that everyone will agree that only God is perfect, so, therefore, how can we *not* "fall short of the glory of God"?

Take a minute and read again the next to last sentence in the paragraph above. What I said was this, we are not perfect and most importantly of all, *we were never intended to be perfect when God created us.* Think about that for a second, because it leads us to the next fallacy of Calvinism, that of the "rebellion of the fall." What the Calvinists are talking about is our supposed "fall from grace" in the Garden of Eden. Listen closely. The "fall from grace" is in itself a fallacy. If we had fallen from God's grace, then God would have had nothing more to do with us.

The human race has never lost God's grace. We have never lost His care. We have never lost His love, and above all we have never lost God's forgiveness. We have never lost the first place in God's heart, and those who say that we have, don't know and don't understand God. Think about this. If God did not still love us (meaning that we still have His Grace), then He would not have sent His Son to save us from our human failings. The foremost verse in Christian doctrine, John 3:16, states, ***"For God so loved the world, that He gave His only begotten Son, that whoever believes in Him should not perish, but have*** *eternal life."* Does that sound like we and the world "fell from grace"?

The church teaches that we (the human race) "disappointed" God by our decision to eat the forbidden fruit in the Garden of Eden, yet in the same breath the church teaches that God knows everything that has happened and ever will happen. Does anyone see the disparity? If God knew what was going to happen (which He did) how could He have been disappointed? We must learn to open our minds to accept the fact that God knew what decisions those two innocents would make before He even created them. Only then can the actions at the Garden of Eden be considered consistent with what we are taught about the foreknowledge of this all-knowing God of ours.

As a point of fact, the decision to eat the forbidden fruit was not the first "disappointment" realized by God after He created Adam. In my opinion, God's first disappointment came when Adam felt "lonely," even though he had God as a companion.

The church has been following in Adam's footsteps ever since as it tries to find the perfect politician (in the place of God) to lead the world. Does anyone recognize the similarity? Let's take a moment and go back to the beginning. God has created the universe; He has created all of the plants and animals and last of all, He creates man. Man was not created to reside in heaven with God. Man was created to live on this earth. Man was given dominion over all the plants and animals. Why? So that he (man) would have food. A god doesn't need food. Only man needs food. A god is perfect. He doesn't need to eat. Man was never intended to be perfect; therefore man needs to eat. Get it? Even when the first couple, Adam and Eve, resided in the Garden of Eden, they needed food and sleep. They weren't gods, nor were they intended to be gods, and therefore they were not perfect.

I think that it is hilarious that some people (even some Christians) question the "perfection" of God when bad things happen, yet they insist that when Adam and Eve were created, they were "perfect." Only one being within our sphere of knowledge can be considered to be perfect, and that is our God. If you need further proof, then let's take a minute and look at angels. Are they perfect? Sorry, but the answer has to be NO, that is, if you believe the Bible. How can I say that? Well, remember the brightest of all angels, whose name was Lucifer. He was supposedly the favorite angel in God's heaven, yet he betrayed God and became the one that we know as Satan. There were many other angels who made grave errors and brought the wrath of God upon themselves. The purpose of my argument is this: If even the angels are not perfect (and we have proof of that), then how can we expect (and even demand) that humans were once perfect. Maybe the Calvinists would have us believe that the angels are also "totally depraved." After all, more than one of them sinned against God, just as did Adam and Eve.

Let me give you just one more thing to think about regarding the subject of "falling from God's grace" and whether we humans did indeed fall from grace, and, furthermore, whether anyone can fall from God's favor (grace). Consider this. Satan (the former Lucifer) has, repeat has, fallen from God's grace! In other words, Satan's betrayal of God's trust was so horrendous that there is no way he could ever be forgiven. If God will not forgive him, then there is no way that Satan can ever be redeemed. Could this happen to one of us? The answer is no, and the reason for this fact is that Lucifer was given a much higher position of trust and authority than any human can ever hope to attain.

Keep in mind that the Bible states that the more that you have been given, the more will be expected of you. No human being has ever been given the power and authority of one of God's angels, and thankfully no one of us ever will. For that reason, God always reserves His Grace for us humans, the favorite, yet the weakest of His creations. I always find it a source of wonder when I consider the fact that we, of all God's creation, are considered favorites above even the angels.

Knowing that fact, the people who worship, pray to or venerate angels might want to consider redirecting their adoration back to God the Father and His Holy Spirit.

Let us investigate further this abomination that the Calvinist's call "total depravity." According to the Calvinist's, every aspect of man's being was altered through what is called the "original sin" of Adam an Eve in the Garden of Eden. Every Christian leader acts as though this "original sin" was a surprise to God, yet if it were a surprise, then that would refute these same leaders' teachings about the very power and nature of our God. Remember that we are taught (and I firmly believe) that our God is Omnipotent (all powerful), Omnipresent (existing everywhere) and Omniscient (all knowing). My all time favorite analogy concerning God gives us a "view" (pun intended) of just how powerful this God of ours is, as we picture Him seated in a high place, perhaps the Empire State Building, watching the Macy's Thanksgiving Day parade proceed from its starting point to its end.

The point of the analogy is to be able to visualize the fact that God not only sees everything going on in the present, He is able to see where and how the parade (the world) will end. In other words, God saw the creation, He sees what is happening in the present and He knows (sees) what will happen at the "end" of time itself. If He can see how the world will end, then He *knew* when He created Adam and Eve that they would "fall" (another pun intended) into temptation. Some people think that it is a stretch to believe that God knows when and how the world will end, but Jesus Himself, when asked when the end would take place, answered that it was for only God the Father to know.

Since God created the world, He knows everything as, and even before, it happens, and He obviously knows how and when it is going to end. So doesn't it make sense to recognize the fact that He knew ahead of time that Adam and Eve were going to fail? Why do all of the intellectual Christian "thinkers" fail to give God credit for knowing this one simple (and obvious) fact, i.e. that humans, when given the choice to act on their own, can and will be tempted to fail. Read this next statement carefully, because this is what God is all about. We (the human race) were created in love and given the freedom to choose. We were also given an intellect to think, reason and learn from our mistakes; but most importantly, we were given knowledge of right and wrong and last, we were given the knowledge of the great God that created us. Think about it. Every animal can learn from its mistakes, but we are the *only* animal that has been given the knowledge of our God, the Creator. Have you ever seen a rabbit or a lion erecting an altar in the forest? I didn't think so. When Adam and Eve failed to follow God's orders, there was no "fall from grace." That simple act was just one more part of God's great plan for His favorite creation, the human race. Why? Keep reading. I will get to that in a later chapter.

There is one part within the doctrine of Calvinism upon which I agree to some extent, and that is the belief that none (or very few) of us naturally hunger to know God or to serve Him. I have to admit that this agreement stems from a totally personal experience, in that in my younger days, I wanted to accomplish everything by myself. I graduated from engineering school and rose to the top of my profession totally through my own abilities and hard work (or so I thought). I thought that I didn't need God. Oh, sure, I accepted the fact that God existed, but I thought that He was too busy to be bothered with me. Like most people, I didn't want to be bothered even thinking about God (except when I wanted something), and I sure didn't want God claiming credit for my success.

It wasn't until I lost everything that I decided to let God into my life in a personal way. I can now see so clearly that God allowed hardship into my life purposefully in order to bring me to recognize Him. In other words, God put me into a situation where I was pressured (not forced) to make a decision of whether to allow Him (God) to have control of my life. Only someone who has seen true hardship can recognize just how grateful I am to the one God who loves us so much that He will do anything to get our attention. Was that decision forced? No, I had the choice; I still had the free will to make the right, or even the wrong, choice.

This is a good place to proceed to the next letter of our acronym TULIP. The letter "U" in the acronym stands for "unconditional election," and this second step in the grand scheme of modern Calvinism is somewhat more difficult to comprehend. Personally, I not only find this step more difficult to understand, I find it much more difficult to comprehend how the originators of this theory even arrived here, given our overall knowledge of God Himself. The primary reason for that statement is that nowhere in any knowledge of who our God is and how this God works is there any mention of His great love being in any way "conditional" toward His greatest creation, yet that conditionality is the primary idea behind this belief of "unconditional election."

Even the words "unconditional election" are themselves at odds with the theme of Calvinist doctrine. By that I mean the words "unconditional election" say to me that God elects all to salvation "unconditionally"; yet that idea is diametrically opposed to Calvinist doctrine, in that this doctrine proposes that God has "predetermined" who will and who will not be given salvation. Think about it for a second. This dogma totally negates the idea of what we understand as "free will," and this alone is bad news for the entire Christian faith in that some of us don't stand a chance, regardless of whether we decide to follow God or not. Wow. A person can turn from a life of sin and corruption and still not be accepted for salvation by a very quirky God; or some person can follow God all their life and still be rejected.

The advent of Calvinism and the accompanying idea that is known as "unconditional election," a concept which accepts the falsehood that some people may be eternally damned, accelerated the downfall of what we recognize today as organized religion and marked the beginning of the justification for ignoring, and what is even worse, rejecting those fellow members of our human race who for some reason have not yet come to the existence of a belief in God. You see, we Christians love to hate anyone who does not believe exactly as we do, and the notion of "unconditional election" allows us to ignore anyone who has not accepted God, because we now "know" that these people are part of "God's rejected." Personally, I think that most Christians are so wrapped up in their own feelings of superiority at having been smart enough to accept God that they enjoy looking with disdain at the rest of the human race when instead they should be reaching a helping and loving hand to others who are not as fortunate.

This would be a perfect time to look at the actions of Jesus Himself as He lived and interacted with the people of His time. If you will take the time to read through the Gospels, which are the stories of the life of Jesus, at no time will you find Him rejecting **anyone**. This in itself is surprising, given the "type" of people with whom Jesus associated. Think about it. Jesus Christ's friends and associates were the very people with whom no modern Christian would allow themselves to be seen. As a matter of fact, these are the very same people with whom the modern church tells us to **not** be associated. Jesus' friends and associates were prostitutes, tax collectors, cheats, liars, thieves and who knows what else. Jesus Himself was called a "drunk" by the leaders of the church.

The point that I am making is this; Jesus Christ never told anyone that they were predestined to burn in Hell, despite the fact that He associated Himself with the scum of the earth of that day. If Jesus Christ did not believe in predestination, how can we? As a matter of fact, there is one story in the life of Jesus, as He confronts one of the chief tax collectors that refutes for all time the idea of predestination. As Jesus calls this scoundrel out of his seat in a tree and converses with him, this man changes his entire life and vows repentance and repayment to any person whom he has wronged. Jesus' next words are so important as He says, *"Today, salvation has come to this house...."*

Consider, for a moment, Jesus' statement, because it destroys forever the theory of predestination. As Zaccheus repents and promises repayment to any person whom he has cheated, Jesus starts His statement with the word "today," which in itself identifies the fact that our status regarding salvation can be changed. Furthermore, Jesus' words confirm the fact that every one of us has the *free will* to change our status. If such an idea as predestination existed, Jesus might have said, "Even though you have repented, God previously chose you to burn in Hades."

Since the Calvinists denial of the concept of "free will" is at the heart of their entire doctrine, let's take a minute and try to ascertain whether God did indeed give us the ability to think and act "freely." The first place to turn in an attempt to ascertain the answer to this question would logically be the very first book of the Bible, and in Genesis we find Adam and Eve being instructed by God not to eat of the fruit of the tree of knowledge. I wonder whether God had a twinkle in His eye as He said this, because He certainly knew what was about to happen. By the way, if you don't believe that God knew what was about to happen, then you have just negated the entire concept of God, because you have placed limitations on His almighty abilities. Think about it.

O.K. God has "instructed" Adam and Eve not to eat the fruit of a certain tree. Look in some depth at what has just happened here. God has given an instruction, and that is all that He did. Doesn't that sound like something that you do to your (over toddler age) children? God didn't place an angelic guard around the tree. He didn't make it impossible for Adam and Eve to get to the tree. He didn't make the fruit poisonous so that they would die if they ate it. God gave an instruction, and He stopped there. In other words, just like every parent, He instructed His children as to what was right and what was wrong, and then, He **let them choose for themselves!** He (God) gave them free will and to this day we are given the free will to choose. Freedom of choice does exist. Yes, of course there is a punishment for going against God's wishes, but He still loved them. They didn't lose God's grace, and by that same reasoning, we haven't lost God's grace either.

Every good parent will immediately understand the concept that we can't chain our children in their room (even though we want to). We have to give them the freedom to choose, because making mistakes is a large part of the learning process, and that is exactly what God allows us to do. Let's face it, who is the supreme parent? God, of course, and Jesus confirmed that through His teachings. Let me ask you a question here: What child do you know that, because they made one mistake, lost forever their parent's love (read grace)? Of course, the answer is NONE, if their parents loved them in the first place. If no human parent would stop loving their child after that child made a mistake, why do the Calvinists believe that God would stop loving all of us after our forbears made a mistake. Let me repeat myself when I say that there is no such thing as the fall from grace of the human race. If God had not wanted Adam and Eve to make the wrong choice, then why did He allow the serpent to tempt them? Do you (or does the church) think that God didn't know what was happening. If you think God didn't know what was happening and what would happen, then you had better stop singing the hymn, *OUR GOD IS AN AWESOME GOD*, because you don't believe the words.

I think that it would be appropriate to use my own experiences as an analogy here. I was a very rebellious teenager (my own dad who is now with God is probably jumping up and down yelling "AMEN" at that statement). I went to a revival as a teenager and went to the altar. Did I find God? No, I chose to reject Him and depend upon myself and the world for happiness. Get this. I was given the choice. God didn't force me to follow Him. He gave me free will. It wasn't until age 51, after I had exhausted the resources of myself and the world, that I chose to follow God and find true happiness.

Freedom of Choice? Yes, it exists and God wouldn't have it any other way. If freedom of choice doesn't exist, then I want you to immediately do two things: 1. Stop working for God or praying to God or even being concerned about God, because you are probably saved anyway and what does it matter, because you have no say in the decision. 2. Stop witnessing for God or Jesus Christ because God has already made His decision regarding the salvation of everyone else, and your efforts aren't going to change anything. You certainly can't offer salvation to anyone because God has already made up His mind! Are you beginning to understand how the concept of Calvinism contradicts most of the other teachings of the Bible and the practices of Christianity? Why would Jesus Christ give us the great commission of going out and teaching the world if God had already made the decision as to who would and who would not have salvation?

To more fully illustrate the confusion of this heterodoxy they call "Calvinism," some proponents believe in something called "double predestination," which asserts that God also specifically chooses those (of His own creation) who are to be eternally damned. In other words, God systematically chooses the specific members of His human race whom He will send into eternal damnation, and (according to the Calvinists) He has already made that choice before those persons are even born. Talk about hopeless! What is even the use of living if we are to believe in something this outrageous? We all just might as well commit mass suicide so that we can reach our (pre)destination sooner and not have to put up with the troubles of this world. **The church has failed!**

FAILURE!

The church has failed because it has allowed itself to attempt to "intellectualize" God through the teachings of certain so-called "deep thinkers," who in their own attempt at self-glorification, have to come up with human level reasons for God's decisions. These same people fail to realize that in attempting to compartmentalize a God that is so far beyond our comprehension, they are attempting to usurp the power of God Himself.

The first two letters of the acronym TULIP present almost the entire definition of Calvinism, and the last three letters are, for the most part, repeating, or perhaps we can, with over generosity, say clarifying, certain beliefs. The "L" in TULIP stands for the concept of "limited atonement," which does nothing more than repeat the concept of "unconditional election." "Limited Atonement" advances the theory that because of the fact that God has "prechosen" those whom He loves, there are certain specified people among God's great creation that are forever destined, with unchangeable finality, to burn in Hell. Now, I am sorry, but I just don't buy that! I just can't even begin to consider worshiping a supposed "God" who purposefully destroys, in the most horrible way, His own creation. Can you? If you can accept a "God" like that then you had better start feeling very insecure in your own salvation, because you just might be someone prechosen to be delivered to a very warm retirement.

"Irresistible Grace," the "I" in TULIP, is very simple in concept, and very easily refuted through the words of the Bible. Stephen, the first Christian "martyr" told the Jews that were prosecuting him that they were always resisting the Holy Spirit, just as their fathers had in the past when they persecuted and killed God's prophets. Jesus told of the Jews killing the prophets and "resisting" God's messages. The Apostle Paul talked of "quenching" the fire of the Holy Spirit. We have to look no further than the Old Testament to find the Jews repeatedly resisting the instructions of God relative to worshiping "idols" to be able to easily ascertain that God gives every one of us "free will" and that God Himself **can** be resisted.

Why is this concept so difficult to understand? Stated simply, it is because the church has attempted to "oversimplify" a God that they do not understand, and they have attempted to rely upon their own wisdom in order to present a God as **they** would like Him to appear. Can anyone truly "understand" our magnificent God and know how He thinks and works? It is impossible, and if you take just a moment to think about it, that is the reason that He is our God. I look forward with great eagerness to the day in which I will be with this wonderful God of ours so that I can be given an understanding of His works and plans. In the meantime, it is not my place to attempt to outguess Him; my place is to complete the work which He has given to me during my time on this earth.

    I want to pause at this point and return to the originating theme of this book, that of each person having an individual responsibility to read the **entire** Bible. Although I have stated it before, it bears repeating that the Bible is the most complex book ever written. That is the way that God wanted it, and that is the reason that no human being can attempt to "teach" the Bible to anyone else. Because of its great complexity, the words of the Bible are easy to misuse and to twist into self-serving ideologies. Think of it this way. If the Bible were so easy to understand and obey, why are there so many church denominations? Even the Catholics cannot agree among themselves, to say nothing about the Baptists, so how can we even begin to think that God's word is simple to understand?

    In spite of this fact, every Sunday, thousands of Sunday school teachers will stand before thousands of Sunday school classes, and pretend to "teach" an understanding of the Bible, when these so-called teachers have never even read the Bible for themselves. These "teachers" are not leaders in studying the Word of God; they are, in fact, only "followers" in passing along the accepted dogma of a particular denomination. The primary reason that I left my home church, First Baptist Mauldin, was that in the entire church, I could not find even one "teacher" who had read the entire Bible from cover to cover, and that statement includes every one of the pastors. This is, in my opinion, a shame, and it is a gross crime that the church allows even its leaders to be ignorant of the Word of God. The first question that should be asked of any applicant to a Bible college or seminary is, "Have you read the Bible from cover to cover?" The same question should be asked of any pastor before he is allowed to preach.

At this point, I want to return to the last letter of the acronym TULIP, which stands for "perseverance" within the context of those preordained to salvation. While this is the last letter of the acronym and may have been added as an afterthought or simply as a means to come up with an understandable word to use as a memory device, this idea of personal "perseverance" is the most detestable of all to anyone who understands the relationship of man to his God.

The Calvinists would have us believe that those who have been chosen by God for salvation have also (at the same time) been given the superhuman strength to resist temptation or any sort of "falling away" from Godliness. This is the worst kind of fallacy and subverts the dependence that we should and must have upon our God in order to have a meaningful relationship with Him. Believe me when I state that anyone who believes in their own strength or ability to resist temptation is opening the door to their own downfall, and here again is another reason for the failure of the church. Just look at the recent history of the church. Pastors of every denomination who have sexually abused children. Church leaders practicing homosexuality. Theft and misuse of church funds. Even worse, the ignoring of these acts by those responsible. How can anyone say or even think that the "chosen" can persevere, when the sad fact is that no one can persevere on their own? Even as I am writing this book, a well known local evangelist has been indicted for several instances of child molestation. So what are we to do?

You probably realize that I like to use myself as an example. In my younger days, I pictured myself as invincible. I was young, smart, athletic and egotistical. I boxed and swam for the U.S. Army (Germany) swim team, and if I was only half as great as I thought I was, I would have been wearing a cape and blue tights.

When we are young, it's OK to think this way, but God has many ways to bring us to our senses, and then those of us that are smart enough can see ourselves for what we really are. As I indicated earlier, God gives each of us the choice of allowing Him into our lives. The problem is that some of us (me) are too dense to listen until God grinds our noses into the dirt.

The first thing that I had to realize as I brought God into my life was that I really didn't have *any* power, and I certainly wasn't in control of anything, least of all my own life. This was a painful revelation at first, but after I learned to accept this new knowledge, it began to give me great pleasure. I had thought that I was in control of my own destiny for most of my life, but as I looked back, I began to recognize that I had spent most of my life in a state of frustration and anger simply because I couldn't control anything. However, I had steadfastly refused to recognize that fact, and as I see frustrated and angry people today, I can instantly recognize the reason(s) for their frustrations, and I see myself as I was before I allowed God to be in charge. "Road Rage" happens to be one of the popular terms of the day to describe people who aren't really angry at other drivers; they are really angry and frustrated at themselves for not being able to be in control of their own lives. What these people are failing to realize (just as I did) is that no person in this world can ever be in control **of anything.**

The point that I want to make here is this: If I can't control *anything*, how am I going to be able to "persevere" in the Godly life without help? It is impossible, that is without the daily help of God Himself in the form of the Holy Spirit. The Holy Spirit is, after life itself, and after the sacrifice of Jesus, the greatest gift that God has ever given mankind. The Holy Spirit is nothing less than God the Father within each of us, yet so few Christians recognize that gift. The Holy Spirit, that forgotten and much ignored third member of the Trinity, is the one part of our

God that actually lives within us and is available to us at any time.

The fact that the Holy Spirit is misunderstood and ignored was brought home to me when I led a prayer at a Baptist service after I had talked about a summer New Testament reading program. My prayer began like this: "Holy Spirit we ask you to guide us and teach us as we read the New Testament...." I finished the prayer and was followed to the podium by our assistant pastor who, before I was even seated, made the statement, "Jesus is the God that we worship!" I sat down and thought to myself, "What ignorance, and from a man who has graduated from divinity school. What are they teaching?" Here was an assistant pastor of a Baptist church, a divinity school graduate, who had no idea of the fact that the Holy Spirit is the presence of God with us.

FAILURE!

If you learn nothing else from this book, then learn this one fact. God recognizes each of us as weak and unable to control our lives, because that is the way that He created us. Think about it for a second. If we could control our own lives, then why would we need or even want a relationship with God? Yes, we are weak. Yes, we succumb to temptation. Yes, we make wrong decisions, and our great God created us with this built in weakness so that we would *need* His strength. After all, why did God create us in the first place? He wanted our companionship, our love and, yes, even our dependence. Read this carefully. God **wants us** to use His strength, not our own. Our God did not intend to create other Gods (although that is what some of us consider ourselves), and, on the other hand, God did not intend to create little automatons who could not think for themselves.

God, contrary to Calvinist dogma, created humans who could think and make decisions, even if those decisions were wrong. Why? The answer is this. God wanted to know who would make the right decision, and those are His "chosen people." You see, God allows us to make the choice. He even allows us to make the wrong choice. I don't know about you, but that is the kind of God that I want. I don't want a God that is so insecure that He can't allow us to have options. Have you ever seen an insecure person in a relationship? How do they act? For starters, they don't allow their "significant other" to have *any* freedom. They watch that person every minute and their relationship is totally devoid of trust. Those kinds of relationships never last and that is not the kind of relationship that God wants for us. Remember, Jesus Christ was Himself tempted so that He could come to the aid of us, who are also tempted. Does that sound like Calvinism?

So far, I have discussed Calvinism and the five points known by the acronym TULIP, which serve to explain this misplaced dogma. My arguments have originated strictly from common sense as derived from knowledge of our great, kind and loving God. Now it is time to take a look at what the Bible says about whether a person who considers himself "saved" can be in danger of falling away from that state of "salvation." The Bible states: *"For if we go on sinning willfully after receiving the knowledge of the truth, there no longer remains a sacrifice for sins."* This passage is quite clear in refuting Calvinism, because, first of all, it recognizes that all men have *free will* when it refers to "sinning willfully." This obviously recognizes that each of us has the ability to make the choice of whether we will sin or not. I am not talking about *strength* here, because not one of us has the *strength* to resist sinning. I am talking about the choice of whether to continue living in sin or choosing to use the strength of the Holy Spirit to resist our previous lifestyle. In my own case, my lifestyle did not change overnight. It took years of walking with the Holy Spirit and in His strength to change not only my lifestyle but my entire outlook on life itself.

This passage also clearly recognizes that there can be only **one** sacrifice for sins, the sacrifice of the Son of God dying upon the cross, and if we continue *"willingly"* in sin, then we have thrown away that sacrifice. The operative word here is *willingly*, and we must recognize that it is the word that defines the entire meaning of the passage. From the previous discussion, most readers will agree that God gave all of us what is called "free will." This so-called "free will" is what defines us as human beings, and it also gives us the ability to accept or reject the knowledge of God or anything else in our world; and it also gives us the choice of how we will live our lives. In other words, we can choose to obey traffic signs and stop lights, or we can choose to live in disobedience, but we had better be ready to pay the consequences. Did you understand the last part of that sentence? Just like the passage cited above, we can choose to obey God's law or we can choose to disobey God's law. Which will it be for you?

Let us go back to that Bible verse one more time: "***For if we go on sinning willfully after receiving the knowledge of the truth, there no longer remains a sacrifice for sins.***" Let's dissect this sentence so that we can understand exactly what is being said. The sentence contains three distinct phrases and they are: 1. For if we go on sinning willfully, 2. after receiving the knowledge of truth, and 3. there no longer remains a sacrifice for sins.

As I stated earlier, the key word in the sentence is the word "willingly," and it serves to forever separate "willful" sin, or sin by choice, from what I would term "inadvertent" or accidental sin. Obviously we all sin accidentally every day and even hundreds of times in a day when we get frustrated, impatient, angry, hurtful, etc., but this is not the type of sin that the Bible is talking about. Don't forget (as the Calvinists have) that our loving God did not intend for us to be perfect at all times and in every way. If we were perfect then we would be Gods ourselves, and that is not what our God intended. Instead, God, in His supreme wisdom, allowed us to be (a lot) less than perfect so that we would look to Him, as a child looks to its father and mother for guidance, love, help and encouragement. If you think seriously about that concept for a minute, you will begin to understand just how wonderful it is.

The world we live in has always been a dangerous and complex place well beyond the understanding of even the most sophisticated intellectual. Dangers of which we are not even aware face us every day. How can anyone know whether or not the automobile coming toward them at 60 miles per hour is driven by a drunk who has just fallen asleep? How can anyone know that the airliner which they are boarding was or was not maintained properly, causing an engine to fall off as it begins its flight? Before I deviate too much from the point that I am trying to get across, the word "willingly" carries so much weight because God has given us the intelligence and the ability to make decisions and to recognize right from wrong. Even Hitler in the 1930's and Saddam Hussein in the 1990's had the capacity to recognize right from wrong, and each of them made the calculated decision that ultimate power was to be their "God." They made their decisions, and each one of us has to make our decision.

The second phrase of this Bible passage, "after receiving the knowledge of truth," is a conditional statement, similar to those found (at least implicitly) in most Biblical promises, and refers to our knowledge, and necessarily, of our acceptance of Jesus Christ and His sacrifice for us. Most Christians will remember another passage that states, "The truth shall set you free." And the "truth" referenced by both passages is the fact of the sacrifice of the One whom we call Our Lord, as He died to free us from our sins. So what does this phrase tell us? This part of the sentence tells us very specifically that when we have accepted the "truth" of Jesus Christ into our hearts and lives, that we must now make a decision and begin a new life. Is this tough? Yes, and perhaps that is why so many Christians and the church itself choose to ignore this teaching in their misguided efforts to "collect" converts. After all, who wants to join an organization that is going to make impossible demands? Are these demands really impossible for us? The answer is YES, but if you think about it, this is not a bad thing and turns out to be one of the greatest parts of God's magnificent plan.

Yes, I can see the person who is asking the question: "If God's demands are impossible for us to meet or achieve, how can we ever hope to succeed?" In answer, I will explain something that took me five years to recognize. It is impossible for me (or you) to change your life.

The analogy I like to use is the fact that it is impossible for a tiger to change its stripes. In the same way, it is impossible for me to change my life into something acceptable to God. So what to do? Pay attention now. Here is the best part of all about this great and wonderful God of ours. You see, He already knows that we are too weak, troubled, tempted, etc. to ever be able to change our lives, and He has the solution immediately available. That solution is called the Holy Spirit, yet most Christians refuse to recognize the Holy Spirit as reality. So how do we get this "holy being" to help us? Again, let me tell you how, from my own experience.

When I first came to Christ, I was as bad as or worse than most people. I had failed in every facet of my life. I hadn't been a good husband or a good father. To be honest, I wasn't good at anything, but like most humans, I refused to recognize the facts. How in the world God came to choose me is still, to this day, beyond my comprehension. After I took Christ as my Savior, I continued to live as I had before, but something began to happen. I began to receive thoughts that certain things within my lifestyle were no longer acceptable to God. Of course, I resisted those thoughts, but gradually I began to try to change. What I soon found out was that changing my life was impossible! Had I reached a dead end? An impasse? Listen closely now. Yes, I had reached a dead end, **if I continued to try to change on my own,** and this is the point where most Christians fail and where the Church continues to fail.

You will remember my telling you earlier that when I decided to become a Christian, I took it seriously, and I began reading the Bible. When I started reading, I had no idea that this one book would become such a tool in my life, and how it would become the direct road to a relationship with God's Holy Spirit. As I fought my daily battles with anger, frustration, and temptation, I began to realize that I just wasn't going to be able to succeed. I also came to recognize something else, something much more profound. I began to realize that whenever I took even a few minutes to read the Bible, I no longer felt the tribulations of the world. Gradually, I began to *use* the Bible as a tool whenever life, or my desires, became more than I could handle. No matter how angry, frustrated or tempted I was, it usually took less than five minutes of reading to bring me to a state of calm and peace in which I knew for certain that I was within the presence of God and He without a doubt was holding me in His hands, strengthening me, calming me, protecting me. What a wonderful feeling. Try it, and you won't be disappointed if you will just let go and let His Holy Spirit into your subconscious.

Are you getting the picture? Neither you nor I can change our lives. Not one of us can become the person that God wants us to be. We cannot change **BUT** (to coin a phrase) we can *be* changed, by our loving, ever caring God, if we will just give Him a chance to talk to us. The best way to let God talk to us is by reading His word. Having troubles in your life? Read the book! Having temptations in your life? Read the book! Problems in your marriage? Read the book. Yes, I am not lying or exaggerating. It really is as easy as that. Let me take a moment here to laugh at myself, because a Christian lady recently told me that I was "way over the top," and she now refuses to even talk to me. Is she correct?

Yes, without a doubt, I am the most "over the top" person that I know, and you can be too. I look back at my life of 51 years, and there is no way that I would ever go back (to the world). I am happier than I have ever been. I have a peace that I never knew existed. I can resist every temptation, through the strength of the Holy Spirit. I have even surpassed that supreme deity of all philosophers, Alfred A. Neumann (What Me Worry?).

Have you received that "knowledge of truth"? The knowledge that the Son of God willingly died for **all** the sins that you committed in your past life. But are you having trouble taking the next step, stopping the continuation of those sins? Keep this in mind. Neither you nor anyone else has the strength to resist sin, but God's Holy Spirit is a real entity whose sole purpose is to provide the power to change your life and provide a direct communication link to God Himself. I just have one last statement to make on this subject and that is to the point of anyone who thinks that he is being tempted by Satan: **forget it.** Satan was defeated when Christ died for our sins. Any temptation that we feel is strictly from our own desires, regardless of what Flip Wilson said. (Good old Flip; he was one of the great comedians of our time) If you are having problems, forget about playing the "blame game." A person's problems are caused by themselves and can only be solved by dependence upon the Holy Spirit.

It took long enough for me to get here, but we have now arrived at the point where we are able to analyze the last phrase of our chosen Bible passage. To refresh your memory (if it is as short as mine), let's review the entire sentence, *"**For if we go on sinning willfully after receiving the knowledge of the truth, there no longer remains a sacrifice for sins.**"* This phrase makes a powerful, and the church would have us believe, untrue statement.

Obviously the "sacrifice for sins" referred to here is the death of Jesus Christ upon the cross. Keep in mind that the purpose of Jesus' sacrifice was to cleanse us of our sins. If that sacrifice no longer applies, then someone is in a heap of trouble. So why would the church try to have us believe patently false doctrine? There are several reasons, they want your membership (the numbers game), they want your finances (the money game), they want your allegiance, (so they give you an easy lifestyle where you don't have to give up anything) and they (the church) want control of the world. By the way, this is as true for the Muslim religion as for the Christian, as anyone can see by watching the news. Even the Jews want control of the Holy Land over the Palestinians. But what is especially sad about that situation, is that they were *given total control* only to have it taken away when they refused to worship God? Here is a question for you: Will the United States eventually lose its leadership role because the Christian faith refuses to recognize the Word of God?

The bottom line is this. If you recognize the Son of God as your savior, then you had better change your lifestyle, because you are going to be kneeling in front of Him at the final judgment.

If that example was not enough to convince the most hardened Calvinist, then let's look at another passage. This example will consist of three verses and gives an even clearer picture as to its intent: "*It is impossible for those who have once been enlightened, who have tasted the heavenly gift, who have shared in the Holy Spirit, who have tasted the goodness of the Word of God and the powers of the coming age, if they fall away, to be brought back to repentance, because to their loss they are crucifying the Son of God all over again and subjecting Him to public disgrace.*" Notice the words, "if they fall away," because that is the key phrase and the subject of the three verses. Why has the church failed to teach the truth? It could be that they just might have to get rid of some of the wealthiest deacons, and no one would want that. Personally, I feel that the primary reason is that the church leaders are afraid that not one of their members (or their clergy) would stick around if they felt that they had to travel the "narrow road." Is the narrow road easy? Yes, and no. If you try to travel the narrow road by yourself, it is totally impossible, but utilizing the power and strength of the Holy Spirit, the road is easy.

I once belonged to a church where the assistant pastor was caught in a motel room with a parishioner. Was he traveling the narrow road? Somehow, I don't think so, and he is going to have to pay a heavy price. We all know the names of Jim Jones, Jim Bakker and others who prostituted the Holy name of God for their own greed and gratification. Ask yourself this question: "How many potential Christians have these people forever turned away from salvation?" I promise you, their price will be heavy.

Let me paraphrase one last verse in the words of Jesus Himself when He said that there will be many that have called my name, yet I will say that I do not know you. Will Jesus know your name at the proper time? Or will He turn away? Following the Christian way is truly easy. Even Jesus said, *"My way is easy and My burden is light."*

Don't allow anyone to tell you that you are worthless. God did not create the human race as "totally depraved." God does not arbitrarily pick and choose the person that He will save and the person that He will cast into eternal damnation. That is our choice. You had the choice to read this book or not to read it. Never allow an organization to control you, whether through fear or through the promise of an easy life.

The church continues to teach that we, who were created by God Himself, are totally depraved, totally unworthy and totally worthless. My question to the church is this: "How can anything created by our great God be considered any one of these things?" Is it any wonder people have trouble believing in, or, more importantly, loving a God who creates depraved, worthless and totally unworthy creations? Everyone has at one time or another seen "art" that should never have been created. As you looked at this "art," what did you think of the artist? Did you respect that person? Did you think to yourself that this artist really had talent? Did you think that maybe he just had a bad day? No, the answer is that you not only rejected this particular piece of work, you were in no way even interested in seeing anything else that the artist had created.

The teaching of the "total depravity" of the human race works the same way. As we begin to believe that we are totally worthless, we cannot help but believe that everyone else is also "totally depraved" and therefore worthless also. Because we cannot love and respect ourselves, we cannot even for a minute hope to love and respect another member of the human race, and by default, we can never hope to truly love and respect the God that created this "mess." No wonder so many self professed "Christians" continue living in sin. They feel that there is no hope, so why bother. No wonder so many "Christians" are so nasty and hateful. They can't love themselves, so how can they love anyone else? The stain of Calvinism has permeated the whole fiber of the church, and it will take years to remove that stain so that Christians can begin living the life that Christ intended.

The church has got to stop teaching this utterly false doctrine and begin teaching the true fact that God has chosen every one of us who are His creation to be blessed and fulfilled in this human existence. God loves every one of us, but it is our decision and our choice to recognize that He (as God) in fact does exist. This is the first choice (but not the last) that our loving God gives His people. There is a long road of choices that we are given as we proceed from childhood to maturity, and this journey of choices, as I call it, will be covered in a later chapter.

4

WHO *REALLY* KILLED JESUS?

The person (yes, I can call Him that, for during His time with us, He was a mortal man) that Christians everywhere call their Lord and Savior, died by crucifixion almost two thousand years ago. Since that time when He hung upon a cross, uneducated and misinformed people have been searching for a scapegoat to blame for Jesus' death. Ever since the time of the very first Pope, Christians have blamed the Jews for Jesus' "murder," and I think that it is time to put the record straight. For almost two thousand years, pogroms, hatred, murder, genocide, discrimination and you name it have been committed against the Jewish race, all in the name of blame for the death of Jesus Christ.

Once again, the Christian Church has failed in its duty to educate those members of its own congregations about who was truly responsible for the death of this man that we call our Savior, so let's take a short look at the time surrounding Jesus' death. This is the shortest chapter of this book because the answer is so obvious that it is not going to take a detailed explanation. First of all, two things are patently obvious: 1. The death of Jesus Christ was the single most important act that has taken place since the original formation of the world we live on, and 2. Jesus' death was the greatest gift to humankind of all time and should be recognized as the gift that it is. If Jesus' death *was* a gift, and we insist upon blaming the Jews, then why isn't every living Christian walking around *THANKING* the Jews for enabling this wonderful gift to be given instead of trying to fix blame?

Why should we consider the death of our Lord and Savior a gift? The answer should be obvious; however, the church again has ignored the intent of God the Father, because without the death of God's only Son, Jesus Christ, we would not and could not have forgiveness for our sins. Therefore, it is obvious that Jesus' death was not only a gift; it was the supreme gift and the greatest gift of all time.

The answer, of course, is the fact that people are not really concerned about Jesus' death so much as they are concerned with envy and greed toward a people whose work ethic has brought them wealth and power. After all, wealth and power (and control) seem to be what everybody from the Pope to Pat Robertson to Jesse Jackson really wants.

If we are going to assign blame for the death of Jesus, then we must discover how that death was accomplished. Of course, we know that Jesus died by being nailed to a cross, but that doesn't explain how He got there in the first place. My point is this: If someone, a person, an organization, a government, wants to take the life of any human being, it must be in possession of two attributes. The first is "power," and for the sake of this discussion, the definition of power will be simply the physical ability to overcome the intended victim and so end their lives. Just so you, the reader, understand, "power" is easy to obtain. A gun, a knife, a club, overpowering numbers, or even simple strategy can result in the death of even the strongest person; but let's move on to something much more difficult to obtain, "authority."

Even a government (unless it operates outside societal laws) must acquire the authority necessary to eliminate a person, as evidenced by the fact that when a policeman, in the line of duty, shoots an alleged lawbreaker, that policeman is removed from active duty until valid authority has been established through a review of the circumstances. Furthermore, if the action taken by the policeman cannot be justified, authority will not be granted and the policemen themselves will be prosecuted for a criminal act. Here in the United States, even the President does not automatically have the authority to "remove" even the worst madman.

All right, let's return to the time of Jesus, but take a moment to reflect upon the fact that times have not really changed. No matter what period of history we consider, any nation must have established both the power and the authority before an act can be safely accomplished. Certainly, "authority" can be accomplished through raw power, and many examples of this have taken place including the rampages of Genghis Kahn and the conquest of the civilized world by the Roman Empire. But my point is this: The Jews of Jesus' time had neither the power nor the authority to murder Jesus Christ.

As a matter of fact, the Jews of Jesus' time didn't have either the power or the authority to do *anything.* The Jews of Jesus' time were an enslaved people who were totally subservient to the Roman Empire. The Jews were governed by the Romans, they were occupied by the Roman Legions, they were forced to pay taxes to the Romans and they had to obey Roman laws. In short, the Jews had absolutely no power and no authority. They had lost everything from their country to their government to their right of free speech, and, needless to say, they weren't happy about it.

The status of the State of Israel (i.e. enslaved by the Romans) is the primary reason that the Jews could not accept Jesus. They wanted a military messiah riding a white charger who would lead them into battle to regain their leadership of the world, but that wasn't going to happen. Anyone who has read the Old Testament knows the reason why the Jews lost their land, their leadership and even their freedom. The only organization (toothless as it was) that the Jews had left was the "church," (their Temple) and the Temple controlled the life of every Jew. Why did the Romans allow the Jews to continue to worship as they wished? It was a matter of practicality, because when the Jews were allowed to practice their religion, there was less reason to try to overthrow the Roman government, and I suspect that there was no small matter of collusion between the Roman government and the Temple authorities.

I grant you the fact that the leaders of the Temple *wanted* Jesus dead, because this man was, if left unchecked, about to change everything. The problem here is the fact that *wanting* someone dead is totally different from having both the power and the authority to accomplish the act and get away with it. We must remember that Roman law was totally different from Jewish law where a man could be stoned to death if he "looked" guilty. Roman law was very strict about allowing a fair and (for those times) impartial hearing and the Jews had no choice but to obey Roman law. Why else would the rulers of the Temple have brought Jesus before Pontius Pilate? Simply because they did not have the authority to put Him to death.

So if the Jews, who wanted Jesus dead, did not have either the power or the authority to do the job, who *did* have both the required power and authority to murder the declared Son of God? The Romans? Sorry, wrong again. But wait a minute, the Romans were the conquerors; they controlled everything. They ruled the entire civilized world. Am I saying that they did not have the power and the authority to crucify Jesus? That is exactly what I am saying, and to prove it let's go back to a statement that Jesus made to His disciples.

Jesus told His disciples that if He wished He could call twelve "legions" of angels to protect Him. Consider that statement for a moment. The footnote of my Bible tells me that one legion contained 6,000 soldiers; so if Jesus could call upon twelve legions of angels. He then had 72,000 angels at His disposal. How powerful is an army of angels? Well, consider the fact that only ONE angel killed 185,000 of the world's greatest fighting men in JUST ONE NIGHT. Given the ability of just one angel, a little simple mathematics will show that those 72,000 angels could have wiped out the entire population of the Roman Empire.

O.K. It has been established that the Romans, despite their magnificent army, did not have the power to kill Jesus, but how about the authority? Think about it and you will realize that the Romans didn't have that either. After all, who has the authority to kill the Son of God, because after all, who has authority *over* God? No one that I know!

So far we have established two facts. The first is that the Jews could not have killed Jesus because they had neither the power to do so, nor did they have the authority to commit such an act. Yes, the temple leaders wanted Him dead in the worst way, but they just couldn't accomplish the fact; so they went to the Roman court. The Roman court was indeed the law of the land at the time, but when we think about it, it's clear they didn't have the necessary requisites either. Yes, the Roman army had conquered the entire civilized world, but they had not yet conquered the Heavens (thank God). So the question remains: Who had the authority to crucify Jesus? I know that somewhere someone will cry out, "Satan did it!" But they will also be incorrect because even Satan is subject to God's authority, and if you don't believe that, read the Book of Job in the Old Testament.

Since no one on earth or in Heaven above has authority over God's only Son except God Himself, we have the answer as to who "killed" Jesus. I use quotation marks around the word killed, and you will understand why in a moment. Yes, God "killed" Jesus by allowing Him to be killed through the act called Crucifixion, i.e. being nailed to a cross so as to fulfill the prophecies of old, and that act is the single greatest act of love of all time. An act of *love?* Absolutely! Let me repeat myself. The death of God's Son, as allowed by God Himself, was the greatest act of love of all time, because God, years earlier, had shown us the precursor to Jesus' death through the story of Abraham.

Most of you remember the story of Abraham and his wife, Sarah, who were childless for many years and how they prayed to be given a child. Finally, their prayers were answered and Sarah delivered a son to the elderly couple. As the boy grew into a fine young teenager, God made a seemingly strange request of Abraham. God demanded that Abraham sacrifice this young man who was so loved and cherished by his elderly parents. But let me take you to the critical part of the story. Abraham has built an altar to God, he places his only son upon that altar and, as he is about to slay Isaac, God stays his hand.

Let's examine that exact instant as Abraham's knife is raised. What is going through Abraham's mind? There is anguish, of course, at the thought of losing his only son, but what else? The overriding feeling going through Abraham's mind is *LOVE!* First, there is love for his only son for whom he waited so long, but there is also an overwhelming love for this God who has granted his every wish. Yes, there is an overwhelming love and trust running through Abraham's very core being; but look for a moment at the direction of the love, because it is very important.

The direction of this love goes from Abraham to his God. Abraham, at that very moment is proving to his God that his love for his God overrides his love for anything or anyone on this earth, including his family. Is that powerful or what? Now, fast forward several hundred years and listen to Jesus as He tells us that we must love God over even our families. The Bible translates the Greek into the word "hate," seeming to mean that we must "hate" our families; however, the true meaning is that the love for our families will *seem* as hate only when compared to our love for our God.

Sadly, again, the church (at least *my* church) has failed to teach another one of God's most important lessons, and that lesson is that our love and trust for this entity that we so loosely and easily call our God must be an *overwhelming* love. The love for God must overcome and overwhelm EVERYTHING else.

We have now finally reached the point where we can examine the exact moment that our Christ is hung upon the cross. Let's look directly into the face of God at this important moment. What do we see? Sadness? No. Does our God have to turn away as is preached from most Christian pulpits? No. God never has to turn away from anything, because what we will see in the face of our almighty God is nothing less than the mightiest love that the world has ever known. A love so powerful that Satan is forever defeated in one mighty stroke. A love – an overwhelming love – for us, His most loved creation.

Look closely now at the direction of this love. In the story of Abraham, the love flowed from Abraham to his God. In the story of Jesus Christ, God's love flows to His people. How beautiful. As I write these words, I am overcome with joy. As I write these words, I have a warmth that I know is from God's Holy Spirit. As I write these words, I pray that when you read these words you will feel the love that God has in His heart for us, a love so great that He *SACRIFICED* His only Son just as Abraham offered to do.

That most favorite Bible verse of all Christians comes to mind, John 3:16. **"For God so loved the world that He gave His only Son that whosoever believe in Him shall not perish but have everlasting life."** I humbly propose one small change to that verse, and I believe that it should read like this: "For God so loved the world that He *sacrificed* His only Son…"

Yes, God sacrificed His only Son because no one else could do it. No one else had the power. No one else had the authority. Yes, there were those, the leaders of the church of the time, who wanted Him dead because He was interfering with their agenda of control, and that is exactly what would happen if Jesus were to return to earth today. His message of love, humility, sacrifice and servitude would be rejected by the leaders of today's Christian churches because He would refuse to run for President.

As I write this book, I repeatedly admonish the reader to pick up the Bible and read it. Why? Because only by reading the Word of God will any person be able to discover for themselves the overwhelming love of God, and His intentions for this world that He has created. By reading the Bible in a humble frame of mind, and under the guidance of the Holy Spirit, anyone can discover the beauty of our creation and our salvation under the plan of our loving God. Stop right now and read the story of Abraham in the Book of Genesis. You will see the finest example of one man's love and trust of Almighty God.

As I close this chapter, let me make one thing clear, and let there be no doubts about what I am going to say. God, in all of time, only asked one other man to demonstrate his love and trust by murdering his child, and even then that murder was stayed by God Himself and not allowed to happen. That request will never be made again because it doesn't need to. The example of sacrifice has been demonstrated for all time through Abraham as a precursor for the death upon the cross of Jesus Christ. Let no parents think that they are demonstrating love for God by hurting any child, because I promise you that God's wrath will be swift and horrible to bear.

5

THE GREATEST OF ALL COMMANDMENTS!

The subject of this chapter is pertinent to the Christian world today, because as I write these words, the Supreme Court has agreed to hear a case involving the placement of what we know as the Ten Commandments in a government building. If anything can be considered a "hot button" issue in Christianity in America today, it is the issue of allowing, or even forcing, the Ten Commandments to be displayed in public. Christians seem to feel that removing the Ten Commandments from public display in a government building is tantamount to introducing Devil worship into our churches, yet not one in one hundred Christians can identify those same Ten Commandments and undoubtedly fewer than that obey them.

While the facts of the previous paragraph give cause for sadness, the real travesty involving the failure of the entire Christian religion rests with the fact that the church ignores the most important Commandment of all. As a matter of fact, the church even refuses to recognize the specific words of their (supposed) leader as a commandment, despite the fact that this same leader, Jesus, was very specific in identifying His charge and this particular teaching as a commandment.

You will have noticed that I rarely identify the location of specific Biblical verses which I reference, and the reason is that I want the readers to become curious enough to read the Bible and especially the New Testament for themselves. However, in this case, these two verses are so important to the success of Christianity that I am forced to identify them so that their importance will be recognized by everyone, and even more importantly, this chapter will attempt to change the entire paradigm of the Christian church as we know it today. The verses are John 13:34 and John 13:35. The translation of the Bible that I choose to use is The New American Standard Bible, and the reason that I want to use this particular translation is that the NASB is purported to be the most accurate and the most literal of all the translations from the original Koine Greek.

Please be aware while reading this chapter that I have not picked out some obscure passage nor am I trying to skewer the church for not following its dictates. I am identifying what is the most important single teaching that Jesus Christ ever gave. Not only did Jesus give a particular and very specific instruction, He, contrary to most of His teachings, gave us the specific and important reason why He wanted it followed. Within these two simple-to-understand verses can be found almost the total source for the failure of the Christian Church.

The scene is the Last Supper, and everyone can agree that this moment is one of the most important occasions in Jesus' short ministry. We will begin at the point where the meal has ended and Jesus is talking to His disciples. He knows that His crucifixion is imminent, and He has chosen this time and place to announce His departure, but He wants to pass along the one final (and certainly the most important) element of His three years of teaching, one which He knows will define what we identify as the "Christian" religion. In verse 34 Jesus states emphatically: *"A new commandment I give to you, that you love one another, even as I have loved you, that you also love one another."*

This is without a doubt a declarative sentence in the strongest sense, but pay particular attention to what Jesus has defined as the subject of His declaration. "Commandment" is the word that Jesus chooses, and "commandment" becomes the subject of His sentence. Notice carefully that Jesus does not place Himself first in the order of the sentence. He does not say, "I" give you a commandment; He specifically places Himself second, and therefore He relinquishes His own importance to the fact that this "commandment" is of primary importance within the context of the declaration. You will have noticed that I do not capitalize the word "commandment" because it is not capitalized in the original sentence.

This emphasis upon the word "commandment," the subject of the sentence, is worthy of our consideration, since Jesus Christ is recognized as the founder, leader, teacher and the Son of God by the Christian Church. If we, as Christians, are to recognize Jesus as the Son of our God, and of primary importance to our religion, shouldn't we also recognize His teaching as the foundation of our faith? What is troubling to me is the fact that while we recognize Jesus as the Son of God and God in His own right, we refuse to accept His teaching unless it suits our needs. Here, in this moment of time, almost immediately prior to His crucifixion, Jesus is handing those of us who choose to follow Him the **KEY** to the establishment and the identification of the Christian faith; and yet we choose to ignore His words, or at the very least the *importance* of those words, because we refuse to give those words the priority that Jesus placed upon them and that they deserve.

The Christian faith, even from the earliest time of the establishment of the formal church has refused to recognize the fact that a new Commandment has been given. Why? Should Jesus have made a trip to Mt. Sinai and carved a new tablet of stone which would then have been handed to Peter to carry down and be read before the other disciples? Is that what must happen before we can recognize a Commandment? The rational answer is, of course, NO; but that is what the leaders of the earliest church seemed to think, and that paradigm continues today.

It sometimes seems to me that the Christians of our generation have become exactly like the Jews of the Old Testament. You see, the original Ten Commandments of the Old Testament were given specifically because the Jews were a "perverse and unbelieving people," *Jesus' words, not mine.* Note also the fact that the original Ten Commandments would seem to be self evident to any God-fearing Jew of that or any other time; yet God felt it necessary to bind them to the hearts of the people by formalizing them as "Laws" because He knew that every one of His Commandments would be broken.

We Christians of these "modern times" have become exactly like the Jews of old in that while we "hear with our ears (and see with our eyes) yet we do not believe." I have sat through sermon after sermon on the subject of the *TEN COMMANDMENTS*, yet I have never once heard even one sermon or discussion about the one commandment that Jesus himself gave us. I ask every church leader and every Christian this question: If you recognize Jesus Christ as the head of your church, and if you recognize Jesus Christ as the head of your life, and if you recognize Jesus Christ as God Himself, why can you not and/or why do you not recognize the Commandment that He specifically gave immediately prior to His death? After all, the next sentence that our Lord uttered gave the very reason why this Commandment is so important. *"By this all men will know that you are My disciples, if you have love for one another."*

FAILURE!

The title of this book is FAILURE. The preceding paragraphs describe the primary reason why the Church has failed. If there were no other reason for the failure of the church (and the failure of each of us as Christians) it would be reason enough that we have *failed* to recognize not only the one commandment that the Head of our church gave, but we have also failed to recognize the only sign that Jesus gave us that will enable all men to *recognize* us for what we claim to be: "Christians." Is it any wonder that people all over the world fail to recognize Jesus Christ? It is because they cannot recognize us as His disciples. You see, Jesus Himself gave us the key not only to being His disciples; He also gave us the key by which everyone else can recognize Him.

Hanging on my refrigerator door is a scrap of paper. It has been hanging there for ten years, and at least once a week my eye falls on it and I say Wow!, how true. The first sentence of that scrap of paper says this: "The other day I heard the song, 'You're the Only Jesus Some Will Ever See.'" My question is this, How can you be Jesus Christ (or His representative) when you are only concerned about yourself? Have you had a conversation with a self-styled "Christian" lately? The subject of the conversation was probably about electing some official or paying fewer taxes or complaining that the world is going to the dogs or about abortion or about their latest aches and pains or why the U.S. should or shouldn't go to war.

Speaking of going to war, this book is being written as a war rages in Iraq and thousands of young people and innocent civilians are being maimed and killed. It is really too bad that Christians in the United States no longer believe in God, because if we did, we wouldn't need all of those troops, tanks, jet fighters, ships, missiles and on and on. How can I say that? Do you believe the Bible? If you do, then read about a man named Gideon. Yes, you remember him; he is the one that puts all those Bibles in your motel room. Just kidding. Gideon was the youngest son of the least respected family in Manasseh when the Lord called him to serve, and this young Gideon defeated a people described as "innumerable" and "like locusts for number" with only three hundred men and, get this, NO WEAPONS. Of course, if you want to count water pitchers as weapons, then you can describe them as well armed, for they each carried a pitcher and a torch.

One of the more interesting facets of the story of Gideon is the fact that he had recruited about 33,000 fighters, but the Lord allowed him to "do battle" with only 300 men. I ask you Mr. or Ms. Christian, is your God dead? Is He asleep? Is He senile? Could it be that you just do not believe in Him, or is the real problem that you don't really even believe that there is a God and you are just hedging your bets regarding death? By the way, before I go back to my original subject, the story of Gideon can be found in the Book of Judges, but don't worry, not five in one hundred readers of this book will bother to read it, and not even one in one hundred will believe it. It's as if many Christians think that the Old Testament is some kind of fairy tale.

Yes, I know the Old Testament is history, but a famous and intelligent man once said, "Those who do not know history are doomed to repeat it." Is America doomed to failure, just as the Jews failed to keep Israel, because they repeatedly strayed from believing in God? If I were a prophet (which I am not) I would predict that, yes, America will be conquered and we will lose our precious freedoms, but it won't be because of the people who do not recognize God. America's failure will be due to all the so-called Christians who believed in God with their mouths but not with their hearts, those same Christians who stand in Church and sing, *OUR GOD IS AN AWESOME GOD*, and then worry about who will be our next president.

Let me return to my subject. The verse is John 13:35, and Jesus has just told us how we are to be identified. ***"By this all men will know that you are my disciples, if you have love for one another."*** Jesus has just given us a new Commandment (which we refuse to recognize) and now He tells us that by this Commandment (only) we will be recognized as Christians. For those of you who are not aware of this fact, being or defining yourself as a Christian assumes that you are attempting to be a disciple of Jesus Christ. That is the definition of the Christian Faith – being a disciple or follower of the Son of God, the Messiah who died for us.

Let's look at this sentence closely (v35). The subject of the sentence is again the word "commandment," referring to the specific commandment which He has just given. By this commandment, "all men," the object of the sentence "will know that you are My disciples...," the objective of Jesus' entire time on earth. Do you see the importance of what Jesus has just stated? He has just defined in one simple sentence what we are to do if we are to call ourselves "Christians," and He has just defined, again, with one simple sentence how we "Christians" will be identified by the rest of all the people of the world.

Do you see it? If you do see it, you now have the key to Christianity in all its entirety. There is just one problem. If you see it, you can now see why the Church in all of its self-proclaimed glory has failed.

Allow me to tell you two stories. The first concerns the saddest thing that I have ever heard stated within the confines of a church. It happened in a Sunday school class, and the discussion was about the love of Jesus and how we should love our fellow man. Someone stood up and said, "I may have to love them but I don't have to like them." Does anyone understand the sadness and the failure of that statement? I think that anyone who understands the mechanism of the human mind and its inherent frailty would understand the fact that the person who made that statement has not only failed as a Christian, but has failed as a human being.

I am going to step up and make a bona fide, blanket, bottom line statement here, so listen closely: If people cannot bring themselves to even *like* other people, they have failed the entire reason for their existence. They have failed themselves and they have failed their God. Ask yourself this question: "Why were you put upon this earth?" Do you think that it was to become wealthy and have fun, or maybe you think that you were given life so that you could sing meaningless and worthless praises? Somehow, I don't think so. For those of you who refuse to recognize it, our (short) life on this earth is nothing more than a test, designed by God Himself to see if we are worthy or capable of handling the job that God has planned for us in the next life. I am not, repeat NOT, talking about reincarnation. Reincarnation (here on earth) does not exist. I am stating that God, during this life, gives us total freedom to choose whom we will serve and how we will act. I promise you that you will pay, or you will be rewarded, for the choice that you make.

The second story that I want to relate happened to me just last week, and while the story itself is straightforward, it gives a good example of how God works in our own, as well as others' lives. I have a friend whom I will call Bob (because Bob is easy to type on a keyboard). Bob is a genius! Bob could have a job doing anything, but Bob's entire life is a failure. Bob is one of those guys whose intellect I admire beyond belief. Bob can read and speak several languages, including Latin and Greek, and Bob has read the Bible in each of those languages because he wanted to understand exactly what was being told prior to a translator's input. The problem with Bob is that he just doesn't get it. You see, Christianity is so simple that Bob, like most other Christians, just can't understand what it is all about. Anyway, to continue my story, I got a collect call from a detention facility. Now, since I don't know anyone in jail, I hung up. They called back. This time, my curiosity was aroused and I listened to the operator (a recording) tell me what the call was going to cost, and in time a voice came on screaming, "Don't hang up. It's me, Bob. I need your help!"

Let me go back in time for a moment and explain. I have known Bob for twelve years and I have seen the conflicts in his life. We had just renewed our friendship a couple of months before, and I had been trying to explain to him how he could put his life together, but he couldn't understand my reasoning because my words were being blocked by his ego and his intellect. Have you ever met someone so intelligent that his own mind creates limitations on his reasoning powers? That is Bob. But you had better not underestimate the powers of God, because if He wants your attention, He will do whatever it takes to get it. (Sounds like my own story.) Anyway, God had grabbed Bob's attention by putting him in jail over Christmas with no way to get out.

Yes, when we don't pay attention, God will do what it takes. Make no mistake about that. Anyway, Bob needed $3,600 to get out of jail. I don't have a spare $3,600 lying around, do you? Of course not! It was the end of the fiscal year, December

27 to be exact, and I had set aside $3,000 to put in my IRA, and I had a few bucks left over to purchase some stock that I knew would be a winner when the economy picked up. Isn't it just like that darn God? Just when I have my life all together, He goes and throws a monkey wrench into the works, and I have to make a choice.

Want to be a true Christian? The choices that God brings into your life are what it's all about. You see, I had to choose whether my retirement here on this earth is important (and so build up my IRA) or whether my retirement with God is more important (forget the IRA for this year). I had to choose whether to follow the Commandment of Jesus and love my fellow man or follow my own greed. After all, it was Bob's own fault that he was in jail wasn't it? I certainly didn't have anything to do with this person's downfall. But wait a minute. Isn't this the very person whom I had been trying to teach about the ways of God, and the love of God? OH, FORGET IT. IF GOD WANTS HIM OUT OF JAIL, THEN HE CAN DO IT HIMSELF! God has all the power, right? Why doesn't He just open the jail doors like He did for Peter? (There is a good story, but you might have to read the New Testament and its all fiction anyway.) What is all this crap about love anyway? Does love mean going out of my way to help someone? I sure hope not. I don't want my cozy life disturbed. Does love mean spending some money that I have allocated for important stuff like my retirement? Does serving God mean serving my fellow man when he is crying for help? The answer is YES to all questions.

Listen closely. The only way that we can serve God is by serving our fellow man. What will my own choice be? I don't know about you, but I have to work hard for my money and I am not going to waste it. I know what every Christian reading this book is thinking right now: "If I 'loan' out this money will it be a waste? Will I get it back? Will this man finally listen to me? Will he come to know God? Will his life change?" Those questions are not my concern, and I am certainly not smart enough to figure them out. But let's take the time to address each one of those concerns because I know that someone is voicing them.

  First of all, forget about the word "loan." If you truly want to serve God by serving your fellow man, then put the word "give" into your vocabulary and forget about loaning anything. When you "loan" something, you are not "giving" anything. A loan must be repaid by the recipient; a gift may never be repaid (except by God Himself), but WOW how God pays. Secondly, quit wondering whether your gift will be wasted. That is God's concern. Remember God gives all of us total autonomy, and he does that so we can make our own decisions. Will this man decide to change his life? That is not my worry. I will be here when advice is needed, but I am not here to "force" anything, and I certainly can't "bring" someone to God. Only the Holy Spirit can do that; I am just the catalyst. Has this man repaid me? Well, as I write this, it has only been two weeks since the call, so I certainly would not expect it. Is God repaying me? I don't know, but my income over these last two weeks has more than doubled what I made last year. You tell me.

  O.K., I have given some money to a person to get him out of jail. Now what? Do I now "own" that person and now have the right to dictate their life? Here again is where most Christians will be mistaken, because they don't believe in God or God's power. Bob is now out of jail, but what is important for me to realize is that God has not stopped working in his life. The Holy Spirit is working with Bob every day, and I must not interfere. What I must do is continue to demonstrate my love for Bob by maintaining communication with him and just being there if and when he needs me. Notice the word "communication," because to most Christians "communication" means witnessing, and witnessing means talking when we should be just listening. Listening is without a doubt the most important thing that we can do, and listening is the *most* important, and sometimes the most powerful aspect of communication.

When we listen, we allow someone else to speak. When someone else speaks, their mind is working in an attempt to identify and resolve their own problems; plus we are now able to get an insight into their own thinking. Oh, what wonderful things could be accomplished if we Christians would just shut up and allow someone else to talk. Take a note here; if we would shut up, then maybe, just maybe, God could talk with us. Oh, just one more thing. When someone is talking to us, I promise you that God is talking to us.

I want to tell you another story, one that I read in an industry newspaper. The story is told by the manager of a health club and it struck me as a perfect example of how we are to love God's people. Now, I have no idea whether this health club manager is a Christian or not, but he is a lot closer to God than most of us who profess to be Christians. Let me tell the story and you decide. Late one evening, this club manager is in the process of closing for the day when an obviously overweight, middle aged woman tentatively *limps* through the door.

This lady looks like she is in unfamiliar surroundings and she obviously is not a candidate for a health club, but our club manager interrupts the closing process, shakes her hand, and asks her name. The lady replies, "My name is Doris, and I see that you are closing, so I will come back another time." Our manager, in a moment of intuition, senses that he will never have another chance to talk to this lady, so he tells her to go sit in his office where it is cool, and he will join her shortly and they can talk. Do you see the first "Christian" action that this manager has taken? He has put his personal desire to be home with his family second and he has put this lady first. Would you do that? Not me.

Our club manager speedily joins this lady in his office and as they talk, she starts crying. After giving her time to compose herself, he asks her to tell him about herself, and he learns that her husband has just died, her children are gone and she has gout, depression and is overweight. She doesn't even know whether she can get a job. Tell me Mr. or Ms. Christian, what would you do at this point? If you are a typical Christian, here is exactly what you would do. You would tell her about Jesus, give her a tract, pray with her and show her to the door so that you could get home before dinner got cold. On the way home you would be congratulating yourself on having a "witnessing opportunity," and you would be oh-so-smug in the warmth of making *yourself* feel good. Our manager was obviously not that kind of Christian, because he took the time to let her tell her story, then he took even more time to tell her how he and his club might help. Let me ask you a question. Do you think that God had a hand in bringing this lady to this club at just that moment? You had better believe it.

I am going to interrupt this story of the club manager for a minute to tell a short story about myself and my early years as a Christian. I was attending an evening church singles Bible study, and afterward a young man who had been in the class approached me and wanted to talk. This young man obviously wanted some advice but I was in a hurry and I gave him my phone number. Why was I in a hurry? I was meeting a lady, and I put myself and my worldly priorities first. To make a long story short, this young man never called, and TO THIS DAY, I remember that I wouldn't take the time to talk to someone who wanted help. Is this memory painful? The answer is YES. Here was a learning experience, and I will never make that mistake again. My point is twofold. First, even a sin can teach a lesson and make us better people in God's eyes; second, when someone needs your help, drop everything, because God is giving you an opportunity to serve Him through serving others.

To get back to the story of Doris and our club manager, they talked for two hours. WOW! I would like to meet this guy, because he knows what life is all about. This raises an interesting question, and I want to specifically address the wives here. Would you be angry if your husband came home two hours late because he was doing God's work? Be honest now, because this is important; if you consider yourself the Godly wife of a Godly man, then it is just as important to God's work that you put your own feelings and anxieties aside and let God's work get done. This works for both men and women, but one note of caution, don't allow yourself to get into a "temptation situation" where the intentions of doing good end up compromising God's credibility. Too many pastors have fallen into this trap. Why not call that wife/husband to join you and help with whatever problem is being addressed. Anyway, back to my story.

Our club manager, after spending some time with Doris had a revelation, which, although he doesn't say it, probably changed his life forever. Let me tell it in his own words, "At that moment, after more than a decade in the fitness industry, after managing three clubs, after selling thousands of memberships, I realized for the first time what I was doing in the business." What do you think it was that this man suddenly realized? Did he realize that the fitness industry changes lives? No, I don't think so, because he already knew that years ago.

What he recognized, as he was talking to a lady who was having big problems with her life, was that his purpose in life was helping people. Is this a huge revelation? You bet that it is. That revelation is so huge that most self-professed Christians still haven't gotten that message. Here is a man, who probably was not a Christian (I just don't know), yet he has learned that last and, in my opinion, greatest Commandment given by our Lord and Savior prior to His death on the Cross: *Love and serve your fellow man. (*My paraphrase). Why can't the church begin to recognize that Jesus tried to teach this one message above all others?

FAILURE!

What did Christ mean when He told His disciples to love one another? Did He mean for the disciples (only) to love each other (that is, the other disciples, only)? This seems to be what most churches are teaching and thereby sealing the fate of their own failure as followers of Christ. As a matter of fact, this is exactly what is being taught by a supposedly "Christian" university right here in Greenville, South Carolina.

I have heard several radio sermons in which the students and faculty of that university are admonished to "separate themselves" from anyone or any group that does not believe or practice their faith exactly as they do. What ignorance and what arrogance. Listen to this, because it is important and it is the foundation of the Christian faith – Jesus Christ never separated Himself from ANYONE. Jesus went out of His way to find unbelievers, both rich (the tax collector) and poor (the woman by the well). Should we do any different than the man to whom we owe our allegiance? I think not.

Why is the church of today failing? The answer is emphatic; it is because they are failing to teach their own believers how to emulate the life of their own professed Lord. Because of that one important failure, Christians everywhere compromise their own "witness" every day. Do you remember my telling you about the fact that when some businessman declares himself or herself to be "Christian," a red flag is immediately raised in my own mind, and I am far from being alone in that thought. To return to this supposed Christian university for a moment, the students of that university are so lacking in integrity that they were banned from my business for several years, because they would repeatedly make reservations and then not show up. Think about it, these are the very people who are walking around telling everyone else how to think and worship. Is this a sad commentary on the Christian religion? You bet.

Again, what did Jesus Christ mean when He told His disciples to *"love one another"*? Whenever I want to verify the meaning of some word I go to my trusty little CD Rom dictionary, and when I did that just now, I found that the word "love," within the context of Jesus' message, means, *unselfish, loyal, and benevolent concern for others*. This definition seems altogether appropriate, and I would like to further analyze what it would mean for a Christian who wanted to follow Jesus' orders. First, let's look at the word "unselfish." I think that a person who is unselfish, is a person who could be characterized as being more concerned with the well-being of others than with the well-being of themselves. Notice that I said *more* concerned with others, because God would not want, nor would He expect us to totally disregard our own well being. After all, total disregard for oneself would lead to sickness and/or death, and how can we serve others if we are too sick to get out of bed?

Notice that I just said, "How can we serve others." What I didn't say was, "How can we serve God," and there is a particular reason for my stating it that way. That reason is this: serving others (and I mean everybody, not just someone from your own or another church) means serving the people that you might not like and or would not normally associate with. I mean the people who are sick, impoverished, mentally ill, nasty, ungrateful, hurtful or uncaring. In other words, people just like the ones that you find attending most churches.

Listen to me. Serving others is serving God directly. I have said it before and I will say it again. Singing in the choir, tithing, being a deacon (the most egotistical of all) or ushering is (get this) NOT SERVING GOD! All of these jobs serve the church. Please don't misunderstand; all of these jobs need to be done. Everyone should and must tithe of their income in order to prove to God that He (God) is more important to them than riches. Everyone who has even a barely good voice should sing in the choir because it helps lead the rest of us in praising our God. The point is that God doesn't really *need* any of these things. Does He need our money? No. Does he need our choir? No. He has a choir of angels.

Most Christians confuse their service to a particular church as serving God. You see, most of these people aren't concerned about being of service to God (themselves), they expect someone else i.e. the church, to go out and perform the actual work of service.

Hear the words of Jesus as He is giving a parable of what will take place at the final judgment. These are His words:

Then the righteous answer Him, saying, "Lord when did we see You hungry, and feed You, or thirsty and give You drink? And when did we see You a stranger, and invite You in or naked and clothe You? And when did we see You sick or in prison, and come to You?

"And the King (God) will answer and say to them, Truly I say to you, to the extent that you did it to one of these brothers of Mine, even to the least of them, you did it to Me."

Serving God is not about serving yourself and not about serving the church. Serving God is about serving the people of this world who need help, and that is everybody. Did you hear what I said: EVERYBODY. Serving God can be as simple as serving the man in the next lane who needs to be in your lane to make a turn. Do you see that by such an easy and simple act you have served someone?

Last evening I had to go to town during rush hour. As I was trying to make a left turn, there was a line of cars blocking the oncoming lane. When a gentleman who was blocking the drive into which I wanted to turn saw me with my turn signal on, he checked his mirror and BACKED UP so I could get through. Question: Could this be classified as a Christian act or just common courtesy? Answer: Both. Any act that gives any help, shows any care, demonstrates any love, is without a doubt Christian in origin whether the person performing the act knows it or not, because that is exactly what Jesus taught us and what He repeatedly demonstrated throughout His life.

God doesn't *need* us to sing in a choir. God *needs* us to demonstrate His love for His people that we meet every day. Remember the words of Jesus: ***"By this all men*** (and women*) **will know that you are My Disciples, if you have love for one*** *another."* Let me return to the gentleman who backed up so that I could make a turn; how do you think his small act of kindness made me feel? Yes, I felt good and I felt kindly toward this man. If I had known whether this man was a Christian, I would have felt open to Christianity as a whole. I would have been open to any witness that a man such as this would want to give.

Do you see where we Christians have failed? Most of us are so egotistically tied up in our own knowledge of salvation that we don't recognize that it is now the other person who is important in God's eyes. Why do I say this? Who did Jesus say that He came to earth to see? Not us. We are already His. His concern, as He said, is for the "lost" sheep. Does that mean that God no longer cares for us, His followers? Of course not. Believe me, God takes care of His people in a mighty way; it is just that His first priority (if I can describe it that way) is bringing those "lost" sheep into the fold so that He can care for them also.

Let me return to that Southern "Christian" university. Can anyone now understand why their policy of "separation" is so patently abhorrent to God and so contrary to the life and teachings of Jesus Christ? Jesus Christ, whom they claim as Lord and Savior, never, repeat, never, separated Himself from ANYONE. How can anyone claim to love Jesus and then totally ignore His life and work?

The misguided doctrine of "separation" is in direct conflict with Jesus' teachings: **"And if you greet your brothers only, what do you do more than others? Do not even the Gentiles do the same?"**

FAILURE!

The Christian Church is failing every day, and it is failing because of misguided policies such as this. Do you remember studying in school about the middle ages when the Catholic Church was in total power? The church of that time ostracized *anyone* who refused to believe as they, the church, decreed. This ostracization extended to the point of forcing people from their homes, from their ability to make a living, and even to the point of death. Thank God that the church is not controlling the government, although they would like to.

Travel with me to rural France around the 1500s. The church dictates everything. Have you heard the little French song entitled, *"FRERE JACQUE"*? It goes like this, and it was sung to me by my aunt as she was trying to teach me French: "Are you sleeping Brother John? Morning bells are ringing, morning bells are ringing, Brother John." Just who do you think was ringing those morning bells? It was the church. The church told you when to get up. The church told you when to go to bed. The church even told you when to eat. This is what some modern Christians are advocating today by electing the "correct" politician, enacting the "correct" laws, enforcing "correct" decisions on our lives. Where is love? Where is love shown when my only interest is forcing someone else to live as I dictate? Where I am going now is the key to changing the Christian religion into an organization that exemplifies the teachings of Christ.

I was raised on a ranch in Texas, so believe me; I know what I am talking about as I give an example that is so true that it is going to hurt. If you love horses, you will recognize immediately the truth of what I am saying and, as a matter of fact, I'll bet that some of you will already have guessed where I am going. How many of you remember the old adage, "You can lead a horse to water but you can't make him drink." Isn't that what we Christians are trying to do? We are trying to get everyone to drink of that "living water" that Christ spoke about.

The problem is not with our objective; the problem lies with how we go about achieving that objective, and here comes my example. Lesson one: How to make a horse do your will. If you want to make a horse come with you, you have to LEAD it. Get it? I want all of you self-professed Christians to go to the nearest stable, walk into the first stall, and try to push even the gentlest horse to the water trough. Better yet, get your Congressman to pass a law that requires horses to drink. They just won't go; yet that is what we are doing when we pass laws telling other people how to live their lives. We are "pushing" them in the direction that *we* want them to go. Is it any wonder that they resist? Am I saying that people are like horses? Absolutely!

People can be just as stubborn as the most recalcitrant horse or mule. This is exactly what the Catholic Church did in the middle ages when they forced everyone to toe the "church" line. Would you want to live that way? I somehow don't think so. Back to my example, why do you think that a horse will follow you? It is for only one reason. He "trusts" you to lead him, and he knows that wherever you lead good things will follow. Does that sound like the way that God treats us? You bet, but let me ask this: What are you doing to "earn" someone's trust? Are you telling them how to vote? Are you telling them what they can't do? Are you showing them a loving person who is at peace with God and the world, or are you showing them an angry, controlling person who "demands" their allegiance and forces your values upon them.

What is love? What did Christ mean when He told us to "love" everyone? Let's take a moment to see if the word "care" can be an appropriate synonym? What does "care" mean? The word "care" can have the simplest meaning for us Christians because it can mean nothing more than *taking an interest in* whatever person we happen to be associating with at the moment. Most Christians are so involved with "the big picture" i.e. world problems, that they forget two things: the first concerns the fact that God Himself is taking care of the "big picture." No, I'm sorry, God is not dead, as much as most Christians seem to believe. God is alive and well, and he is firmly in control of this world.

The second thing that we Christians forget is that God didn't tell us to be concerned with politics or world affairs. He told us to be concerned (to care) about His people, our brothers and sisters. Why would God tell us that? After all, He *is* God and He can take care of them Himself, can't He? Of course, the answer is YES, and He *does* take care of all of us, even though we don't want to believe it sometimes. The reason that we are to be concerned, to care, about His people is to ultimately be able to visually demonstrate God's love, as we demonstrate *our* love, to each person with whom we come in contact.

Remember this: God in His infinite wisdom has given us complete and total freedom whether even to believe in Him! Isn't that awesome? God gives every one of us total freedom to choose. If that is true, then why is it that once people begin believing in God, they want to take away everyone else's freedom to choose? WOW, am I glad that not one of us Christians has been chosen to BE God. If that were the case, the entire world would be like Afghanistan under the control of the Taliban. No movies, no TV, no Internet and on and on. Think about the Taliban for a moment; they forced everyone to do only what *they* thought proper and moral. Does this sound like some of the Christian community today?

Do you remember my telling you about the vote for a lottery here in South Carolina? Every pastor of every church in this State railed unceasingly against the lottery; yet here in a State that is 80% Christian, the lottery passed. Does the lottery concern me? Absolutely not! As a Christian, I must allow God to be in control. As a Christian, I must not be concerned with the problems of the world. Listen to me closely – I am to be concerned ONLY with the problems of God's people, because that is the job that He gave me, and it is the job that He has given you. Do you accept it? Will you accept it?

Why is the job of caring for people so difficult? The answer is that most Christians don't like people. Oh, yes, I can hear the cries of rebuttal and indignation, but look around. What does the church have to do in order to get us "loving Christians" to care enough to bring someone to church? The church has to, once a year, have a "visitor's day," at which time we are encouraged to bring someone to church. Look around at "visitor's day." How many of your fellow members cared enough to bring someone? Not many. In my church, I was the only one who regularly brought someone to the service that I attended.

There are two points that I want to make here. First, you must be in a caring relationship with some unchurched person before you can invite them to church and expect any sort of positive reaction. Second, you don't have to wait for "visitor's day" to invite someone to church, but you DO have to have established a relationship of love and caring. I want to tell you a particularly sad story about the day I took a male friend of mine to church. This guy was an attorney who was doing some work for me at the time, and we had become friends, so I invited him to my church.

After the service, we went to Sunday school in the singles class which was taught by a lady who had obviously never read the Bible. This lady, during the lesson, allowed her own personal hatred to show through, when she made the comment, "Men are such jerks...." Not only did I take offense, my unchurched friend stood up and walked out. Do you see that this church is allowing hateful and untrained people to lead their classes? What a shame. My friend has never been back to ANY church, and rightly so. Do you see the fact that this man is now a candidate for any cult that comes along, and all because of one lady who could not separate her hatred of men from her duty to teach Christ's love.

Why do churches not train and evaluate their teachers? I will tell you why. It is because these same churches are not training their members about Christ's greatest Commandment. Another reason is that the churches of today are desperate for workers. Because the church is not teaching their members about

Christ's greatest Commandment, that of loving and serving their fellow man, they will never have enough people devoted to service. Did I just repeat myself? No. Christ's greatest commandment tells us to love (care) for one another, and if we truly cared about other people, we would be BEGGING to serve them in some way.

I'm not a poet and I have never in my life written a poem other than one of the *ROSES ARE RED, VIOLETS ARE BLUE* genre; however, I believe that God has given me one which I would like to share with you:

ARE YOU SHOWING THE WORLD,
ONE WHO IS STINGY AND MEAN,

OR ARE YOU SHOWING THE WORLD,
GOD'S CARING MACHINE,

ARE YOU SHOWING THE WORLD,
ONE WHO IS STINGY AND BLUE,

OR ARE YOU SHOWING THE WORLD,
A CHRIST WHO LOOKS JUST LIKE YOU?

We Christians forget, or we have never been taught, that as we go about our daily activities, we are in effect waving a banner that tells everyone with whom we come in contact who we are and what we are.

Do you get the picture and the message of my poem? We Christians have lost our love for our fellow man because the church just isn't teaching us not only TO love, but HOW to love. Why do you think that Christ would give us, just before His death, a message that He deemed so important, that He called it a COMMANDMENT? You are aware, of course, that nowhere else in the Bible is any statement called a Commandment. Not even when the original Ten Commandments were brought down from Mt. Sinai were they called commandments. So why did our

Lord and Savior, whose word we supposedly follow, call this one particular instruction a commandment, and why also did He give us the only KEY by which we would be known as His followers?

Did you notice what I just said? I said that Jesus Christ, in these two statements, not only told us what we are supposed to do if we are to call ourselves Christians but He also told us that in following this particular instruction we would forever be identified as His people by everyone else in the world. *"By this all men will know that you are my disciples, if you have love for one another."*

Is anyone out there getting the message that Jesus Christ intended? Anyone? Certainly not the leaders of the church. They are too busy running the world, telling everyone else how to live, voting for the right political party, passing laws that mandate how everyone else is to live and building monuments to themselves, to worry about something so elementary as *LOVE* and *SERVICE*. While I am on the subject of "pastors" building ever larger monuments to their own ability to pontificate, I have to tell you how much I admire Billy Graham. Here is a preacher to the world in the finest sense of the word, one who could have built the largest cathedral in America, but who instead chooses to let his words be his only monument.

I want to make just one more statement that is directly related to the paragraph above and it is this. Christ told us what to do and why to do it, but more importantly there is an implicit message within His instruction. That implicit message contains the fact that by this instruction, and how and whether we choose to follow it, Christ Himself will measure us at the final judgment. How do you want to be judged? Are you going to kneel before Him (as we all will) and say, "Aw, gee, I didn't think that you were serious," or, "Well, I voted (name your party) all my life," or "I worked hard for my money, and I certainly deserved to keep it." Maybe you will want to make up your own excuse for not following His commandment, but just keep in mind that you will either pay the price or be rewarded accordingly.

So what are we supposed to do? Run out and give away all of our money and live in poverty, or be a missionary to some foreign land? I'm sorry but the answer isn't to be found in any of these, but let me tell you about one of my neighbors. Fred isn't a Christian. As a matter of fact, Fred refuses to even talk about God and whether He exists, but Fred is the closest epitome of a true Christian that I have ever met. How? If you met Fred, you would immediately know. Fred is always smiling, and Fred is always helping someone. Got your truck stuck in the mud? Call Fred and he will be over with his tractor and a chain. Need some firewood? Call Fred and he will bring his log splitter.

Last winter, we had one of the worst ice storms ever. My electricity had been out for four days when Fred showed up at my door with his generator so that I could get my freezer back down to temperature and save the food inside. Take note here, I had not even called Fred, because even though I knew that he had a generator, I felt that it would be unfair to ask for it because I knew that he had his own family to take care of. Fred showed up with the generator anyway, and when he did, he apologized for not showing up sooner, because, as he said, "I had to take care of the other neighbors." Can you believe that? This guy owns a generator and he is taking care of the entire neighborhood! You tell me, who are the *real* Christians?

I have a question for you. Why do churches have to designate and assign greeters to meet you at the church door on Sunday morning? Pay attention now. The question was not *why* churches designate greeters; everybody knows that. The question was, why do churches HAVE TO designate greeters, and the answer is because no one else will bother to greet anyone other than their own friends. You see, the Christian church has become a big social club. You are either *in* or you are *out*.

FAILURE!

Allow me to return to our health club manager and Doris, the lady who showed up at the club's door right at closing. If you remember, this manager had given this lady two hours of his time, and let me say right now that time is one of the most valuable gifts that anyone can give. The date is now approximately a year later, Doris has been a regular member of this health club and she approaches our manager and asks to see him in his office. Doris is a happy and changed person, and now allow me to quote from the original story: "Beaming from ear to ear, she answered. Well, I've lost 35 pounds! I don't take medications any more! My doctor says it's a miracle. I tell him, 'No, it's just exercise.' I have a great job...I met my boss here in the club! I'm getting married again...I met him here in the club too!" Doris continues talking and then she says, 'What I really came here for is this. To thank you. To thank you for giving me back my life.' It was then our manager's turn to cry, and the old Conway Twitty song came into his thoughts: 'That's my job. That's what I do. Everything I do, I do for you, 'cause that's my job.'" Isn't that a beautiful story? Isn't that what Christ meant when He told us to "love" our fellow human? Isn't that what our lives should be about? ISN'T THIS WHAT THE CHURCH SHOULD BE TEACHING? Again *FAILURE!*

Here is a documented case of a person's life being totally changed, and all because one person took the time to listen. How do you think God is going to look upon people who give of themselves to help others? How many readers of this book are members of a church participating in a WWJD program? If you aren't familiar with the letters WWJD, they stand for *What Would Jesus Do?* Let's stop a moment and ask ourselves, "What *did* Jesus do while He was here on Earth with us?" The answer is that Jesus helped almost everyone with whom He came in contact. In other words, Jesus "served" people, and if there was a one word description of Jesus Christ, that word would be "servant."

The church in its self-induced failure mode only focuses upon three aspects of the entire life of Jesus Christ: His Birth, His death and, to a very limited extent, His "miracles." But why did Jesus perform all of these miracles? Was He showing off? Was the entire thrust of His life dedicated to proving that He was God? Absolutely not. Not only did He NEVER take credit for performing any miracle, He gave ALL of the credit to God the Father. So the question remains: Why did Jesus perform all these miracles? And the answer is that He did them to *help* people. Let me repeat myself: the objective of EVERY miracle that Jesus Christ performed was to help people – NOT to build His reputation.

What I find amusing is the fact that the only people that Jesus became angry with were the leaders of the church; and I am willing to bet that He would be just as angry today with the leaders of our largest congregations, such as Pat Robertson, who use the Word of God to further their own self interest and political ambitions.

If Jesus' ENTIRE reason for coming to earth was to help people (and it was), shouldn't those of us who call ourselves followers of Jesus Christ do the same? If we worship Jesus, shouldn't we try to emulate Him? If Jesus' entire life was devoted to helping people, shouldn't we follow Him and do the same?

Very probably the first thing that some Christian will say right now is this: "Well, Jesus was God, so of course He could do miracles, but I am just some poor human being." The first thing I would reply to a comment such as that would be this: if you are a human being, then you are God's greatest creation, and not only that, you are (can be) just like Jesus. Remember, Jesus Christ didn't perform any miracles either; they were all performed by God Himself at Jesus' request. If you want to argue with that premise, then read what Jesus said about the work that He was doing.

Jesus repeatedly stated that He could do nothing without the Father. Was He lying? I don't think so. Why have I repeatedly tried to make this point? It is because the church has again failed to tell us that we can be just like Jesus. We can perform miracles. Actually, I think that if we just got some of these so-called Christians off their complaining backsides, that would be a miracle, or maybe if we got some church to work with the hurting people of their own city that would be a miracle, but maybe, just maybe, if God were to get all those pampered preachers off the golf course, that would be the greatest miracle ever produced.

All right, I have had my fun, so let's get serious. Can you and I actually perform miracles with God's help? You bet. Remember Doris and our health club manager? Her whole life was changed by a two-hour conversation. If that isn't a miracle then none have ever occurred. When was the last time that you changed someone's life? The church loves to teach about the miracle of Peter being released from jail in the Book of Acts. That's no big deal, I did that too. I released from jail a man who was contemplating suicide, a man who thought that Satan had control of his life, a man who had no hope, and I (read God) gave him another chance. Can you perform miracles? The answer is an unqualified YES. But you must do two things: stop being concerned about the world, and start being concerned about (loving) God's people.

As I close I just want to answer what I know will be the first criticism made of this chapter. The title of the chapter is *The Greatest of All Commandments,* and I want to answer those who will say that I am ignoring or belittling the original Ten Commandments given to Moses. That argument would be totally baseless, because the original Ten Commandments were given by God Himself and they, by themselves are the key to reaching a relationship with God. The reasons I call this particular commandment the greatest Commandment (besides wanting to get your undivided attention) are twofold. The first reason, as I have said before, is that this is the only Commandment ever given by Jesus Himself; the second reason is that if we were to believe and follow this one Commandment, the first ten would be followed automatically. Think about it.

Why should this so-called commandment even be considered a commandment? After all, if God had wanted this declaration to be considered a commandment, or if He had even wanted it to be a commandment, He would have included it among the ten originally given to Moses on Mt. Sinai. God gave us the commandments by which He wanted us to live, didn't He? Why do we need another one? If God wanted to add another commandment, then we have to believe that God forgot something and this last "commandment" was an afterthought. Given the perfection of God, we know He doesn't need afterthoughts like we humans do.

The answers to the above comments are evident as one reads the Bible and discovers how and why the Israelites failed. They not only failed God; they failed individually, and they failed each other. Please don't misunderstand me. God knew that it would happen. The failure of the Israelites was a foregone (and a planned) conclusion and was the reason that Jesus came to earth to rescue us from our sins.

Consider this: if the Israelites had not failed, there would have been no need for God's Son to be sacrificed upon a cross, and there would have been no reason for the addition of this final commandment. Most importantly, consider the repeated parables that Jesus gave that had as their subject the mistreatment of our fellow human beings. Among those parables are the parable of the Good Samaritan who came to the rescue of an injured Israelite and the parable of the beggar Lazarus who was ignored by the rich man. Ask yourself these questions: When the rich man died, where did he go? When you die, where will you go? Don't be too sure unless you are living by the words of Jesus Himself and you are also living the life of the modern day Good Samaritan.

6

FIXING THE CHURCH

So when you spread out your hands in prayer,
I will hide my eyes from you,
Yes, even though you multiply prayers,
I will not listen,
Your hands are covered with blood.

The words of Isaiah as given to the Jews of the Old Testament are as true today as they were during the reigns of Kings Uzziah, Jotham, Ahaz and Hezekiah of Judah. The church of the time (i.e. the Temple), had failed in understanding the true intent and teachings of God the Father, just as the Christian church of today has failed in following the teachings of Jesus Christ, His Son.

Listen to the prophet Isaiah as he cries out the word of God: **"Bring your worthless offerings no longer. Incense is an abomination to me."** To the church of today, those words say that our tithes, used to build ever larger buildings when 800,000 people, including 200,000 children, sleep under bridges, are repugnant to God. Incense, as used in the Temple services, were a form of what we know as "praise and worship," as practiced today by the singing of hymns and anthems, and are just as worthless to God when we selfishly worry about politics and taxes while ignoring and mistreating our fellow man.

The church of today has failed because the leaders of the church want to be in control of every facet of the world, including finances, politics, the making of laws and the enforcement of those laws; and they pretend to want all those powers "in the name of" God, when in fact that very God is already in control of this world, but the church doesn't recognize and refuses to understand how God works.

Think back to the New Testament and you will remember that the *only* people with whom Christ ever became angry were the leaders of the church and, of course, the money changers, whose tables He overthrew. Sadly, those same money changers exist today in the form of those pretend Christians whose only priority is self-enrichment through the deprivation of the less fortunate and the elimination of any tax upon themselves. These are the people who want a free ride through life, and they justify their desire for that "free ride" through the fact that they purport to believe in God. If they truly believed in God, they wouldn't be concerned about something as unimportant as money.

The modern Christian church does one thing well. It teaches of the birth, the life, the death and the Deity of Jesus Christ, but it stops right there and thereby assures the failure of the entire Christian religion. The closest parallel that I can make would be that of sending your children to school for twelve years but not allowing them to leave kindergarten. Week after week, one hears sermons about the life and death of Jesus, but almost never is the story of that life applied to the life of the very ones who call themselves "followers" of that same Jesus. How can people call themselves "followers" of the Savior, when they refuse to acknowledge and practice in their own life the attributes of the one whom they pretend to "follow?"

Possibly the single most telling example of the failure of the church and the existence of what I call "kinderchristians," or professing Christians who have no idea of what Christianity is all about, came to me as I was listening to a secular radio station located right here in the Bible belt. The announcer began talking about the illegal downloading of music and movies from the internet. Now I really didn't have much interest in the subject since I have yet to download anything except some of the interesting things that my friends send attached to their e-mails, but when the announcer asked what was the single most downloaded movie of all time, my curiosity was piqued. Do you know or can you even guess? Try it; take a guess because the answer will blow you away if you are a true Christian.

No, you are wrong, it isn't *STAR WARS*. The single most illegally downloaded movie of all time is Mel Gibson's *THE PASSION OF THE CHRIST*. Can you believe it? Millions of so-called "Christians" think nothing of breaking the law (in the name of Christ?). The announcer went on and began a tirade about the hypocrisy of people who call themselves Christians, and I began to feel ashamed that so many of us have again betrayed the name above all names. What are we thinking? The answer is that we aren't thinking because the church doesn't teach us to think and as a matter of fact, doesn't even seem to care. Don't Christians understand that whenever they cheat or steal even music or movies, they are giving witness (especially to those who don't know God).

FAILURE!

The announcer then made a statement that has rung in my ears every day since I first heard it: "Do these people (Christians) love Jesus Christ so much that they will justify stealing for Him?" Let me ask you, the reader, a question. Do you know anyone who has illegally downloaded this movie or anything else with a Christian theme? Go to that person or that church and remind them that they are sinning and, even worse, blaspheming the very name of the One whom they purport to follow.

I know for a fact that whenever the largest Baptist churches have a Christian concert, within hours, dozens of illegal copies of that particular artist's CD's are being distributed to friends. What is going on when we betray even our own fellow Christians?

Most Christians will look at the title of this chapter and ask, "Gee what could be wrong with the church? After all, church is the place where we go to worship God, and He demands our worship, doesn't He? Church is also where we go to meet our friends and gather in an effort to make this world a better place. And don't forget, we have one evening set aside for outreach, a time when we go visit with anyone who visited our church last Sunday. What could be wrong with that?" The answer is that *everything* is wrong with that.

In his New Year's address, the Pope calls for a "fair and just world" and a world where there "will be peace." If that statement isn't naive and indicative of a total lack of understanding of the purpose of this world, then nothing is. In case anyone was wondering, this wasn't meant to be a fair and just world. God intentionally didn't create it that way. He didn't mean for this world to be fair and just, and if you don't believe me, then search the New Testament for any place where Jesus said that all things would be fair or just, or even peaceful. While you are searching, look for where the Bible says that Christians are supposed to "get a better deal" than everyone else. If God had wanted this world to be fair, just and peaceful, then He, in His infinite wisdom, would not have created evil in the first place. Oh, yes, God, our loving God, created evil and it is in the Bible. Of course, if you haven't read the Bible then you won't know that, because the church doesn't teach it.

The title of this chapter is "Fixing the Church," and that is a tall order, so where should we start? I would like to start by throwing out all those self-proclaimed "ministers" and "pastors" who have never read the Bible from cover to cover, but I know that is impossible, and in their defense, they are just repeating the mistakes of the previous generations and absorbing the (no less than) heresy taught at our seminaries; so let's start with a clean slate and take a positive direction.

We humans have become accustomed to the mindless acceptance of any dogma taught by any persons or group that represents themselves as being "educated," and therefore whatever is taught at our institutions of higher learning by those persons who have the letters "PhD" after their name is accepted as the word of God. The problem with this is the fact that most educators, while they have studied the Bible diligently and perhaps for many years, fail to recognize the *intent* of this God of ours. Oh, yes, these people can tell you the particular meaning of every word of the Bible, they have researched the sentence structure of every discourse of Jesus Christ, they can read the Bible directly from the original Greek, and they can expound for hours about the life and times of the Greek and Roman Empires, yet they don't have even the first clue as to God's intent and reasons for creating this world and the real purpose behind the life of God's only Son. It is my humble opinion that too many PhD's within the church and our seminaries have been educated far beyond their own intellectual capacity to understand what they have learned.

The first step that any organization or individual must take in attempting to worship or serve anyone or anything is to gain knowledge and understanding of who and what that entity is. The failure to accomplish that task is the reason that so many innocent people have been taken in by the Jim Joneses, the Pat Robertsons and the Jim Bakkers of this world. The only way that we can understand this entity that we call our "God" is to look at His actions throughout history. We can start with the fact that He created **everything,** including the human race, and if we can accept that He created everything, then we have to accept the fact that He is still in control of everything, but that last step is where the church fails because we humans have a lazy streak and we want, as the Apostle Paul said, "to be spoon fed."

The first action that the church must take in order to make itself pleasing to God is to begin recognizing that **GOD IS, IN FACT AND WITHOUT ANY DOUBT, IN CONTROL OF THIS WORLD!!!** This seems so simple and so elementary once a person establishes in his own life that God exists that I cannot understand why the church won't accept that fact. After all, don't we sing those wonderful hymns and songs about our God being an awesome God, and mighty and powerful is He? Yet the people in the church do not seem to believe it, because in the next breath they talk about politics, the necessity of having a strong military and, of course, that bane of all self-proclaimed Christians – taxes and abortion. We have only to look back in history, as we review the repeated rebelling against Roman authority by the leaders of the Temple, to determine the futility of resisting the will and the plans of God. What did that rebelliousness achieve? It resulted in the total loss of the land originally given to them by God. Is that the very thing that we wish to accomplish today? Why do we Christians constantly worry about what is happening in the world? Do we believe that God is dead (or maybe just sick or weak or forgetful or maybe He has Alzheimer's)?

Abortion is undoubtedly the foremost cause which has diverted the church from its sacred mission of saving souls into the secular world of mainstream politics. The single issue of abortion has caused a monumental rift of such proportion that many potential Christians have turned their backs on even the consideration of the existence of God, and in consequence, the church has become its own worst enemy in the accomplishment of its original mission. Is abortion good or even allowable? Of course not. The real question is whether abortion will always exist, and the answer is (sadly) yes; however, abortion or the need for abortion could be reduced to almost nothing if only the church would stop trying to change the laws and start loving and caring for people.

The real question about abortion that the church fails to recognize isn't whether abortion should be legal. The real question about abortion is whether abortion would be even considered by a person who has made the wrong choices and is now in trouble if they had been befriended by someone who knows God. Remember, God gives us the freedom to make choices every day because He wants to see which choices we will make. That is the exact reason that God gave us a mind to reason and think like no other animal in existence. The ability to choose is God given and He gave it only to us human beings. Are we Christians making ourselves into God as we take away the right of everyone else to make a choice? I think so, and not only are we attempting to usurp God's power, we are creating a chasm between the real God and those who have not made up their mind about the existence of that very real God.

So why has the church chosen to wage the battle of abortion in the political arena? The answer is so sad because it is due to the fact that it is so much easier to campaign for a politician than it is to get out of your pew and love, help, support, befriend and teach a fellow human being *before* they begin walking down the wrong path. The bottom line is the fact that the church leaders really don't care about loving and helping their fellow man; they care about building an ever larger church and eventually controlling the world.

I recognize that any argument about the subject of abortion is controversial, but the argument of how to go about the resolution of that subject can be taken directly from the life and example of Jesus Christ. Nowhere and at no time did Jesus ever charge His followers to change the laws of government, even though He lived in a time of wars and strife which included slavery and murder. Think about this as you sit listening to the next sermon; could the time, commitment and a little bit of love of a single person change the life of someone who is facing temptation? You bet! Will you be one of the people to change the world, or will you be like most Christians and expect the government to change the laws and thereby eliminate all things "bad." Will you be the face of Jesus Christ to someone who doesn't know Him? We can't exemplify the face of our Savior as we carry a picket sign and block the entrance of an abortion clinic. I ask you, how can actions that project "hate" show the life of love of our Savior?

While we are talking about Jesus Christ, let's take a look at this person who lived two thousand years ago and who was sent directly by God Himself to show us how to live. We readily accept that Jesus Christ was the Son of God but we have no idea why He came here. If you were to ask any Christian why Jesus came to earth, he would tell you that His purpose was to be our Savior, and while that was indeed what He did for us, there was something even more important that had to be accomplished first before He could die upon the cross. I have discussed earlier that during His life and ministry, Jesus' job title was that of "servant," and I want to repeat that His actions as a "servant" were even more important than His death on the cross, because even in His death for us, He was "serving" us, the children of God. If you will read through the New Testament, you will understand that every message that He gave, every action that He took, every miracle that He performed, served the people of His time, yet Christians today who walk around mumbling the letters WWJD (What Would Jesus Do) do not give a second thought (or even a first thought) to the opportunity to serve a fellow human being as the life of their Lord and Savior exemplified two thousand years ago.

Why do I emphasize Jesus' servanthood over His sacrifice as our Savior? The answer is very simple, before Jesus could become our Savior, He had to demonstrate to His disciples His very nature – that of being a servant to all. So why don't Christians today understand what Jesus is demanding (yes, demanding) of every Christian? There are several answers, the first being that neither servanthood nor humility is being taught in today's Christian church. When was the last time that you met a Christian whom you could describe as "humble"? The second answer is the fact that over ninety-five percent of practicing Christians have never read the New Testament from cover to cover, so how can they know anything except what they hear from the pulpit. Think about this. The disciple Peter, after spending three years following in Jesus' footsteps didn't know either. Remember the one commandment that Jesus gave to every one of us who claims to follow Him? He told us to *love* our fellow man, yet how many Christians equate that command to love with the word "serve."

The third answer to why Christians do not understand what Jesus was all about stems from that abomination known as Calvinism which I discussed in an earlier chapter. By extension, Calvinism leads to a subverted Christian paradigm known as the "It's all about Me" Christianity. After all, the church teaches that once I have achieved salvation, no matter what I do (or don't do), I cannot lose my ticket to heaven. If I have been saved, I can continue living a selfish or self indulgent lifestyle in which I don't have to give a hoot for anyone. Remember, its all about **my** salvation. ME! ME! ME!

FAILURE!

So far in this chapter I have identified three specific changes that the church must make. The church must start teaching that God really does exist, that He really is in charge of the world even today, and we Christians do not need to be concerned about politics or law. Second, Jesus Christ's entire life was totally about serving, and third, we should drop the virus which has sickened the entire Christian church (i.e. Calvinism).

The fourth change that must be acknowledged if the church truthfully wants to follow in the footsteps of its leader, Jesus Christ, is to initiate a program of "educating" Christians on how to actually become Christian. The church has to begin accepting the fact that most of us have no idea how to follow in Christ's footsteps. Joining the church today is exactly the same as joining a social club; we make the commitment to join and, voila, we are in with full status as a practicing member and we think that it is now our job to change the lives of everyone else while we leave to God, the job of changing our own life. Doesn't that sound like most of the "Christians" that you know? They want to change everything that they don't like about everyone else's life, including the law, yet they seem to totally disregard their own imperfections while shouting to everyone the slogan,

"Christians aren't perfect, they're just saved!" Is that a cop-out or what?

On one of the first pages of this book, there are two statements. One of them states, "There is only one way to please God." Pleasing God has nothing to do with worship and praise as we sit in our weekly entertainment called a church "service" on Sunday morning. I find even the word "service" humorous when describing the weekly gathering of the faithful. Who do they think they are serving? It certainly isn't the people who need help in their lives, and therefore it certainly isn't God. Let me say it again. There is only one way to please God, and (listen closely now) it is by changing *our own lives through the power of the Holy Spirit*. Forget about changing everybody else: change yourself. Changing our own lives is what God wants, and He demands no less from anyone who claims to follow His Son.

How many people reading this book have ever been lied to by a practicing "Christian"? How many have ever been cheated, mistreated, gossiped about, stolen from or even sexually abused by persons masquerading as "Christians"? The sex scandal in the priesthood of the Catholic Church, where over 4,000 homosexual and pedophile priests abused the very children that were put in their trust, exemplifies the laxity that is pervasive in not only the Catholic Church but **every** other Christian denomination. In my own city, the largest Baptist church had a deacon that was found guilty of child abuse, yet that same church has yet to change or even review its policy of selecting deacons or training its membership.

While we are on the subject of child abuse, let's look at the problem of homosexuality in the modern church. More and more denominations are accepting the practice of homosexuality, not only within the laity but within the priesthood, in an effort to bring these people within the Christian fold. While every Christian should applaud and endorse any effort to bring **everyone** into acceptance and knowledge of the love of God, the church has failed to recognize the fact that while God loves even (and maybe especially) a person who has homosexual tendencies, God does not and will not accept the **practice** of homosexuality. Do you understand the difference? Perhaps the leaders of the church will understand the words of the Apostle Paul when he said, "Everyone who confesses the name of the Lord must turn away from wickedness."

Every one of us, whether or not we are "Christian" has desires that are not acceptable to God. Those desires may take the form of lust, greed, covetousness, anger, frustration, or whatever, because not one of us was created in perfection, and God purposefully created us with the ability and even the desire to be less than perfect. God's purpose in creating us in imperfection was to give us the decision and the opportunity to use His strength to change, but the church seems to think that this change is God's responsibility, not ours, and therein lies the problem.

The continuing fight over "gay" marriages sheds a bright spotlight on the present day thinking of those who would call themselves "Christian," and, again, the fault lies squarely on the lack of teaching by the leaders of the Christian church. We hear time and again that through allowing homosexuals to legally marry, marriage and perhaps the entire institution of marriage will be ruined. So whose marriage will be ruined? Not any one that I know. Will your marriage be ruined by the gay marriage of someone else? Not likely! The fact that professing "Christians" are even concerned about gay marriage again points out the fact that these same "Christians" are not as interested in bringing people to Christ as they are in telling everyone else how to live. I just can't figure out why Christians everywhere have this seemingly unquenchable thirst to *force* everyone to toe "their" line.

God has not given us, as Christians, the task of deciding how everyone else should live. If even Jesus Christ didn't do that, then it should be obvious that we do not have the mandate to deny anyone the right to be involved in a "gay" marriage.

Instead, we should be demonstrating through our own lives and happiness and success that a true, meaningful, and working relationship with God is the only path to true happiness and fulfillment. It probably wouldn't be appropriate to comment on the fact that "gay" marriage might be more desirable than some of the "Christian" marriages that I have witnessed. (Yes, that was a pun)

Let me make sure that everyone understands the fact that not one of us has the ability or the strength to change their lives to that which is acceptable to God. Is this bad? Should we give up or become discouraged? The answer is no, because (and this is where God's plan is so wonderful) we can change any problem that we have through God's strength *and only* through God's strength. We all want to forget that God created us as weak and frail beings, because He wants us to depend upon Him for our strength. Frankly, this was a great problem for me as I first became a Christian. There were some things that I didn't want to give up, such as control of my life or my farm, which I felt was the only thing that I had left.

The story of my finally being able to give up control of my dearest possession at that time, my farm, provides a perfect example of just how hard God will work in order to bring us to Him. At the time I decided to give God a chance in my life, I had gone through a nasty divorce and I didn't have a job. In short, I had nothing except my farm, and, consequently, that farm was the most important thing in my life. I can remember worrying that I would lose that farm, which was my only home. I worried about getting sick and having to go to the hospital and losing the farm because of medical bills. This worry probably became an obsession with me and God decided that enough was enough.

I came down with a cold and took some over-the-counter cold medicine which was out of date, but I didn't have money to buy more. Within twenty-four hours the cold had settled in my chest and I had a full blown case of pneumonia, or so I thought. When I reached the point where I couldn't wait any longer, I asked my dad to drive me to my doctor's office so that I could be admitted to the local hospital. As we drove out the drive, I remember looking at my farm in the knowledge that I probably wouldn't have it much longer, but not caring any more. We drove through the woods to the road, and I told God that He could have my farm. I wasn't going to concern myself with it, and I just put everything in His hands. If God wanted to take my farm away then so be it, because I had to make the decision to put Him first instead of a piece of property, and, frankly, I had come to the decision that I needed God's help in my life above all else.

Let me make sure that everyone understands what is happening here because it is important to understand how God works. Remember that I have brought God into my life but I still want to hold onto certain worldly goods, such as my farm, and this concern about worldly things is interfering with the growth of my relationship with God. One thing that we had all better understand about this God of ours is that He does not want to be in "second place" in anyone's life, and He will do anything that it takes, including placing hardship and even sickness in our life in order to accomplish exactly what He wants, *being first* before anything or anyone else.

To continue with my story, the doctor examined me and could find no sign of pneumonia. When he learned that I had taken an out of date cold medicine, he told me that I had an allergic reaction. He then prescribed something and instructed me to go home, sleep and call him that afternoon. Immediately upon waking, I felt great, the pneumonia symptoms totally gone. The lesson? God wanted me to stop worrying about losing my farm and trust in Him. Being the hardheaded person that I am, God had to take drastic action to get my attention. The result? This story took place ten years ago, but I still own my farm and, in fact, have added to it since that time. The moral? If you truly want to put God seriously into your life, give everything to Him and don't be concerned with the things of this world. Why worry? If you take care of God, believe me, He will take care of you.

We are still on the subject of the fourth change that the church must make if it truly wants to follow the teachings of Jesus Christ, and that change is to initiate a program whereby every person who desires to call themselves "Christian" enters into a formal program of education with the goal of learning how to become a true Christian in the pattern of Jesus Christ. A logical first step would be to train a core group of Christians who believe in God deeply enough to take Him at His word and read the Bible, New Testament first, from cover to cover. While this seems like a very simple task, as I have said before, very few Christians, including most pastors, have ever taken the time or had the initiative to read the entire Bible.

I remember one conversation that I had with a self-identified "Christian" who was using his purported Christianity as a lever to sell a product. When I suggested that he read the entire Bible from cover to cover, he exclaimed, "You mean sit down and read it like a novel?" My reply was this: "That is exactly what I mean, because it is the greatest book ever written and if you want to use the word "novel," the Bible is just that, the most novel book ever written because there is none like it." His reaction? Negative, because like most Christians, he was too busy being concerned with "worldly" problems to be bothered reading the Word of God and he was using his "Christianity" as a marketing tool.

It took me a long time to figure out why most churches don't want their parishioners to read the Bible, and there are several reasons. Let's look at the Catholic Church and the Church of Jesus Christ of Latter Day Saints first. I'm not sure that either one of these denominations even believes in the Bible because they both have originated books that are supposed to "explain" the Bible, but the real reason is fear of a loss of control of their congregation. After all, if people were to actually "read" the Bible, they might understand that some of the teachings of their particular denomination were false. Notice that I said that "some" of their teaching is false. I am not accusing any Christian denomination of being a cult or of spreading totally false teaching or dogma. What Christians need to understand is the fact that almost *every* denomination has strayed from the intent of God the Father and the direct teaching of Jesus Christ, His Son, and it is for that very reason that this book is written. Let me say with utter clarity and without reservation, I do not advocate starting another church or denomination, nor do I attempt to create a schism within any church or denomination. What I do advocate in the strongest possible terms is for Christians everywhere to read the Bible and begin to understand the intent of our God in creating this earth and our responsibility to Him.

I find it so strange that millions of professed "Christians" who have never read the Bible have embraced works of fiction such as the *Left Behind* series and the more recent *Da Vinci Code*. It is obvious that people are fascinated by the life of Jesus Christ, but perhaps they refuse to read the Bible because they don't want to become like most of the other Christians that they know, who continue to lie, cheat, and steal as a supposedly God-given right.

Another reason that churches do not require their parishioners to read the Bible is that it would possibly compromise the prevailing "social club" atmosphere. "Church," as most of us know it, has become both a place of entertainment and a social club where we meet and greet our friends, sing hymns and praises, and listen to the same sermon we heard last year, but not much else. How many people reading this book can honestly say that what they have learned at their church in the past year has brought them into a closer understanding of God?

The last reason that churches do not want to change their existing paradigm is that they have convinced everyone that the ultimate goal of Christianity is to build ever larger church buildings to hold ever larger congregations. This is nothing more than the ego of the pastor at work and accomplishes nothing except enriching construction companies (and the pastors) at the expense of the people who could really use some help. Everyone has seen the bumper sticker that reads, "He who collects the most toys wins!", but I think that in their minds, the pastors of these mega-churches have a bumper sticker that reads, "The pastor that builds the largest church wins!"

So what is wrong with bringing more people into a particular church, you ask? Reason number one is the fact that Christian churches are, in many cases, doing nothing more than stealing members from each other. The modern version of what is called "outreach" has become simply a game of Monopoly where each church tries to collect the most players. The problem is that once new members are collected, they are ignored, and soon they begin to feel disenfranchised and move again, having learned nothing and not growing as a Christian.

This particular paradigm was brought home to me by my own experience with Christians as a teenager. A high school classmate of mine, who at that time was active in his local church and was trying to be a good Christian, took me to a tent revival. I was naive enough to raise my hand when several leading questions were asked by the preacher, and consequently I was brought to the altar to "be saved." Is this bad? Of course not. The problem here is the fact that after this classmate brought me to Christ, he forgot all about me, and my conversion became nothing more than a notch on his belt. It goes without saying that I forgot about that conversion experience and it was not until thirty years later that I came to God, as a last resort. One last note regarding this story concerns the fact that this former classmate and I renewed our friendship several years ago and he has been an invaluable help in writing this book. To him I say "thanks."

This problem of not educating or "growing" Christians is the single biggest problem of the church today and parallels the practices of the Temple of Christ's time when He told the

Temple leaders that they would travel to the ends of the earth to win a convert, and then they would make those converts twice as much a servant of Hell as before. Aren't the churches of today doing the same thing when they bring people to Christ then immediately send them out to "win" others without them even being aware of what it takes to be a Christian?

    I am going to make a seemingly contradictory statement here and it is this – It is very difficult *to become* a Christian, yet it is amazingly easy to *be* a Christian. Remember that Christ said that we must "enter by the narrow door," but then He said that "my burden is light." What did He mean when He made those contradictory statements?

    Becoming a Christian could be compared to joining our Armed Forces. Every new recruit is required to go through a fairly difficult process called "basic training." "Basic training" is exactly what the name implies. Each person must learn the basic skills that are required of every member of that branch of the service, and that training course usually lasts about eleven weeks, six days a week, for a total of about 528 hours. Remember, here we are talking about just learning only the most basic skills. When recruits leave basic training, they aren't given an M-1 tank or an F-16 fighter jet, which takes even more training and practice to operate effectively. Why then does the church feel that becoming a Christian is so much easier that it requires no training whatsoever? The truth is that the church does not in fact *care* whether people become "Christians." The church only cares whether people become giving ***members*** of their organization (i.e. the bottom line is money because "church" has become a business).

    Let me make another comparison between learning to become a soldier in the Army (which I was) and becoming a soldier for God, because this is so important, yet the concept is ignored by the Christian church. One of the first things that a new recruit learns is to forget civilian life. Ignore it! What that person did or was as a civilian is no longer important. Whatever is happening in civilian life is now of no concern to any person serving in the military, and by the same token, whatever is happening in civilian life is now of no concern to any person who has made the choice to join the Army of God. If you don't believe that, let me quote the Bible directly: *"No one serving as a soldier gets involved in civilian affairs – he wants to please his commanding officer."* Those words were written two thousand years ago and they are as true today as they were then. In case anyone didn't understand what that Bible passage said, let me paraphrase the second sentence. **Anyone who serves Jesus should not be concerned with worldly problems if they want to please God.**

Do you see why I said that it is difficult *to become* a Christian? This is the primary instruction that we must follow. No longer are we to be involved in politics. No longer are we to worry about money and taxes. No longer are we to be worried about some promotion, because (listen closely now) we are now working for God and He will be our employer. God will now take care of our income, our family, our very health, even as He is taking care of the world.

Now let me tell you why it is so easy to *be* a Christian. We don't have to worry about our own lives. Consider this carefully because it is so important. When we work for God, *He works for us!* That last statement will be considered blasphemy by some misinformed churches, but Jesus frequently referred to The Father as being even better and more caring than any worldly father. Jesus so stressed the "Fatherness" of our loving God that He warned us to never call anyone else "father," only God. (Pay attention Catholics.) I will never forget that one of my instructors of freshman English in my first year of college called me "naive." Was she right? Am I naive? You bet, and maybe that is the reason I have been so successful in my relationship with this great and loving God of ours. As I gave my life to the work of my God, I found that I didn't have to worry about my own life and success. I don't have to worry about money, and I don't have to worry even about my own health. Wow, what utter and absolute freedom. How many Christians do you know that are living a freedom like that? Are you?

I have tried for years to figure out why the church doesn't teach that God will take care of us, and the answer is that they do, but only half-heartedly, and as a result, no one believes it. Wholeheartedly trusting God to take care of us has become like some pie-in-the-sky dream that everyone only half believes. Why is this so? The answer is that so few people have tried it. An even more important answer is that almost no one has made the concentrated effort to 1. Forget about worldly things, 2. Read the Bible from cover to cover (repeatedly) and 3. Make the service of God the number one priority of their life.

I have asked myself (and God) a thousand times, "Why me?" Why did God choose to pick me up out of the ashes of my life after I had lost everything, and why has He blessed me beyond even my own wildest dreams? I want to give you something to think about, so I need to ask myself a question. The question is this: Can I prove to any person other than myself, beyond the shadow of a doubt, that God has done this? In other words, could this be some kind of fluke that would have taken place anyway because I happened to be in the right place at the right time? The answer is no, I cannot *prove* to anyone that my success is due totally to the hand of God in my life. Anyone who does not know God cannot have any idea of His power and will, and this is why the church has failed, because so few church leaders have truly experienced God themselves, they don't know how to train anyone else to experience God.

You see, I could not prove to you or anyone else that God exists, and neither could you prove to me that God exists, even through the most persuasive arguments known to man. God can be proven only through our own personal experience, yet the church expects us to suddenly "believe" without teaching us how to develop a relationship with God. The problem becomes the Catch 22 that no one can experience God without developing a personal relationship with Him. Forget the idea that once you have decided to accept the fact that there is a God and that He had a Son, God will come running to you and change your life into some Nirvana. Accepting God and His Son is only the first step, and a new Christian is exactly like a new recruit in the Army, totally ignorant of what is now required of them.

The fact that the church does not teach, or even require, new Christians to begin developing a relationship with God is the chief reason for the rise of cults and alternative religions, and it is time to define a program whereby Christians can begin growing to the point that they can establish their own personal relationship with God, and I want to identify certain steps that can be taken toward that end.

Let me first give several warnings and guidelines. This program cannot be undertaken in a large group setting. Group size should be limited to a maximum of five people and groups should be segregated by classifications such as age, length of church experience, educational level and depth of problems in life. This last item may take some study and a good working knowledge of human behavior but it should be given serious consideration prior to making group assignments. The program that I am going to describe is almost exactly what God guided me to do on my own; however, I have to recognize that most people will not be as lucky as I was in not having a job or a family at that time. Did you notice that I called myself lucky at *not* having a job or family? It was just that for two reasons. Since I did not have a job, I could spend my days reading the Bible, and since I had lost my family, there were few distractions. Yes, I recognize that sounds awfully hard-hearted and self-involved, but neither condition was my choice, and because I was at the bottom of the barrel so to speak, my commitment was serious.

I talked about not having a family to create a distraction, but a husband and wife can make a terrific team that can and must support each other in the learning process. I cannot emphasize enough that criticism has no place and must not be allowed in this program. Each person is a unique individual and will learn at their own pace, and this learning process provides a great time to learn patience, how to support someone else, and acceptance of the thoughts of others without criticism.

The warnings are out of the way and we are now ready to begin, so where do we start?

STEP ONE: ESTABLISH QUIET IN YOUR LIFE

Yes, I know that you have a job and a family, but there are many times when shutting out the world can conveniently be accomplished. When you drive to or from work are you listening to the radio? Turn it off. Commuters who ride a train, bus or airplane are especially blessed because they don't have to concentrate on the road. Do you have a cell phone? Establish times that it will be turned off, no matter what (what is your first priority – God or your friend with the latest gossip). What do you do for lunch? Lunch time is recognized as personal time, so what are you going to do with it? If you have to, make a sign to put outside your office or cubicle that says "QUIET TIME – SEE ME AFTER LUNCH UNLESS THE WORLD IS LEAVING ITS ORBIT, AND IF IT IS I DON'T CARE ANYWAY!!!

Most people will respect your wishes and the ones who don't are the people who don't want to see you succeed. A quiet, preemptive word with your boss, your mate and your kids is appropriate here, along with an explanation of what you are trying to accomplish. The people who love you will support you. The greatest bosses that I had during my engineering career were the ones who wanted me to succeed.

Why do I want you to shut out the world? Because you are trying to establish a relationship with God, and if you aren't able to listen to Him, He can't communicate with you. Actually He can communicate anytime; it's just easier for us to hear Him when we aren't concentrating elsewhere. Most Christians forget the axiom that we are to be *in* the world but not *of* the world.

STEP TWO: START COMMUNICATING WITH GOD

Notice that I didn't tell you to get on your knees and start praying. Here again is a gross error perpetrated by an unwitting church, because we can talk to God through the Holy Spirit anytime and anyplace and I guarantee you that He is listening. Most Christians walk around judging their own piety by the amount of time that they spend on their knees, but in a few minutes I am going to tell you the real way to judge the success of your relationship with God.

So what do I have to do to talk with God? Nothing, just start talking. It's nice to start by saying His name, but don't worry; He knows to whom you are talking. As you start this little communications project, it will seem as though it is only a one way street. However, if you keep it up, you will soon discover that He is not only listening but talking right back to you. So how will you know that He is answering you? Well, there won't suddenly be an angel perched on your dashboard. Keep in mind this isn't Hollywood. This is real life and God communicates in many ways. Did a problem suddenly and very quietly (so much so that you might not even notice) resolve itself? Did you get to that appointment on time in spite of traffic or a flat tire? Did your exhaustion suddenly disappear?

Let me take a moment and talk directly to anyone reading this book that refuses to believe that God exists. Start the same thing that I discussed above in steps one and two, but add one more thing. Say this to God: "God, I don't believe that you exist, but I am willing to have an open mind on the subject. If there really is a God as in the Old Testament of the Bible, will you talk to me? No, I don't expect you to pop up as I am walking to my car. I just ask that you, in your own way, begin talking to me and help me to listen to what you have to say." Do this every day for a month and see what happens.

There is one final test for unbelievers, but you had better have courage and be prepared if you want to try it. If the attempt at communication described above doesn't work for you or if you just can't bring yourself to believe that it worked for you, make the following statement to God in the strongest possible terms: "God, I refuse to believe in you and I want you out of my life right now." My suggestion is for you to yell this at the sky in the greatest anger that you can muster. Oh, I almost forgot. It's O.K. to throw in a few curse words too so that He understands that you are sincere. Just so you know, I did it, but you can bet that I won't do it again, because I don't want to go through the Hell that can happen when God does step back out of my life.

I told you a few paragraphs back that I would tell you the real way to judge the success of your relationship with God, and here it is. About what do you talk to God? Do you find yourself asking for something? Is something troubling you, or is there something that you or your family needs? Are you sick? Listen closely, because I want to make this so simple that everyone can understand. The success of your relationship with God can be judged solely by what you talk to Him about. If you suddenly find that you are happy and really don't need anything, you can bet that you are doing His will. You have got a great relationship going with the Big Guy Upstairs, and you have discovered what Christianity is all about. Let's see now, didn't Jesus say that He came to give us life even more abundantly? Why won't the church believe His words?

STEP THREE: DEFINE *WHY* YOU WANT TO ESTABLISH A RELATIONSHIP WITH GOD!

Take a careful look at your own life. Where are you and what have you accomplished? Are you where you want to be? Are you happy? Are you wealthy, broke or in-between? Do you have a great job and family? Are you lost and miserable? Are you sick, hurt, hating, angry, frustrated, dying? Do you have friends or are you misunderstood by everyone? Does everyone depend upon you, or are you dependant upon everyone else? Does your life have meaning and purpose, or are you just slogging onward from day to day like a person walking across Antarctica who doesn't like the scenery? As you look in a mirror and evaluate yourself, are you a success or a failure?

I see people every day who are angry and frustrated, or are physically ill, and if you asked them, they would tell you without a single doubt that they are "good" Christians. Look around you as you drive to work. Do you see the person ahead of you who refuses to yield his lane so someone can pass, or do you notice a person weaving in and out and in a great hurry to get somewhere? I use the example of what we see every day on the highway, because it is a perfect microcosm of how various people spend their lives. People don't suddenly change their personalities when they get into a car. Their actions on a highway give away what is happening in their lives. To return to the examples above, that person who refuses to give up their lane to another driver is a typical Christian who, in truth, dislikes people and feels superior to everyone and wants to be in control of the entire population. That person weaving in and out and in a great hurry is probably another typical Christian who has no respect for anyone else and whose life is out of control.

The answers to the questions I gave in the first paragraph don't matter in the least. Where you are or what you have accomplished to date is totally irrelevant, no matter what your age. Remember, at age fifty-one, I was a total failure. The purpose of the questions is for you as an individual to begin to know yourself, how you feel about yourself, and to decide where you want to go from here. I am going to make a statement that will seem rather strange, but it comes from my own experience. If, when you take a look at your life, you are hurting in some way, you don't like what you see, or you are at the end of your rope, you are among the most blessed people of the world. Why? If you are having a difficult time with life, I can guarantee that God is using those circumstances to call you to Him, and that you have been designated a very special person for which He has a use. Second, those same difficult circumstances will serve to give you motivation beyond what others can even dream, and if you stay the course, I guarantee you happiness beyond your wildest dreams.

Go down to one of the office supply stores and buy yourself a cheap spiral notepad. Make it your own personal book. The definition and answers to the questions asked above should take up at least two pages. When you have finished, remove those pages from the pad and either put them in your wallet or somewhere you <u>will</u> read them every day. Keep the notepad with you at all times so that you can write questions and make comments on what is happening. An even better idea would be to purchase a journal and write something every day. To be honest, I was never good at keeping a journal, but I did keep a journal during those years of trial, and when I look back, I can readily see what an awesome God we all have.

Keeping a record will give you a great perspective of where you started.

STEP FOUR: START READING THE BIBLE

WARNING! Before starting this step, you should have been practicing the first three steps for at least a month, and you should have many entries in your notepad or journal.

Before you start reading the Bible, it is imperative that you establish communication with God in the form of the Holy Spirit, because it is the Holy Spirit alone that is going to instruct you as you begin to read God's word. After making that statement, I can hear the howls of protest echoing through the very walls of churches everywhere. Throughout the land, preachers of every stripe (and some with prison stripes) will howl to the heavens that they are the only elect that have been given authority to teach the Word of God. After all, they wouldn't want you to find out something that might question their omnipotent authority, or in the case of the Pope, his infallibility.

To be serious for just a moment, the Bible is, as I have stated before, the single most complex book ever written. It was written that way for a reason and the reason is that God wanted it that way. Why? Because within every page of this most marvelous of books is a specific message aimed at each one of us who takes the time and makes the effort to read it. The specific message aimed at each of us can only be taught by the Holy Spirit, because the Holy Spirit is the only one who can look into the heart of each one of us and correctly time the delivery of the message. Does this sound silly? It won't to those of you who have read through the Bible in the past.

You will remember that I stated earlier that I have read the Bible from cover to cover five times. Does that mean that I know all about it? Absolutely not, and that is what is so wonderful about the Bible. Every time that I sit down and read it, the Holy Spirit brings something to my attention that I never noticed before. As I write this book, a Bible sits by my side, along with a yellow pad covered by notations about passages. As I have looked for a particular passage to go along with the subject about which I am writing, the Holy Spirit will sometimes guide me to something entirely different and I will be amazed at His timing and intuition about my innermost thoughts.

If you have followed the steps outlined above, then it is time to start reading the Bible. Now, I have no preference as to which Bible translation you should use; however, I do strongly suggest that you purchase a NASB (New American Standard) translation because it is written in the plainest English possible and it is supposed to be the most literal translation from the Greek and Hebrew manuscripts. At this point, I am going to make a suggestion that will seem quite strange. During your "first" reading, don't take notes or underline anything that you read. Why? Let your mind be open to what you are reading, and let yourself be submerged in the whole story rather then some part or idea. If *any* person, whether they believe in God or not, just sits down and reads the New Testament as though it were a novel, they will be awestruck by the story, and that is what should happen to anyone reading it for the first time.

So where should we start? Turn to the Gospel of Mark, the second book of the New Testament. Why Mark? The Gospel of Mark is the first story of the life of Jesus ever written. It is both the simplest and the shortest of the Gospels, and because it doesn't carry the "agendas" of the other Gospels, it is easier to read and understand. Don't forget, because this is very important, to ask the Holy Spirit (if there is such a thing for you non-believers) to open your mind and open your understanding of what you are about to read. Don't read for more than thirty minutes at a time, and actually, I really recommend that most people read for only fifteen minutes at a time, because as I stated earlier, this is the most complex book ever written.

O.K., I finished the Gospel of Mark, so where do I go now? Well, this is going to be a surprise. Go back to the beginning of Mark and read it again, but this time you may take notes or underline or highlight anything that suits your fancy. When you have finished Mark for the second time, go to Matthew and do the same thing. When you finish Matthew for the second time, start through the rest of the New Testament using the same method, but skip Romans until last because it is quite deep. Even though I have an engineering degree and have been reading extensively all of my life, when I tried reading Romans for the first time, I became totally confused and the Holy Spirit guided me to stop reading. Three months later, when I again picked up the Bible and started from Matthew, I was able to get through Romans, but still without a great deal of understanding.

I am not going to follow the reader through the New Testament chapter by chapter because that is entirely beyond the scope of this book, but I do have a word of warning for everyone. While anyone may choose to read the Book of

Revelation, don't even try to understand it. The Book of Revelation was given to John while he was "in the spirit" and it is not meant to be understood. If you want to think of being "in the spirit" as being in a dream or written in code or as prophesy totally beyond our comprehension, you won't be far from correct, and I have total disrespect for any "preacher" who pretends to know how or in what sequence the world is going to end. The most important thing that I can say about the Book of Revelation is that it is not important to us as Christians today. Yes, it is an insight into God's plans, but on the whole, it is not relevant to what we Christians should be concerned about in our daily lives.

I have only one more word of caution for those who wish to call themselves Christians, about reading the Bible. Don't read the Old Testament until you have read the New Testament at least three times and you have begun to understand the intent and the love of God the Father for the entire human race.

Why do I advocate not reading the Old Testament until you have read the New Testament at least three times? The answer is that there are too many "Old Testament Christians" in the world today whose lives are filled with hate, vengeance and a refusal to acknowledge the part that patience, love, humility, and selflessness play in God's ultimate plan. You have met them. They are the people whose favorite Bible passage is the one about "an eye for an eye, and a tooth for a tooth." One of the most despicable preachers that I have ever met once made the statement, "Well, Jesus told me to turn the other cheek when someone hits me, but He didn't say what to do after he hit me the second time." Is it any wonder that the church has failed, when its very leaders refuse to understand God's purpose?

When are these self-designated "preachers" going to get off their backside and stop playing God, because "playing God" is exactly what they are doing when they refuse to endorse the planned reading of the entire Bible as a necessary part of learning to be a Christian. Everyone is familiar with the old real estate axiom that states that the three most important considerations when purchasing real estate are location, location and location; well, the three most important considerations when reading the Bible or preaching a sermon are "application, application and application." In other words, Christians must say to themselves as they read or as they prepare a sermon or a lesson, "How do these words apply to my life **today.** The church in its endless quest to gain ever more members has ignored the words of Jesus when He said, *"And everyone who hears these words of mine and does not act upon them will be like a foolish man who built his house upon the sand."*

STEP FIVE: CHANGING MY OWN LIFE

Let me give you a word of warning, and this is very important so listen closely. As you continue your New Testament reading program, don't rush out and tell everyone else what you have discovered or what *they* are doing wrong in their lives. Developing a relationship with God is a very personal experience, and if you want to talk about what you have discovered, talk with God, because not only is He listening, He is willing to discuss it and I guarantee that He will provide the insight that will relate your new discoveries to your own life. The single worst thing that Christians do is try to get everyone else to change their life when they themselves refuse to look in a mirror. Keep in mind the fact that Christ told us to get the log out of our own eye before we offer to remove the splinter from the eye of someone else. Most "young" Christians seem to feel, and in fact are encouraged by the church to feel, that they should go out and change the world by forcing everyone else to conform to their own narrow beliefs and practices

Now I am going to tell you how to judge whether you are being successful in this program of self study. As you have read through the Bible, and as you have discussed your findings with the Holy Spirit, have you begun to see areas of your life where you are less than perfect? Maybe even a lot less than perfect? Did you have some kind of interaction or communication with another person in which you walked away thinking, "Wow, I really screwed that up." If so, congratulate yourself, because you have begun a communication with no less than God Himself. You see, unless you are the Pope or Pat Robertson or Jesse Jackson, you are not and you never have been perfect. As a matter of fact, none of us is perfect, and the only way that we are able to judge the effectiveness of our relationship with God is to acquire the ability to recognize our own foibles and errors and have the desire to change. Did you get that? When we can recognize that we are not perfect and then desire to change, only then have we begun a relationship with God, and only then have we begun to please God. Let me say it again for those who refuse to believe, **there is only one way to please God,** and that is to change our own life and begin to heed the words of His Son. Yes, worshiping God is acceptable and even desirable, but worship without change, humility and service is nothing more than the mindless burning of incense as performed in the Old Testament and hated by God as useless.

As I go through life every day, I repeatedly see my own actions and interactions as much less than what God wants for me. I look at myself and I say, "How could I have been so stupid or uncaring or misunderstanding or arrogant." And while this self recognition is important, what is really important is the next step when I say to myself, "O.K. I see my mistake and I will do better next time."

If one is to understand anything about Christianity, it must be the recognition that while not one of us can ever become even close to the perfection of God, being a Christian is all about each one of us humbly (now there's a word missing from most Christian's vocabulary) and repeatedly attempting to improve our lives, because as the song says, "YOU ARE THE ONLY JESUS THAT SOME WILL EVER SEE."

Why doesn't the church face the fact that we all have to *learn* to be Christians? I believe that it is due primarily to the "social club" atmosphere that pervades most churches. After all, if we forced our members to recognize the self-serving and sinful nature of most of our practices, we might lose some members. I know of at least one upstanding church where, if the pastor were to talk about lesbianism, half of the choir would walk out. Is this what God had in mind when He sent His Son to die for the sins that would be so easy to give up if we were just willing to make the effort and use God's strength?

I have discussed five steps that a person can take and that the church **must** teach in order to enable Christians to begin having a relationship with God. These steps must be taken by those persons who are to be designated or chosen as leaders to begin teaching the rest of the congregation. Churches must begin choosing their lay leaders more wisely than they have in the past, because in my own experience, most teachers and church leaders either have an agenda other than that of God or they are on an ego trip. I have told the story of the man-hating single female Sunday school teacher who offended every male in the class on visitor's day, so I don't need to repeat it here, but this is just one instance in which a person has been allowed to teach others without having established their own relationship with God. Here is a good question, "How can anyone readily identify someone who does have an active and ongoing relationship with God?" There are two key identifiers that readily identify someone who has an active and ongoing relationship with God.

The first identifier is very simple and easy to recognize and can be exemplified by the word "successful." Anyone who has a successful relationship with God is immediately identifiable as a success in their own life. Whether that person is a mechanic, a mother, a doctor or a retiree, whether they are wealthy or not, if they have that aura of success, then you can bet that they have a great relationship going with God. I am going to talk more about this in another chapter, but I want to quickly tell you about the two favorite ladies in my life. They are both doctors, one an MD and other a Chiropractor, but when I spend time with either one, I know that these ladies not only have a relationship with God but that they are serving Him on a daily basis. If you are blessed enough to have friends like this in your life then you know immediately that people like this are very special. People, who know God, *care* (about people).

The second identifier is much more subtle, but also easily identifiable when you know what to look for. As you talk to a person, notice what they talk about and what are they concerned about? Are they worried, do they have problems that they don't seem able to solve, are they concerned about the things of this world such as politics, taxes, money? Listen closely because this is important – **anyone who truly has a relationship with God isn't worried about anything.** How can that be, you say? Well, I'm going to give you just one example, and it is the Apostle Paul. Remember him before he came to Jesus Christ? He spent his life hurting others who did not believe as he (then called Saul) did, yet after he discovered the truth, he no longer worried about anything, including governments that wanted him destroyed. So what are you worried about? Believe me, it's not important.

My focus in this chapter has been on the subject of individuals developing a meaningful relationship with God and themselves, and the reason for this is that the church must be able to begin establishing a core cadre of lay people that will be able to teach and lead others. Of primary importance is the development of teachers that will be willing to teach the children, because the children will be the "witnesses" of tomorrow for the entire Christian church and they will bear the responsibility of overcoming the mistakes of their parents.

7

FIXING THE CHURCH Part II

Why do you call me Lord yet you do not do what I say?

And let our people also learn to engage in good deeds to meet pressing needs that they may not be unfruitful.

However, the Most High does not dwell in houses made by human hands

Several months ago, a typical church youth group of teenagers visited my farm, and with them was a very pretty young girl who was rejected and ignored by the rest of the group. This shunned little girl, was so desperate for acceptance that she displayed outlandish behavior which, of course, pushed the others even farther away. I made sure that the youth pastor (who was present) was made aware of the situation and made several suggestions before they left. However, when I followed up several months later, I was told quite flippantly that it was no longer his concern because she had left that particular church.

FAILURE!

What a shame! Here was another little girl who would someday be a young lady and who would probably someday turn to drugs, cults, violence and perhaps even prostitution, as a means of obtaining "love" and acceptance, all because of a youth pastor who was too busy or uncaring or maybe just not even trained in identifying youth at risk.

Of all the failures of the Christian church over the ages, the failure to recognize the need for, and to implement programs to "train" Christians about just what it means to be a Christian and what is required of all Christians is the preeminent reason that the church as a whole has failed to follow the teachings of God's designated spokesperson, His Son, Jesus Christ. The church, even from the earliest times, has twisted God's purpose for its own ends and personal gain, even as the Pope promised salvation to anyone willing to participate in the Crusades, the sole purpose of which was to wrest control of Jerusalem from the "infidels.". I ask you, when did God ever indicate that certain portions of real estate were near and dear to His heart?

This perversion of the spirit and the intent of God is evidenced not only in the Catholic church through the acceptance of homosexual priests who prey upon the children of their own flock, but even fundamentalist Protestant evangelists have been found and convicted as abusers of children.

When is the church, every church, going to clean up its own act? Well, it won't happen until the people, not the leaders, rise up and demand it. Remember, the leaders of any organization, whether sacred or secular, don't want change because that change will cost them their positions of power. Even today, as the Pope rails against the policy of zero tolerance toward abusive priests, most of the members of the Catholic Church sit quietly and uncaringly on their hands. Jesus Christ was so right in characterizing us as sheep, because we exemplify sheep as we follow our chosen leaders in whatever convoluted and ungodly path they care to take. The ordination of an openly gay Bishop in the Episcopal Church is a manifestation of the uncaring attitude of most Christians, and especially of the church leaders. While the acceptance of homosexuals as fellow human beings in need of salvation (like us all) is Christlike behavior, the acceptance of practicing homosexuals as leaders or pastors of the church is utterly abhorrent to God, and this abhorrence is manifested in many Biblical passages in both the Old and New Testaments.

> *You shall not lie with a male as one lies with a female; it is an abomination*

> *For this reason God gave them over to degrading passions; for their women exchanged the natural function for that which is unnatural,*

> *And in the same way also the men abandoned the natural function of the woman and burned in their desire toward one another, men with men committing indecent acts and receiving in their own persons the due penalty of their error*

> *..., for murderers and immoral men and homosexuals and kidnappers and liars and perjurers, and whatever else is contrary to sound teaching.*

Yes, there are more passages, but when the Bible compares homosexuals to murderers, kidnappers, and liars, I think that the message is plain enough, although no one seems to be listening.

The bottom line is this. The church, in order to become effective in its mission, must clean its own house. Nothing more needs to be said.

In the opening paragraph of this chapter I told the story of a teenager who was rejected by her peers. This is not an isolated incident, and it brings home the fact that the church is failing in its duty to teach even teenagers how to be Christians. Someone is going to say, "Well, that is the job of the parents." but that will be only partially correct. The failure to teach even their own teenagers isn't the only area where parents are failing, and this is due to the fact that the church isn't teaching the parents either. Therefore, it has to be up to the church to take the lead. Since it is obvious that the parents are failing to teach their own children, Christians must make the difficult choice of who will be willing to stand up and teach our young people what it means to be a Christian. Is this one more responsibility that we are to expect of our public schools so we can blame them when they fail? I think not, but that seems to be the pet philosophy of most Christians who seem to *want* the public schools to fail so they can shout, "I told you so."

For this young girl, or any young person, to be allowed to be isolated, mistreated, and even ostracized by their peers, especially in an organized church setting, is totally unacceptable and should result in nothing less than the dismissal of the persons in charge until they have been properly trained.

Everyone knows the story of the Columbine High School shootings perpetrated by two young outcasts named Eric Harris and Dylan Klebold. The question that nobody has asked is how these two young people *became* outcasts in the first place. The very simple answer is that they didn't become outcasts by their own choice. They became outcasts through the fact that their own peers, including Christian teenagers, refused to recognize, perhaps through a lack of training, their desire for acceptance, and their cries for recognition.

Listen to what I am saying. **No one wants to be an outcast! No one wants to hate and be hated!** Rebellion is a natural act when it is a result of frustration due to the fact that no one will take the time to listen, and, more importantly, to love and even accept a person who has no one to turn to. Doesn't anyone recognize the fact that being "different" is nothing more that a cry for attention and recognition as a fellow human being? Where are all the people who call themselves "Christian"? Where are all the people who attend worship services every Sunday and brag about how much they love God, yet they don't have even one hour a week to give to the people who really need help? As a matter of fact, most of these self-professed "Christians" will not even take the time to listen to someone who just needs a friend.

I am willing to bet that hundreds of people associated with that Colorado town have made a statement similar to this, "I would have given anything to stop those killings from happening!" If you think about it, that statement is a lie, because those same people are the very one's who won't spare even one or two hours a week to work with **any** school or any organization such as the Scouts, etc. These are the same Christians who expect everyone else to be responsible so they can play the "blame game.".

The Christian church has failed because its very goal is to bring people *in* when in fact the goal should be to send trained disciples *out* into the world. Christianity is failing because the church is facing inward when it should be facing *outward.*

FAILURE!

Presently on television is a popular program entitled, *Joan of Arcadia*, which I find interesting and so subtly pertinent to every Christian's relationship, not only with God but with our fellow man, and I will explain that statement later. In this program, God appears to Joan as various people, such as a substitute teacher, a child, a bus rider, a bum, etc. but the disguise I find most appropriate is His appearance as a leather-wearing, facially-pierced, typically repugnant "acid rocker." Why is this particular disguise appropriate? It is appropriate for two reasons, the first being the fact that if God wanted to hide His identity, appearing in the guise of an "acid rocker" certainly wouldn't raise suspicion. Think about it. When most of us see a person like this, we avert our eyes and look away, and most of us walk just a little bit faster. Wouldn't it be appropriate and maybe just like God to take on such a disguise? The second reason I find this particular disguise appropriate is the fact that God just might want us to see the fact that He is in all of us, even the most socially repugnant. Whether you want to accept it or not, the fact is that there is no person in this world that is "repugnant" to God. Even the most lost of any of us can be redeemed, and that is what God wants us to help Him accomplish. Did you get that?

God wants our help. Does He need it? No.! He wants it, and, listen closely now, He is demanding it, if we are going to pretend to serve Him.

I think that having God take on the appearance of an "acid rocker" was a stroke of pure genius of the part of writers of the show, or just maybe they were led there by God Himself. Think about this, all you "Christians" out there. Who were the people with whom Jesus hung out? They were for the most part the dregs of society of two thousand years ago. Jesus befriended thieves, lepers, tax cheats, prostitutes, drunks, people living in sin, and more. Why don't we who pretend to follow Him do the same? Is it because the cults that call themselves "God fearing and God loving churches" teach us instead to "separate ourselves" from anyone who does not believe and act as we do? This is exactly the kind of thinking that encourages the anger and frustration that produces a Dylan Klebold and an Eric Harris. Everyone who wants to call themselves a Christian had better understand the fact that any "church" that advocates "separation" is in fact advocating "selfishness."

Let's take a closer look at what happened at Columbine High, from the perspective of the question of what could have caused two intelligent young men to become so estranged from society and their fellow classmates, that murder and suicide became a viable option. Before I proceed further, I want to establish two points of reference; the first is a disclaimer of the fact that I am not a psychologist nor do I pretend to know psychology beyond the scope of the usual college freshman courses., but I am a good observer, and (this is the second point of reference) I myself was an outcast throughout high school.

This is not meant to be a treatise on adolescence, but from the viewpoint of us geeks, nerds, and dorks; adolescence and the teenage years are pure torture. We look at everyone else and see other young people who have physical beauty, or athletic ability, or social graces, and we don't have the faintest idea of how to fit in. Perhaps we don't even know how to make conversation, and, to put it bluntly, our individual lives become a hell which can, and in the case of Dylan and Eric, did, result in a downward spiral.

Because God made us humans as social animals, meaning that we seek and need the company of others, we all search for fellow humans who will accept us even as we are, and this is where the church has failed. The church, even for teenagers, has become a closed "social parlor" where the brightest and the best can meet and commune. Oh, sure, they "invite" others to join their party, but then they treat those same invitees as outcasts unless they "submit" to the group. How many Christians are taking the time and making the effort to actually become friends with someone who might be socially less acceptable.

The church teaches us to "witness" the life and meaning of Jesus Christ with only our mouths, when, in order to be effective, we must witness with our lives. What does that mean? Just this: the only effective witness that any Christians can make is through their own lives, their friendship, their time, and their help. Keep in mind that every time that we ignore the people who need our time and our friendship, we are sending a message that they are not worthy of us. Well guess what, those people are going to find someone who *will* accept them, and the results won't be pretty.

I would really like to know just how many (if any) young Christians ever offered the hand of friendship to either Dylan or Eric. I'm not talking about inviting them to church; I'm talking about taking time and making an effort to become friends, or at least accepting them socially and intellectually. Who wants to bet that both these kids were at least of average intelligence or above? Listen up, because what I am about to say holds the key to preventing what happened at Columbine from happening somewhere else.

The blame for the murders and mayhem that happened at Columbine High School that terrible day **does not** rest with Eric Harris and Dylan Klebold. The blame rests on the shoulders of every so-called Christian student and every so-called Christian teacher and faculty member of that school and, therefore, upon every Christian church leader, minister, teacher, and lay member in that city. When is the church going to recognize that we must begin teaching even (and especially) our children how to become a living example of Jesus Christ so that those same children will know how to love and befriend even the most unlovable of our fellow human beings.

Removing the blame for the murders at Columbine from Dylan and Eric would seem to contradict my earlier premise that God gives us the freedom to choose, so let me clarify my statement of the last paragraph. Dylan and Eric did indeed have the freedom to choose whether to proceed with their plans and ultimately they alone made the decision to pull the triggers, and the ultimate blame rests on their shoulders.

The point that every Christian and every Christian church must begin to recognize is that we also have the freedom to choose, and every choice that we, either as individuals or corporately as an organization make, affects the lives of everyone. The fact that people who called themselves "Christians" ignored or hated or discriminated against the two young men known as Eric Harris and Dylan Klebold, and that discrimination built every inch of the wall of events that led to that desperate act of murder and mayhem. Listen to me, we individually cause the events of this world by our own actions of uncompromise or rejection or dislike. We Christians have caused and spread hatred from the time of the Crusades to the present day genocide of Muslims in Croatia. When are we going to learn and when will the church recognize that there really is an Eleventh Commandment, and Jesus Christ deemed that Commandment one of the most important parts of His three years of teaching.

FAILURE!

Every time that either Eric Harris, or Dylan Klebold or any other member of their group was shunned, laughed at, gossiped about, rejected, or ignored, one more brick was laid in the wall that separated those two from society and societally acceptable behavior. We Christians must learn that it is *we* that are responsible because it is *we* that have been given the mandate by God to love and care for our brothers and sisters.

Any adult who has spent any time at all in any school setting will remember instances of cruelty and just plain meanness and ignorance perpetrated by both girls and boys on the weaker members of their peer group. Is this normal behavior for young people? The answer is "Yes," because this is a time of learning for all children and they are learning hatred and rejection from their parents and their church. The saddest part is the fact that every Christian mouths the Name of Jesus Christ yet no one seems to be teaching His words and actions. Is there no one who recognizes the obvious fact that behavior that hurts others is behavior that contradicts the teaching, the example, and the very life of Jesus? Eric and Dylan had been ostracized and rejected so many times that they resorted to the ultimate means of getting attention and recognition, murder.

If the church is to be effective, it must begin teaching its young people that recognition by one's peers, while desirable, is not the ultimate goal and, moreover, it isn't even important. The only thing that is important in this life is recognition by God as we work for Him. Notice I didn't say "worship" Him;, I said "work for" Him. The church has made the act of contrition and worship the end objective, when in truth; it must be just the beginning.

The church repeatedly mouths the word "outreach," yet that is nothing more than a meaningless word, the responsibility for which is placed upon someone else. Our young people (and hopefully our adults) must be taught that "outreach" is an individual responsibility and an individual action that is the responsibility of each of us, and it is one that we can easily perform every day as we befriend someone who needs a smile, a touch, a conversation, an acceptance and a recognition to get through the day. Why is it so difficult for Christians to be nothing more than "nice" to our fellow human beings? I can't figure it out. Perhaps if just one self-proclaimed "Christian" teenager or one "Christian" teacher had taken the time to be nice to Eric Harris and Dylan Klebold, the massacre at Columbine High might not have happened. We praise and worship a Savior who was helpful to everyone with whom He had contact; is it too difficult to follow that lead?

I want to share a story that was passed along through my e-mail that exemplifies exactly how anyone who calls themselves a Christian should act toward their fellow human beings. I wish I knew the author of this story, because, as you will see, it is so very pertinent to our society today.

This is a beautiful story and I hope that every reader will take it to heart.

One day, when I was a freshman in high school, I saw a kid from my class walking home from school. His name was Kyle. It looked like he was carrying all of his books. I thought to myself, "Why would anyone bring home all his books on a Friday? He must really be a nerd." I had quite a weekend planned (parties and a football game with my friends tomorrow afternoon), so I shrugged my shoulders and went on.

As I was walking, I saw a bunch of kids running toward him. They ran at him, knocking all his books out of his arms and tripping him so he landed in the dirt. His glasses went flying, and I saw them land in the grass about ten feet from him. He looked up and I saw this terrible sadness in his eyes.

My heart went out to him. So, I jogged over to him and as he crawled around looking for his glasses, I saw a tear in his eye.

As I handed him his glasses, I said, "Those guys are jerks. They really need to get a life!" He looked at me and said, "Hey, thanks!" There was a big smile on his face. It was one of those smiles that showed real gratitude.

I helped him pick up his books, and asked him where he lived. As it turned out, he lived near me, so I asked him why I had never seen him before. He said he had gone to a private school before now.

I never would have hung out with a private school kid before. We talked all the way home, and I carried some of his books. He turned out to be a pretty cool kid. I asked him if he wanted to play a little football with my friends. He said yes. We hung out all weekend, and the more I got to know Kyle, the more I liked him, and my friends thought the same of him.

Monday morning came, and there was Kyle with the huge stack of books again. I stopped him and said, "Boy, you are gonna really build some serious muscles with this pile of books every day!" He just laughed and handed me half the books.

Over the next four years, Kyle and I became best friends. When we were seniors, we began to think about college. Kyle decided on Georgetown, and I was going to Duke. I knew that we would always be friends, that the miles would never be a problem. He was going to be a doctor, and I was going for business on a football scholarship.

Kyle was valedictorian of our class. I teased him all the time about being a nerd. He had to prepare a speech for graduation. I was so glad it wasn't me having to get up there and speak. Graduation day, I saw Kyle. He looked great. He was one of those guys that really found himself during high school. He filled out and actually looked good in glasses. He had more dates than I had and all the girls loved him. Boy, sometimes I was jealous.

Today was one of those days. I could see that he was nervous about his speech. So, I smacked him on the back, and said, "Hey, big guy, you'll be great!" He looked at me with one of those looks (the really grateful one) and smiled. "Thanks,", he said.

As he started his speech, he cleared his throat and began. "Graduation is a time to thank those who helped you make it through those tough years. Your parents, your teachers, your siblings, maybe a coach...but mostly your friends. I am here to tell all of you that being a friend to someone is the best gift you can give them. I am going to tell you a story..."

I just looked at my friend with disbelief as he told the story of the first day we met. He had planned to kill himself over the weekend. He talked of how he had cleaned out his locker so his mom wouldn't have to do it later and was carrying his stuff home. He looked hard at me and gave me a little smile. "Thankfully, I was saved. My friend saved me from doing the unspeakable."

I heard the gasp go through the crowd as this handsome, popular boy told us all about his most desperate moment. I saw his mom and dad looking at me and smiling that same grateful smile. Not until that moment did I realize its depth. Never underestimate the power of your actions. With one small gesture, you can change a person's life, for better or for worse.

God puts us all in each other's lives to impact one another in some way. Look for God in others.

WHEN YOU DIE WILL YOU BE ABLE TO SAY THAT YOU REALLY DID SOMETHING WITH THE LIFE THAT GOD GAVE YOU? IT'S YOUR CHOICE, BUT RECOGNIZE THIS – GOD ONLY GIVES US ONE CHANCE.

We will never know whether Eric Harris and Dylan Klebold truly believed in God or not, but we have a clue about how they felt about the people who called themselves "Christians," because one of them asked a Christian girl a question just before shooting her. The question asked by one of the killers went something like this:; "Do you believe in God now?" It is reasonable to surmise two things from the fact that this question was asked at all during a time of high stress and anxiety. First, the question of God's existence was on the mind of at least one of the young killers, and, second, the person to whom the question was asked was a person whom he knew within the framework of Christianity.

We will also never know for sure just how or in what way this troubled young man knew this young Christian lady. Did Eric or Dylan know her as a kind and loving person who accepted their odd views and dress code but loved them and interacted with them as fellow human beings anyway? Probably not. It is purely conjecture on my part, but more likely than not, Eric or Dylan knew this particular young lady as a member of a typically arrogant "Christian" social group that talked about God and His Son while simultaneously laughing, gossiping, and making fun of those like Eric and Dylan, either openly or covertly. Why is it that we Christians have so much trouble recognizing others as fellow human beings? The answer is that because of the poison of Calvinism, which teaches that certain people are damned from birth, we are allowed to ignore someone crying for acceptance, someone and who looks or acts differently than our allowable norm.

When will the leaders of the church recognize that instead of teaching its members to "separate themselves" from anyone who does not meet their standards, they should be teaching their members to be like Jesus Himself, who never rejected or ignored anyone, and who, in fact, served everyone regardless of their sins?

Let me give an example of the typical "Christian" attitude practiced by the church of today. Many years ago, I went to the funeral of a good friend, held at the largest Catholic church on the East side of Cleveland, Ohio. The service included communion, and even though I wasn't Catholic, I wanted to take communion, because to me it is one of the most humbling events that takes place in our Christian religion. Whenever I take communion, the words from the Episcopal service come back which remind me that, "I am not worthy so much as to pick up the crumbs from under the table....," much less to be accepted and loved by God. As I stood in the line moving toward the altar, I had tears in my eyes (as I usually do during this service); and after a few minutes, I finally stood before the altar and received the communion wafer. At that instant, I happened to glance up at the eyes of the priest who had obviously identified me as a non-Catholic and was gazing intently at me with obvious anger, hatred and rejection. It was as though I had desecrated not only the service but the entire church, and the intensity of the look of that priest spoke volumes regarding my acceptance and the acceptance of anyone who might not fit their "mold." To this day, I am still in awe at the degree of overt hatred displayed by that priest (presumably a "man of God"), and I have always wondered if they had to hose out the entire church after the service because of my presence at "their" altar.

Is this a typical attitude of only the Catholic denomination? Sadly, the answer has to be "No," and every denomination must rethink their attitude and acceptance of those who may not believe or practice exactly as they do.

In my life as an engineer, I have spent a lot of time traveling, but whenever I am on the road on a Sunday morning, I always try to find a church to spend a little time worshiping the God who has been so good to me. One Sunday morning, as I was dressed in my usual traveling uniform of jeans and a sweatshirt, I came to a mainline Baptist church and I went in to join the service. The looks I received at my uncouth "uniform" were, while not overtly hostile as was that of the Catholic priest, certainly not welcoming either and not one person spoke to me or welcomed me into "their" service. At the other end of the spectrum, I stopped at an Episcopal Cathedral in North Carolina just as the service was beginning and dashed in dressed as usual. I was greeted warmly and I sat toward the back of the church. Because the service had already started, I was fumbling with the prayer book, trying to catch up, when I noticed one of the ushers standing at the end of my row. He was watching me trying to find my place in the service with the Book of Common Prayer, and it was obvious to me from the look on his face, that he was standing there solely for the purpose of serving me should I need help.

For those of you not familiar with the Episcopal Church, they have a prayer book that is even more complicated than the instruction book for Windows 98, but the fact that even one man was willing to help me join in a strange service gave me a feeling of warmth, and of the presence of God that stayed with me all day. As I glanced toward him at that instant, I mouthed the words "thank you" and smiled at him to make sure he knew that I appreciated his silent offer of service. In the vernacular of our young people today, I have to say, "Now that's what I'm talking about!"

Some of the practices of our churches today are laughable and I want to share one with you. This practice comes from the Southern Baptist denomination, since that is the denomination which I have been attending for the last ten years and it is the denomination which "encouraged" me to write this book. The practice I'm talking about is that of having a "designated greeter." This is a person who carries a little brass plate pinned to his or her chest with the word "GREETER" emblazoned on it, and their job is to walk around the church shaking hands with everyone and making them feel "welcome." Does that sound as phony to you as it does to me? Why does any church need a designated greeter when every person attending that service should take on the responsibility of greeting everyone else, especially strangers? Oh, well, I guess the reason is that everyone else is too busy talking to God to be bothered talking to a mere human. How many church services have you ever walked into where every person smiled at you and greeted you warmly, even if they didn't know you?

I want to take a few moments to cover one of the more overt departures from the church of Biblical times, even though I have discussed it previously, because this subject contributes so heavily to the failure of the church in general. The subject which I want to discuss is the constant building of ever larger houses of "worship." I put the word "worship" in quotation marks since the predominant use of these beautiful and expensive buildings is nothing more than entertainment. Most Christians go to church on Sunday morning to be entertained. If you don't believe that, then go to the largest church in your area on Sunday morning and analyze the actions and delivery of the preacher during the sermon. Listen to and watch the choir, robed so magnificently, and singing so gloriously, accompanied by an organ of such power and proportion that with the slightest touch of a pedal it could blow out the eardrums of the entire congregation. Like the song says, *"That's Entertainment."*

Let's go back to the time of Martin Luther for just a moment. Remember him? He is the person that started the Protestant movement, but do you remember why? The reason, of course, is that the Catholic church of the time had started selling "indulgences,", and an indulgence was nothing more than a statement of the forgiveness of all your sins in return for money. And why, do you ask, did the church decide to sell the forgiveness of sins? The reason is the fact that the Pope had begun a building program, and he needed money to build what we know today as Saint Peter's basilica and, ultimately, the Vatican. Sound like most of the churches today? As I write this book, I am not aware of even one church that is **not** involved in a building program of some type, many of them spending tens of millions of dollars to further enlarge buildings that are and will be used only once a week.

While the Protestant church isn't so overt that they give out pieces of paper to hang on your wall, the promise is still there. In every service someone gets up and talks about the building fund drive or some such thing. The implication that God will reward your gifts is always present, and my own church went so far as to blatantly state that our latest building program was (in their words), "fulfilling God's dream." Gosh, I wasn't aware that God dreamed about ever larger buildings. In my opinion, the only dreams being fulfilled are those of the pastors who want an ever larger salary while 800,000 homeless people sleep under the nearest bridge and millions lose their jobs to "outsourcing."

Earlier in this chapter, I mentioned that the thrust or the purpose of the Christian church should be directed outward instead of inward. When I talk about the purpose of the church being directed inward, I am talking about the fact that the goal of every Christian church is to gain new members, and thereby be "forced" to expand and build new buildings. It doesn't take much reading of the New Testament to determine that this is contrary to the practices of the disciples and the new Christians immediately after the death of Jesus Christ. The book of Acts describes the establishment of "house churches," meaning that Christians met in each others' homes. Now, I am quite aware of the fact that during that time period, Christians were being persecuted by both the Jews and the Romans and they couldn't just go out and buy or build a "church" and put up a sign to attract converts; they had to worship covertly so as to not be murdered.

The modern church seems to have the sole purpose of building a huge entertainment complex for its members. Most of us remember Jim and Tammy Faye Bakker and their creation known as the PTL Club. I find that name to be appropriate because a "club" is exactly what that organization was intended to be. I visited what they called "Heritage Village", South of Charlotte, North Carolina, one time and I was flabbergasted by the opulence of that which was constructed supposedly in the name of God. I drove up almost a mile long driveway to the Grand Hotel and was greeted by a fully uniformed doorman who ushered me inside to a hotel lobby which could rival even Las Vegas. As I walked inside, a grand piano was playing (entertainment again) and I was in awe of the magnificent antiques, each with its little plaque identifying the donor family, each of whom had probably achieved sainthood for their gift. I sometimes wonder if, when those people die, God will say to them, "You had your reward on earth; (in the form of that little plaque). Depart from Me.".

I have told the story of my own church and its building fund, but few churches can rival the magnificence of another local church, First Baptist of North Spartanburg, South Carolina. As an entirely uneducated guess, I would have to estimate the value of that church's land, buildings, conference center, offices, Christian school, and worship center at around thirty-five million dollars. All that wealth spent on buildings while 800,000 people sleep under bridges and 540,000 American children are housed in foster care facilities with very little, or no hope of adoption (especially by "Christian" families).

Given the fact that there really are 540,000 children here in the United States begging for adoption, I find it totally incongruous that earnest well-meaning Christian families will rush to Slovakia, or Russia, or China, or whatever the country "du jour" is in the hope of adopting some small child when there are almost a half million children right here next door that need a home. What are they thinking? What is their church thinking? Does anyone give a damn or is it one big "collection" game where the parent with the most exotic child wins?

Since we are talking about adoption, there are times that I am ashamed to be an American, and even more ashamed to be identified as a Christian, and one of those times is when the people of one particular race refuse to allow the adoption of foster children of that race into the homes of people of another race or ethnicity fearing that those children might "lose their identity.". Nothing could be more shameful than refusing to allow a child a loving home because of one's own hatred and prejudice. I can make only one guarantee here and that is the fact that anyone who denies a child a home for whatever reason, will find a very special place in Hell awaiting them when they arrive at the end of their life. I have a good question for you. Which is more important, a person's "racial" identity or their identity in Christ?

And what does the church teach about this problem? Nothing!! The church is too busy pandering to its members to hear the words of Jesus.

FAILURE!

It is time for any person who sees themselves as "called of God" to teach and preach, and by that I mean any and every Pastor or Minister or Preacher, to quit worrying about their jobs or their "appointments" and stand up and start teaching the everyday "application" of the life and teachings of Jesus Christ to the lives of those of us who wish to follow. Every Sunday there are thousands of people supposedly "accepting God," yet these very same people refuse to accept God's lifestyle. Salvation (by itself) can't change anyone and, in fact, salvation doesn't change most people. Salvation, as a friend once said in an e-mail to me, brings a change of state (grace) but not a change of personality. The unsaved gossip becomes a saved gossip, the unsaved thief becomes a saved thief, the unsaved homosexual becomes a saved homosexual and no ministers would dare to correct them because they might lose a member (and their money).

Ninety-nine percent of all Christians will remain "kinderchristians" throughout all their lives because their pastors refuse to teach lifestyle application in fear of offending some member of the flock and losing their jobs. What are those pastors going to tell God as they kneel before Him at the end of their lives? "Gee, I didn't want to hurt anyone's feelings?"

These same "kinderchristians" are the ones to whom the following verse speaks: *"They profess to know God but by their deeds they deny Him, being detestable and disobedient, and worthless for any good deed."* This verse speaks to all "born again" Baptists and the members of any Christian church who forget about their fellow man once they drive out of the parking lot. This verse pertains to all Christians who lie to anyone, whether it concerns selling a used car, or representing their intentions.

I have a funny, but sadly, very typical story about the pastor of a local church who brought his old pickup truck to my friend, a mechanic, because the gears in the differential were whining. When my friend the mechanic took the differential apart, the gears were pitted from rust, and it was evident that at one time the truck had been sitting unused long enough to allow the gears not immersed in oil to rust and pit.

When the pastor was told that the differential would require a somewhat expensive rebuild, he told my friend the mechanic to put it back together and fill it with something that would temporarily hide the whining noise from a potential buyer. The exact words that this pastor used, as told by my friend, were, "Put it back together and hide the problem so that I can "'unload'" it on someone." Now my friend the mechanic was an older man who wasn't afraid to say what he thought and let the chips fall where they may, and he rose up, looked at the pastor and spoke rather forcefully, "SAY WHAT PREACHER???" Knowing my friend as I do, I imagine that last part of the conversation was sprinkled with a few (maybe more than a few) words which I wouldn't repeat.

Praise God, another Christian (and in this case, a pastor) has given testimony about what Jesus Christ has done in their life.

Let's take a moment and examine the lives of these two very different men. My friend the mechanic had an intense dislike of Christians and subsequently Christianity as a whole, due to repeatedly being abused by people who called themselves Christians yet who lied and cheated every chance they got. Here is a man who had been "witnessed" to repeatedly by Christians and he wasn't having any of it. This same man, was the most honest and capable mechanic in the entire county and was admired and loved by anyone who needed work done on heavy equipment, because they knew they would be treated honestly and fairly.

The second man is the pastor of a local church, and a "man of god," yet he has no hesitation when the time comes to cheat someone else (probably a member of his own church). You may have noticed that I didn't capitalize the word "god" in the sentence above and the reason is that I certainly don't recognize the "god" that he worships. The God that I worship doesn't accept cheating, and I know that I don't even have to cheat because my "God" takes care of me to the extent (and beyond) that I don't have to cheat someone else. Is it obvious to only me that this pastor's "god" is only money?

When are Christians going to recognize that the God that they worship will take care of them in every way, if only they will follow Him with more than their mouths, and when are Christian churches going to begin teaching that the true path to salvation encompasses more than just worship? I'm going to say it again, and just maybe this time the pastor of some church will be listening: **"The witness of our mouths is more than useless, it is only through the witness of our lives that we can convince unbelievers to open their hearts to God."**

Christians were in the news again this morning as another Baptist "pastor" from a neighboring county was sentenced to eight years in prison without parole for having a sexual relationship with a minor living in his home. Wow, what a great "witness."!!!

Maybe it would be appropriate to review that verse from the New Testament again: *"They profess to know God, but by their deeds they deny Him, being detestable and disobedient, and worthless for any good deed."* It is obvious to me that God is saying that we must clean up our own lives before we can be useful to Him, yet why do so few Christians listen? Because the church has failed to teach it, and the reason is that the church leaders have refused to practice it.

I think that it is time for all "serious" Christians to find new leaders, and by that I mean people who can identify and teach for all time what it means to be a Christian. You will remember that I talked about the National Beta Club and their slogan of LET US LEAD BY SERVING OTHERS. I was so fascinated by that slogan that I visited their headquarters, where I was welcomed and given several copies of their magazine, *THE BETA JOURNAL*. I really didn't expect to find much information in their magazine, since most of the submissions are by elementary school students, but in a free moment, I sat down and read several articles and did I ever get a surprise. A young lady wrote a small article entitled **"follow the leader,"**, and I would like to quote from her article. The subject of her article is obviously leadership and the importance of whom we choose to be our leader, and here are two excerpts from her article, "...the decisions we make in choosing who leads us will greatly influence our whole lives." The second excerpt states, "Choose wisely who leads, choose wisely how you follow and choose to succeed."

Let's examine that first excerpt from the perspective of a new Christian. When we first decide to accept God and His Son into our lives, we naturally give Jesus Christ the place of leadership in our lives, and rightly so. The problems begin when we allow that leadership to be usurped by some "preacher" who becomes, by our own default, God's spokesperson and, therefore, our new "leader." Don't believe me? How many times have you heard about some Christians changing churches because they didn't like the preacher, and how many Christians attend one of the "mega-churches" because they want to be entertained by the best speaker. Let me make this clear, serving God is not about being entertained; it is about reading and study and preparation for the job God has created **just for you.**

The second excerpt which I cited from the young lady's article has a great deal of depth (and wisdom) for one so young, and I want to dissect it at some length. The first word of her sentence is "Choose,", and she is telling each one of us that we have to make a conscious decision regarding exactly whom we allow to lead us. This question of "choice" flies in the face of some misdirected teachings of the church, because some churches would have us believe that we don't have a choice, God decides everything for us, and nothing could be further from the truth. As I stated earlier, most Christians make the right choice, but then they abdicate that choice to the human that entertains them best.

If someone were to ask any (and probably every) Christian they were to meet, whom they considered as their leader, the answer would probably be Jesus Christ every time;

yet over 90% of those same Christians have never read even the New Testament from cover to cover. My question is this: How can Christians *pretend* to follow Jesus Christ when they aren't even interested enough to read about Him? Their answer is this: My pastor interprets the Bible and the words of Jesus for me. How sad, considering the number of incarcerated pastors.

Right here is where the second part of that young lady's sentence comes into play, "...choose wisely how you follow...", and here is where most Christians fail, because they expect God to do all the work. If anyone chooses to follow God, they must work at it every day. Be sure that you understand the fact that God expects nothing less.

The last piece of advice from our very intelligent little friend is to "choose to succeed." Those words are very important to me because when I considered myself to be a failure, I made the choice to follow God and commit myself to Him and His work, and (listen closely now) He has made me the success that I am today solely because I myself chose to succeed by *working* at my own continued growth and commitment to Him.

How does all this relate to the subject of "Fixing the Church"? Every pastor and every church must decide to stop the farce of business as usual, or should I say entertainment as usual, and charge every member with the responsibility of reading the New Testament, understanding and growing in the words of our Savior, changing their own lives, and beginning a life of service to their community and all those others who also happen to be God's people.

I want to stop here for a moment and address that group of people known as "seniors," of which I am a member. I have so often heard an older member of a church say, "Well, I have served my time, and it's time for the younger generation to step up and serve." I will be the first to admit that many of these seniors have served long and well, but they should remember that this earth is not the place where they should desire their reward. It would be wiser to remember the words of Jesus when He told the story of the wealthy farmer and how God said to him, "Tonight your very life will be demanded."

Seniors have the life experience and the abilities to accomplish and give back so much to the younger generation today that they could with minimal effort become the most valuable generation of our entire society. Yes, it is true that we just don't have the stamina that we used to have, and on most mornings, we seemingly don't even have the strength to get up; but just think of the possibilities. Just think about the wisdom that we have acquired through the years that we could pass on so that the younger generation wouldn't have to make the mistakes that we made. No, of course most of them won't listen, after all, we didn't listen either, but think about the possibilities if we could change even one life. If you are reward oriented, think about the reward that you will get from the Father as He says to you, "Well done thou good and faithful servant!" I don't know about you, but that thought motivates me.

We are talking about "fixing the church," and here is the idea that God brought me last week as I was planning to end this chapter. The biggest need in the world today, and perhaps especially in the United States, is for people to act as teachers and mentors to our young people that are in the schools today. What better chance to serve God by serving the youth of today through volunteering in our public schools. Could there be anything more important than the life of a child? I think not, and neither did Jesus when He told His Disciples to **let the little children come to me.** (my paraphrase) If the children were important to Jesus, shouldn't they be important to us? Does it matter that they may be from a Jewish family or an Armenian family? So what that they may not believe in God? Jesus didn't differentiate and neither should we.

Listen closely., I'm not talking about witnessing., I'm talking about helping, mentoring, guiding, listening, tutoring, befriending, because these are the actions that will make a difference when those same young people reach the point where they want to begin thinking about the possible existence of a God.

It is time for all of us Christians to stop worrying about that old nemesis called "theory of evolution" because it isn't important. Really, the theory of evolution does not matter in the least. Let it be taught for what it is, a proposed theory, and remember it is just a theory because it hasn't been and may never be proven. Should we care? No, let God handle the big stuff, while we take care of the job that God wants us to handle. Besides, who of us knows or could understand the mechanism which God used to create the universe?

But shun foolish controversies and genealogies and strife and disputes...

The theory of evolution is nothing more than, as the Bible talks about, a foolish controversy and a supposed genealogy of the creation of the earth. As I said before, it isn't important and it has nothing to do with what we Christians are called to do to serve our God. Each time we make something as silly as this into a point of contention, we are serving the Devil, because we are, in effect, turning away potential believers. Is that our intention? Sometimes I think so when I listen to the silliness that "Christians" argue about. Which one of us was here to witness how God created everything?

I took an old phone book and counted the number of Christian churches listed in the yellow pages, and then I turned to the blue pages and counted the number of public schools in Spartanburg County. There were 302 Christian churches in the city alone, and there were 52 public schools of all grades in the county, for a ratio of 6 to 1. That means that if every church could send just one volunteer, every public school would have 6 six extra helpers. Yes, that would be great, but let's get real, the two largest churches each have around 5,000 members on their roles, and let's suppose that every church tithed (I don't know if you remember that word) just ten percent of its active members, there would be literally thousands of volunteers and the schools would be the best in the country and maybe the world.

What am I thinking? The church tithe? How very backward, I must be dyslexic. After all, we are supposed to tithe **to the church** aren't we? But think about it for just a second. Who does the church pretend to serve? Could it be God? The Bible tells us that God demands our tithe, and what makes up a church? People, of course, so why shouldn't a church, if it purports to serve God, not "tithe" ten percent of its greatest resource, its people, in the service of God's people and, therefore, in the service of God Himself.

I'm not going to even try to speculate on how many people that would entail if every church could get ten percent of its members to volunteer to help, but the number would be overwhelming and each volunteer would only have to spend one hour per week for the schools to be inundated. Can you imagine how test scores would soar if just the Christian college graduates would tutor in a subject related to their degree? We would have the best educated children in the world, to say nothing of the fact that thousands of kids and adults both would have made new friends and developed relationships that just might prevent the next Columbine. Would that be worth it? To find out, ask the parents of one of the kids murdered at that catastrophe.

I have outlined an opportunity for all those Christian churches that say that they are serving God, to actually begin serving their Leader. Will they take the lead? Who knows, as I said before, my college English instructor told me that I was naive. Was she correct? Most certainly, but all of us naive people have a vision which is not seen by most other people because they believe it to be impractical or impossible or both.

In case anyone still cannot understand the ramifications of the project that I am proposing, let me clarify what a project of this magnitude could accomplish. On the secular side, the result could be thousands of kids who might never have had a chance to go to college now being able to pass the SAT and hope for a good job and a successful career instead of a life of poverty and welfare. Another result might be that hundreds of kids who felt abandoned by their parents and by society might find someone who can sit and talk and help them relate to a difficult world, thereby eliminating another potential Columbine. To all of you "Christians" who complain about high taxes, here is your chance to do something about them.

So what benefit would a program like this be to a church or even to God? Didn't someone talk about the harvest being plentiful but the workers few? Think of the potential to show the children of the world that someone cares enough about them to give a few hours of their time. Listen to me – This is witness for our loving God! We have been witnessing with our mouths for two thousand years and where has it gotten us? Islam is the world's fastest growing religion, so it might be determined that we had better change our methods and start caring about people (other than ourselves).

The previous paragraph was supposed to be the ending for this chapter, but God had other ideas, and He gave me another opportunity to demonstrate exactly how He works in my life and how He can work in yours. Last Thursday I was working on the farm; I had eaten dinner early so I could go back to work before dark, and that is what I was doing when I just ran out of energy. I suddenly got so tired that I couldn't continue with whatever I was doing, so I went into the house, fell on the couch, turned on the TV, and here is the story.

I didn't even have to change channels, a rerun of a series that I have referred to before, *Joan of Arcadia*, was halfway finished, and since I had seen it once, if I hadn't been so tired, I would have turned to something else. The story line was about God giving Joan an assignment to help someone (gee, I wonder where they got that idea – does someone in Hollywood read the Bible?). The target person (pun intended- and you will see why) was a troubled teenage boy who had no friends and who was the butt of everyone's ridicule. As He gave Joan the assignment of helping this young man, God told Joan (get this because it is so important), to just *listen* to him.

Understand this, God didn't tell her to go change this boy's life. God didn't tell her to witness for Him or His Son. God didn't tell her how to solve his problems. God didn't tell her how to make him popular – God just said *listen!!!*

Why is it that once 99.9% of "Christians" put God into their lives, they feel that they have to spread the Gospel by running their mouth? "New" Christians have turned more people away from God and His Son, than the devil ever could in a million years of trying. Believe me, no one except the stupidest person will ever be convinced by what someone says. They will only be convinced by what that person *does* in their and with their lives. If you are a new Christian or have been a Christian for any amount of time, (pay attention here), **shut your mouth, change your own life, and start serving others, if by no other means than listening to them and befriending them.** As your own life begins to change, people are going to start looking at you and say to themselves, "Hmmmm, I wonder if there might be something to that Christianity?"

Let's get back to our episode of *Joan of Arcadia*. Joan does as God has asked and sticks with the young man through some harrowing moments, but things don't seem to go very well and she doesn't feel that she accomplished her mission. When God later appears as a "cookie lady," in the school hallway, Joan frustratedly blurts out that she has failed her mission and (as usual) gets angry with God. It is only when God reveals that, through her actions, Joan has averted another Columbine scenario that Joan begins to see that while she was given a relatively simple assignment, God's overall plans are infinitely more complicated than any mortal could ever hope to understand.

I want to make a small comparison here between watching a rerun on TV and "re" reading the Bible. Remember, I had already seen this particular episode of *Joan of Arcadia*, but God chose the time when I was "ready" to receive the message that He wanted to convey. Reading and rereading the Bible works exactly the same way in that God will choose the time that He wants you to receive a particular message that may change your life. The problem for most of us is that God can't communicate His message if we don't care enough to read His word.

The subject of the chapter is "changing the church," and here is the bottom line, so listen closely. The church must begin teaching its own parishioners that just because we have found Him; we have not been given the job of running the world. Running the world is God's job and He doesn't share it with anyone!

So what is our job? Glad you asked – Our job is so simple that even the stupidest of us can understand (that sure includes me). We are to care about nothing else, and, most importantly, nothing less, than our fellow human beings. The government won't care about those less fortunate (because they can't contribute to a political election fund), so it is our job to give of ourselves to anyone and everyone that God puts into our lives. Will you give of your most valuable possession, your time, or even your own life, so that God's plan will be brought to fruition?

I have just one final thought, and it is that the church, in order to become effective in the job decreed by its supposed leader, Jesus Christ, must discontinue its "revival mentality." That is when either the pastor or the leaders of a particular church recognize the staleness of their practices; they bring in some big name evangelist in the hope of bringing "revival" to their congregation, or maybe even their geographic area. The first night of "revival" the entire church attends, everyone is enthusiastic, and hope permeates the air. The second night, the church is half full or less, depending upon the "entertainment" factor of the visiting evangelist, and by the third night everyone realizes that "revival,", as they envisioned it, has not and will not arrive, regardless of the size of the tent, and the amount of advertising.

If I was ever called as a visiting evangelist (perish the thought), the very first sentence out of my mouth would be something like this: "I didn't come here to bring revival, simply because I can't. Even the presence of Jesus Himself can't bring revival! The revival of any organization can only be brought by that organization from within. Revival can only happen through the efforts of each individual member."

The church must begin training and teaching those who purport to call themselves "Christians" that they are the only one's who can make revival happen, and that revival can only happen as those "Christians" teach themselves through reading the *entire* Bible and (only then) begin to serve **everyone else** with more than their mouths.

Listen up, because here is the final paragraph of this chapter. Any church or organization that worries or cares about politics, or money, or taxes, or its own personal comfort, has the devil himself as its pastor or leader. Any church or organization that advocates separation from any other human being created by God, no matter what the cause, can be assured of burning in Hell. Period!

8

PREPARING TO WORK FOR GOD

Jesus saw Nathanael coming to Him, and He said of him,
Behold, an Israelite indeed, in whom is no guile!"

The idea for the beginning of this chapter came to me at 5:30 a.m. as I was waking up and began to think about how good God has been to me. The point that I want to make is that God can and will talk to us whenever we are ready to listen to Him. My own personal problem stems from the fact that I get these revelations from God where every word is so perfect and well thought out, and then fifteen minutes later I have forgotten everything. Consequently, I have learned that when God gives me a message, I am to act upon it immediately; and here I am sitting in front of my laptop at 5:52 a.m. I don't even have my morning cup of coffee yet, although the percolator has just burped and I am going to fix that right now.

Read this next paragraph very carefully because what I have to say is so very important and is also misunderstood by 99.9% of all practicing Christians. Not one person in this world, after they have made their decision to follow Jesus Christ and to take God seriously has the slightest idea of what their job will be. As a matter of fact, we will be given the opportunity to perform *many* small jobs for God as we grow in Him and learn to listen to His direction. At the point in our lives where we decide to take God seriously, we are still "children" in His service; and this is true whether we have been a Christian for the last fifty years or we became Christians yesterday. The fact that we don't allow a six-year-old child to drive an automobile, much less design a bridge across a river, is an appropriate comparison. Keep in mind that the Apostle Paul, a learned and wise man who had been steeped in the religious community and was being groomed as a leader in the church of the day, spent three years in the desert, supposedly under the direct tutelage of Jesus Himself, before Paul even traveled to Jerusalem. We don't know the exact timing of events, but it is estimated that it could have been another fifteen years before he began writing those famous letters that we now read as Books in what is now our Bible. In my own case, I spent twelve years reading the Bible and studying before I could begin this book.

Another valid comparison would be the Apostle Peter, who, after spending three years of his life in the continuous company of Jesus Himself, still "didn't get it" on the eve of Jesus' crucifixion. As a matter of fact, Peter's ignorance and refusal to understand what Jesus had to undergo angered Jesus so much that He called Peter "Satan" and told him to get out of the way. I am going to make a pretty strong statement here, so hold on to your hat. The church today, which by the way was founded by this same Apostle Peter, has allowed itself to become this same devil that Jesus described, because the church, even after two thousand years, still *just doesn't get it!*

A person who does not understand the priorities of God will think that I am insane. The church, our beloved church where we go every Sunday to sing praises and worship our wonderful God, the church with its spire piercing the morning sky and pointing to the heavens, the church with its fellowship and joining of our dearest friends in singing praises to God, the church, with its magnificent buildings dedicated to the service of God, the church, with its private Christian school where its children will never have to be exposed to the ragamuffins of the world, the church with its multimillion dollar mortgage for ever-larger buildings while 200,000 children sleep under bridges, the church, with its outreach program that reaches out only to Christians, the church, that performs great and good works of great sacrifice in someone else's city, has failed? How could that be?

The "church" of the Israelites failed as its leaders became self-serving, self-involved and uncaring of the needs of the people, the same way that the Christian church of today has failed. Yes, we are directly following the Jews of the Old Testament because we have abandoned God for the worship of the politician of the day and the worship of money in the form of having to pay fewer taxes. So how can I work for God? Well, it isn't by trying to elect the correct politician. Forget it. God has already figured out whom He wants in office, and there is nothing any of us can do to change His mind. I have to laugh at the fact that recently a three-star general stated from the pulpit that "God put George Bush in the White House." Does that mean that God *didn't* put Bill Clinton in the White House? I guess so, according to most "Christians." Maybe those same "Christians" think that the devil put Bill Clinton in the White House. That must mean that we Christians have an old, sick, lame, and only "part time" God, who needs our help, and all of us dedicated Christians had better register to vote so we can help this aging and infirm God run the world.

So how *do* we work for God? We have two choices: we can work for God or we can work for the church. Aren't they the same thing? Not always. I remember the lady who thought that she was a dedicated Christian and was continually serving God by singing in the choir. Now, don't get me wrong. This lady had a beautiful voice, but her singing wasn't serving God. Remember, God has all those heavenly angels singing for Him every day, and He doesn't need a frail human voice to please Him. Doesn't He want to be praised? Of course He wants our praise, but there is something else that God needs and wants desperately. Remember what God told the Jews of the Old Testament? He told them that He was sick of smelling their incense (which was their form of prayer and praise) because they were ignoring His people, and that is what the Christian church is doing today. Through our worship, our praise, and the building of ever-larger temples to our own selfishness, we have forgotten His people. I have no doubt that today God is sick of our singing and praise because we have become exactly like the Jews of old.

Remember the old widow who threw two mites (the smallest coin of the day) into the offering and received Jesus' praise? That widow lady exists today, and the church ignores her just as it did two thousand years ago (unless she happens to live 500 miles away and the church can send a team of teenagers for a week to fix her roof).

During Christmas week of 2004, an elderly lady in Greenville, South Carolina died from thermal exposure after Duke Power turned off her electricity supposedly for non-payment of her bill. Golly, there is an example of a company operated by "Christians" right here in the Bible belt. And, oh yes, the churches of that same city should be congratulated on helping widows (provided they live 500 miles away). Please understand, I certainly don't advocate having churches donate money to help a poor widow. That could seriously detract from the building fund or a pastor's new automobile.

So how do we work for God? Do we have to elect the right politician so they can change the world for us? Do we get elected as a deacon so that we can change the church into our own image? Do we tithe to our church so that it can build ever-larger monuments to arrogance? Every one of us Christians wants to change the world. The problem is that we want someone else to do it for us because we are too lazy to do it for ourselves, or (listen to this) the church has failed to teach us that we individually (yes, every one of us) can change the world through our individual demonstrations of the power and the love of God. Can we perform miracles? Yes, indeed. Remember, even Jesus Christ did not perform miracles through His own power, even though He was the Son of God. Jesus repeatedly said that everything that He did was through the power of God. Was He lying or just being humble (falsely)? I think not. Do miracles happen today? Let me tell you, miracles happen all the time. Actually the greatest miracle that I have ever heard of was a sinner like me being brought to Christ in 1991, and if you talked to those that knew me before, they would also think that it was a miracle.

So what is the point that I am trying to make as we talk about "working for God"? Well, you are going to have to wait just a while longer while we investigate and attempt to understand just how God works. Why? The reason that we have to learn how God works is (again) because the church has failed to teach it. Let us first look at the big picture, from the universe on down. Did God create the universe? Of course He did. Does He still control it? Of course He does. O.K., we have that settled. Now let us look at just one little part of that great universe, our world. Do you think that we can suppose that God is still in control of the Universe but He can't (or won't) control the world? No, I just can't picture that. So how do I explain the recent event called 9-11 when three thousand fine and good people died in one act of terrorism invoked in the name of Allah? First of all, let me tell you that God knew from the beginning of time that 9-11 would happen, but the big question is this: How could a righteous and just God allow such a thing to happen, especially if he knew that it was about to take place?

If we are going to question that event called 9-11, let's first question some other events, like the flood a few years back that killed 50,000 people in Bangladesh. Or maybe we should question the earthquake that killed several thousand in Japan. Come to think of it, we should question the 60,000 automobile deaths that happen every year or maybe the 50,000 premature deaths caused by cancer. As this book is being edited, possibly 220,000 good people have died in the Tsunami in Southeast Asia. Do we question God when things like that happen? Yes and No! A good buddy of mine in high school was killed in a one-car automobile accident. I am sure that his parents questioned how God could allow such a terrible thing to happen. Why do we question God and His wisdom when something terrible happens *TO US*? Why did my good friend die when he had just gotten a good job and was beginning to make something of his life? For that matter, why did 3,000 people die in 9-11, or why did 60,000 other people die in automobile deaths last year? The answer is very simple, but the church refuses to teach it.

Each one of us has been given the greatest gift that has ever been given, the gift of life. Think about it. What could even come close to such a magnificent gift? As we are conceived, God gives us not only the great gift, that of life, He gives us (listen closely now) the opportunity to do something with that gift during our short time on this rotating planet. I am going to say something that will probably be considered as heresy by the church. The gift of life is a great gift, and the gift that God gave us in the form of His Son, and the giving that Son's life as forgiveness for our sins is an even greater gift, but maybe, just maybe, the opportunity to do something with our life, such as serving Him, could be the greatest gift of all.

Each one of us has a finite time on this earth, and the span of our life has already been determined by God. Some of us will live long and productive lives and some of us will waste our lives in greed or drugs or whatever, but each of us is given the choice and the opportunity. My dad lived a long and productive life and when he died at age ninety-four, I didn't grieve because I knew where he was going to be and I also knew that I would see him there. While I am on the subject of death, let me digress for just a moment and talk about funerals. I absolutely hate funerals. As a matter of fact, I refuse to go to them, because funerals are the exact opposite reaction that should take place after the death of a Christian. Think about it. There is no death for a Christian who has served God. Our body dies, but we go on to a place with our loving God. What could be better? At my death, I hope that everyone who knew me will have a really big party because I am in a better life. You know, maybe, just maybe, somebody really special will come by and serve the wine if I have truly done the job for which God placed me here.

Just one more note on the subject of death. It seems so sad at the death of a child, because that young person, no matter how old, seemingly didn't have the opportunity of life and service yet. I want you to know that here again, sadness is inappropriate because children are very special to our loving God. Sadness is inappropriate for several reasons, including the fact that God loved that child so much that He wanted that child with Him. Also, that child was not tempted by the sins of the world, and there is no reason to doubt that the child is with God. Yes, the parents and even society feel a loss, and sadness is a part of life. Just remember one final thing: God has a plan. That plan is being fulfilled right now and we are all a part of it. This life is nothing more than a test. Will you pass? It is solely up to you.

How can I state so confidently that this life is a test? For someone who is willing to read the Bible from cover to cover more than once and who is willing to learn from the Holy Spirit, it is pretty obvious. I'm not going to spend a lot of time on this because that is not the subject of this book, but I just want to point out some verses from the Bible that hint at my conclusion. First of all, examine the fact that almost every promise that God makes in the Bible is conditional. By "conditional" I mean that in order to receive the blessings (and there are many) that God repeatedly gives to His people, we have to do something first. It would be appropriate to analyze John 3:16, the foundation of the Christian faith, to ascertain whether my thesis is true or false. John 3:16 states, *"For God so loved the world that He gave His one and only Son, that whoever believes in Him shall not perish but have eternal life."* Obviously, God's promise is one of eternal life, but let's look at the condition.

The condition that we must fulfill is that in order to receive this promise, we must believe that Jesus Christ was indeed the Son of God. Does a statement such as this meet the criteria of a test? Well, I think so, but I will let you make your own decision. Another facet of spiritual life which to me is obviously a test concerns the matter of our tithe (to God). In the Old Testament, the tithe (a tenth of one's income) was a specific requirement of God and was meant to give significance to the fact that everything that the Israelites possessed was a gift from their God. Their land, their crops, their everything, were to be considered gifts from God and, indeed, they were. To me, it is significant that nowhere in the entire New Testament is the tithe mentioned. Does that omission signify that God no longer desires that we acknowledge His gifts through the giving back of the gifts that we receive daily? To me the answer is *no*. This is just God's way of testing each of us as to whether we still credit Him with giving us our daily blessings.

I have told you the story of when I was dead broke and on the verge of suicide and I sat through a sermon on tithing and left the church in tears. It took me three weeks of daily torture before I made the decision that if God wanted ten percent of my money then I was going to give it to Him, because I had definitely proved that I couldn't support myself. You remember, of course, that within the next three weeks, God proved without a doubt that He and only He could and would provide the means for my support. Was that a test? There is absolutely no doubt in my mind that I was given a test. Did I have a choice? You bet! Contrary to the teachings of a moribund church, God gives us choices every day.

I want to make just one more comment to those undereducated leaders of today's church. It is O.K. to test God. Not only is He willing and able to pass any test that we want to give Him, but He is literally pleading with those who doubt to go ahead and test Him, because He wants to come into the lives of every one of us. If God didn't care whether we tested Him, why did He challenge us to test Him in the words of the prophet Malachi?

Let me return to the third chapter of John, and let's proceed on to verses twenty and twenty-one. Jesus is still speaking, and in verse twenty He states, ***"Everyone who does evil hates the light, and will not come into the light for fear his deeds will be exposed."*** You know, a person can go to church all of his life, yet he will never grow because the lessons taught in Christian Sunday schools all around the world are comparable to attending kindergarten throughout one's life. The same old lessons are taught again and again, yet they are never related to everyday life and interaction of the individual Christian. Here is a classic example of an important teaching of Jesus that is for all practical purposes ignored by the church. There is a double meaning as Jesus uses the word "light." We, of course recognize our Lord as the "light" of the world; however, the word light also refers to the exposure of our actions, and here the church again fails to recognize a succinct point of application that Jesus intended as one of the identifying marks of a practicing Christian. What do I mean by the term "practicing Christian"? First of all, a "practicing Christian" is not necessarily someone who attends church. As a matter of fact, in my experience, attending a church usually precludes possession of the title because church attendance seems to instill a sense of egotism and arrogance that enables us to believe that we have been placed into the world in order to tell everyone else how to live.

So what was Jesus talking about as He said, "Everyone who does evil..."? Was He talking about murder, rape, bank robbery? The answer is *yes*, but He was talking about much more than that. Every Christian recognizes those actions as evil, but how about simple examples of evil such as gossip or driving too fast or cheating on your taxes or those just so slightly shady business deals? Are those actions evil? You bet. Let me give you an example that happened last weekend as we were inundated with customers. My cashier sold a $75 case of paintballs for $20. In her rush, she didn't even realize what she had done, but fifteen minutes later, a teenager walks in, places a case of paintballs on the counter and says, "You made a mistake and I wanted to bring these back." **WOW.** Here is a young man who exemplifies exactly what Jesus was talking about. This young man wouldn't even accept a reward, but I offered to give him a free game anyway. Let me ask you a question. Have you ever been given too much change? Did you give it back or did you figure that for once you had beaten the system? If you gave it back, how did you feel? Did you get a warm glow? If you did, that was the Holy Spirit blessing you, but if you didn't give it back, I know for a fact that the Holy Spirit was sad.

Just one more thought, if you kept that change, you will have to pay for that action later. Have you ever watched "Christians" tip a waiter or waitress? They act like they have lost their last dime, and what a shame for two reasons. First, for those waiting on tables, ninety percent of their income is derived from tips, because the restaurant is only paying them around two dollars per hour. Second, any true Christian doesn't have to worry about money because God takes care of His own. Listen to me, because this is important. If you have to worry about money, you aren't working for God.

Everyone knows that women love to gossip, and gossip by itself has turned many people away from the church than almost any other single action that we Christians do. What we often fail to realize is that men love to gossip too, but we just don't admit it. I was reading a magazine at my favorite garage the other day when in walked a stranger and we began talking. This man was a "Christian," because he talked about his church and how he loved the Lord, but he then asked me where I worked. I told him that I was a consultant and I was presently teaching mathematics and electronics at an industrial school. It just happened that this man knew the president of the company for which I was teaching, and he proceeded to tell me that this man had met his wife at a bar in Texas. He implied that this woman had been a less than desirable person and I was aghast that he would impugn the character of a woman that had been married for thirty years. I have made a lot of mistakes in my life, but the mistake that I made here will be with me for the rest of my life, because I let down a friend. Instead of confronting this vile gossiper, I just walked out. The proper action would have been to gently confront this person with the words of Jesus Christ as He said, "Judge not lest you be judged." And I should have pointed out how this person's gossip could hurt a lot of good people. I really wonder just what this man is learning at his church. I think that the answer is ***nothing***, and therein lies another failure of the church. Too many churches are wrapped up in "worshiping" Jesus Christ but ignoring His words and His life. How can the actions of those churches be called "worship" when they are ignoring the message that Jesus came to this earth to give. Even though I have referred to this passage earlier, it bears repeating. Jesus said, *"And everyone who hears these **words** of mine and does not act upon them, will be like a foolish man, who built his house upon the sand."* I have underlined ***words*** because that emphasis is what Jesus desired or He wouldn't have said it in that way.

I don't want to leave the subject of "gossip" yet, because it is the second greatest single action that "Christians" take, that turns people away from Christianity. Well, if gossiping is so bad, why doesn't the preacher talk about it? The reason is (get this because it is important) that your average preacher doesn't want to offend his congregation because he is afraid of losing his job. There, I've said it. Most preachers today have become nothing less than panderers to the lowest common denominator in the congregation and panderers to a misguided dogma of the mother church, as defined by intellectuals who (just like the Israelites), have no understanding of God. We might as well face the fact that any preacher who would dare to confront his congregation with the truth of their actions would have to be a strong believer in the power of that God they supposedly worship.

Let's take a minute and look at the gospel of James on this same subject. Everyone needs to understand that this same problem has been around for 10,000 years, yet no one will take a stand against it, and gossip alone is deeply hurting the Christian message. *"**Do not speak against one another, brethren. He who speaks against a brother, or judges his brother, speaks against the law, and judges the law; but if you judge the law, you are not a doer of the law, but a judge of it.**"* And *"**There is only one Lawgiver and Judge, the one who is able to save and to destroy; but who are you to judge your neighbor?**"* Is there anyone reading this book who does not understand what James just said? Well, it must be so, because every church that I have ever attended allows gossip to flourish and destroy the fellowship of many good people and of the church itself.

FAILURE!

In order to clarify and alleviate a problem, one must provide a succinct definition that will identify for all concerned just what constitutes gossip. I have a very simple definition of gossip and I believe that any but the most dense and mean people will agree with me. Gossip is: *Anything that you might say concerning a person that you would not say to their face and that might make them feel less than good.*

I suppose that at this point it would be appropriate to give examples of gossip, but the concept is so simple and self explanatory that I don't see the necessity and I hope that this book is being read by Christians above kindergarten level. Now I am aware that I have taken away almost eighty percent of all conversations that take place between both men and women inside the church, and by the way, if you don't believe that, keep track of the conversations that you hear next Sunday. So what are we going to talk about? O.K., let's see now. We are in church, right? If we were reading the Bible (fat chance) we might want to talk about what the Holy Spirit taught us over the last week, or we might want to talk about how what we read applies to our own (not someone else's) life. Gee, we might want to talk about what we did last week in the course of working for God, the Father. We might even want to talk about what God is doing in our lives. Let's not forget that greatest of all possible conversations, talking about how we served another person or persons (and in so doing truly served God).

No, I haven't forgotten that the subject is "preparing to work for God," so why am I so concerned about things like gossip and all the other negatives that take place in the daily lives of Christians? I use gossip as an example of a practice that is totally ignored by the leaders of the church and allowed to flourish, but my primary reason is that (listen to this) before we can even consider working for God we must begin cleaning up our own lives to make ourselves and our actions acceptable to Him. In my own walk, I have had to work on many aspects of my personal life. Even now, I am working on and correcting my problems with impatience, especially on the road, and you know what? I am making progress. Whenever I have to drive somewhere, I start at least ten minutes early, and it has become enjoyable as I stay in the far right lane to watch everybody else weaving in and out, jockeying for position like NASCAR drivers. I keep the radio off and spend the entire time just talking with God. You will be pleasantly surprised if you try this to feel the peace and calm that comes into your life. Does that mean that I never listen to the radio or watch TV? Absolutely not. We Christians must never ignore the world, because after all, it is God's world and He has many messages for us as we watch and listen. What we must do is stop trying to run the world or change the world, because I assure you that God has everything under control. It has become a never ceasing source of wonder to me as I write this book to see the messages that God has brought into my life in a timely fashion.

If you were paying attention as I talked about gossip above, you will have noticed that I stated that gossip was the second largest reason for the fact that Christians turn others, including potential converts, away from the church and away even from belief in God and His Son. Christians just seem to not have the slightest idea of the number of people who are hurt through seemingly innocent comments made by people with small, mean and selfish minds. These same people don't have the intellect to hold a conversation on anything but the lowest plane of thought. Well, if gossip is cause number two for the failure of Christians to attract and hold converts, what is the number one facet in our lives that fails to demonstrate the message of God and His Son?

The answer is so simple and so obvious that very few of us can see it, but again the reason that this problem even exists is the failure of the church to recognize it. Listen closely now, because if you get nothing else out of this book, pay attention to what I am about to say, because this can change Christianity in the eyes of the entire world. Our actions defeat our intentions and our very lives. The old saying, "Actions speak louder than words!" is the primary reason for the failure of the Christian church. Has the church been defeated? No, not yet. But most Christians are inadvertently supporting that defeat. Note that I didn't ask whether God has been defeated. God can never be defeated, but those who mouth allegiance to God have become God's worst enemy.

Of all of our actions that defeat our witness, nothing is more compromising than our attitude toward money. I could fill an entire book with examples of how our concern about money demonstrates that we don't believe the words that we mouth every Sunday morning. As a small businessman, I get calls all the time from churches that want to use my services and ninety percent of the Christians calling will say something like, "What kind of discount do you give Christian organizations?" My answer was always, "I'm sorry, but we don't give discounts. We charge the same price to everyone." About half the time, their next comment would go something like, "Well store X usually gives us such and such discount because we are a church." My answer, after a few calls like this, was always, "Well, I am sure that store X can continue serving you well. Thank you for calling."

Then one day the Holy Spirit gave me the answer. Totally out of the blue, the Spirit spoke to me and I told the caller, "I'll tell you what I am going to do. I will give you whatever you want for free as long as you can show me the verse in the Bible that states that Christians are supposed to get a better deal than everyone else." There was a long silence on the other end of the line (as a typical "Christian," this person had probably never read the Bible), then the stammering began. To make a long story short, I continue to have this church's business, but they now understand that God never intended for them or any other Christian organization to have special favors in this world.

Isn't it strange that the church teaches the verse that states that God will meet all of my needs, yet they don't believe it? Why would any Christian ever be worried about money or any other worldly thing when we have a God that will truly take care of us? Do we forget the words of Jesus when He talked about how much better as a father our God is? Come on, all you preachers; get some daily application in those sermons. I'll tell you one thing right now that the average Christian won't want to hear, and that is the fact that if you don't have enough money (or any other blessing) it is because God is trying to get your attention.

      I have a true story to tell you and it would be humorous if it wasn't so sad. A man called last summer about making a reservation and asked the same old question about discounts for Christians. I naturally assumed that he wanted to bring out a bunch of kids, and from the way that he talked I began to think that they might be a group of underprivileged kids. To put it mildly, this guy was so insistent that it was my duty to give discounts to Christians that I became intrigued and relented, giving them a good discount from our normal price. The sad part of this story is that when the group showed up, they turned out to be high priced executives from a real estate investment company. My parking lot was full of Cadillac Escalades, Lincolns, Mercedes Benzes, etc. One member of the group even turned out to be the brother of the former lieutenant governor of South Carolina. ***These guys were multi-millionaires.*** Here was a group of people who probably had more money in their checking account than I will ever see in my lifetime, misusing the name of the Son of God in order to obtain a discount to play a game. Is it any wonder that most of the population is fed up with Christians?

      I saw a bumper sticker the other day that said, **"CHRISTIANS AREN'T PERFECT – THEY ARE JUST FORGIVEN!** Does anyone see this statement as just a little bit arrogant? Certainly we are forgiven, but does that mean that we now have free reign to go on sinning? This bumper sticker sounds like an excuse by the person placing it on their automobile to continue driving in an unacceptable manner.

According to the church, or I should say, according to the lack of training by the church, it would seem that the recognition of Jesus Christ as Lord and Savior is the end and goal by itself. Where are the lessons that begin with the acceptance of salvation and the beginning of a new life and working to eliminate the mistakes of the old life? The problem here is that most Christians are using this label of "non-perfection" as an excuse to continue living their same old sinful, greedy, abhorrent lifestyle. Non-Christians observe this selfish behavior and ask themselves why in the world they would want to become a Christian.

I got the following note in my e-mail basket the other day and it pretty succinctly describes the present day thinking of the church.

A woman was asked by a co-worker, "What is it like to be a Christian?" The co-worker replied, "It is like being a pumpkin. God picks you from the patch, brings you in, and washes all the dirt off of you. Then He cuts off the top and scoops out all the yucky stuff. He removes the seeds of doubt, hate, greed, etc., and then He carves you a new smiling face and puts His light inside of you to shine for the entire world to see."

Most Christians would read this e-mail and say to themselves, "How cute and how true." There are very few Christians in the world today that would recognize the dangerous thinking lurking within this innocent little paragraph, and this same misguided thinking is resulting in the rejection of Christianity by many people. So what am I talking about? Take a moment and analyze the actions that are taking place within the text. First of all, the beginning actions are quite correct. God does pick us; however, He picks all of us. Did you get that? God picks *all* of us to be His children. There is not one person born into this world that God does not pick, yet the philosophy of Calvinism accepted by most denominations teaches that there are those among us that are destined to burn in Hell. The hurdle here is the fact that it is each of us who must make the decision to accept God's grace through His Son. I do agree with the next sentence that talks about God washing the dirt off of us, because if "dirt" is a synonym for "sin" it has to be agreed that none of us can get rid of our sins by ourselves. We just aren't able to make ourselves acceptable to God, yet the death of His Son can do that if we will just accept the gift.

The next two sentences begin with, *"Then He cuts off the top and scoops out all the yucky stuff. He removes the seeds of doubt, hate, greed, etc., and then He carves you a new smiling face...."* Question: Who is doing all the work here? Answer: God. We Christians expect and even demand that God do all the work of remaking us into the likeness of His Son. Sorry, it doesn't work that way.

As you opened this book, I hope you glanced at the fore leaf and saw the sentence that begins, *"There is only one way to please God...."* I am quite sure that statement angered many practicing Christians to the point that they thought that I am quite insane, but we have now come to the place where I will explain that (most foreign) idea. I have talked before about how singing in a choir cannot please God, or the giving of our tithe does not please God (Oh, yes, I admit He requires that of us.) so there is no reason to repeat that reasoning, but now let's discuss the only action(s) that we can take that actually please God. Why would these particular actions that I am going to describe be pleasing to God at the expense of all the others that Christians normally consider to be pleasing to our loving God? Because (listen to this) these are actions that God cannot or, more correctly, chooses not to do Himself. **SAY WHAT?** Listen closely now, because in creating this world, and especially in creating human beings, there are actions and decisions in which God consciously chooses to not be involved or active.

The first action(s) that God specifically chooses not to undertake Himself is the action(s) that we must take in order to change our own lives. Understand this. God, while He has given us the means to be forgiven through the death of His Son, does not suddenly come in, take over our life and remake us into the complete personification of a Christian. That is our job, and our job only, but not only is it our job, it is (completely) our decision. That is the way that God works, and the church has again failed in understanding God and His role in our lives. Most churches teach, as described in the e-mail above, that once we accept God and His Son, God will take over the clean-up of our daily lives, desires and actions. Nothing could be further from the truth, and this fantasy as taught by the church has lead to failure in the lives of uncounted Christians as their expectations are not immediately met.

As President Harry Truman believed, *the buck stops here!* God, in His infinite wisdom, gave us the intelligence to recognize right from wrong, but even more importantly, He gave us the ability to make the decision to change. A good friend sent me an e-mail regarding marriage and the different outlooks that men and women have for each other within the context of matrimony. It went something like this:

When a woman marries a man, she hopes that he will change and he doesn't.
When a man marries a woman, he hopes that she will never change but she does.

I compare the church today with the woman entering marriage in that the church wants God to change His way of relating to His world. The church (and all those new Christians) want God to stop allowing all those "bad" things to happen, like homosexuality, gay marriages, lack of prayer in schools, removal of the Ten Commandments, stamps honoring Muslim holy days, etc. I have been in churches that have repeatedly asked God to bring "revival" to their church and to this country, in total ignorance of the fact that "revival" must come from *within* individual Christians and from *within* the church. How can revival even begin to take place when Christians continue in their own self-indulgent ways and practices?

Yes, God wants us to change our lives, our actions and even our thoughts once we decide to become Christians, but God won't do anything toward that end **UNLESS** we provide the will, the desire and our own willingness to engage in the fight to change our attitudes, lives and priorities. **ONLY THEN** will God, through the Holy Spirit, provide the means and the strength to accomplish what, for most of us, is a terribly difficult and even impossible task.

Why do you think that so many preachers, pastors, etc. have been caught in acts of lust, or child abuse? The reason is that they believe the church's teaching that God will change their lives and their perverted desires, and they are waiting for that to happen. Let me state it one more time – God will change nothing (for you). That is the bad news. The good news is that God will provide you the strength to accomplish the task if you will just step up to the plate with the commitment, the desire and the willingness to fight. Will it be easy, even with God's strength? No, because Satan doesn't like to lose a customer, but just remember that God's strength is always greater than Satan's.

So, now let's answer the question: "What is the only way to please God?" The answer, as you may have guessed, is that in order to please God, we must change ourselves into persons whose lives follow the pattern set by Jesus Christ. Can God do this for us? Of course, but He chooses not to do it. Why? Remember, God made us the highest form of life on this planet, and in so doing, He made us responsible for our own actions. You see, that is the wonderful, but difficult, difference between us humans and the animals. A tiger attacks anything that comes within its range because it is doing nothing more than what its genetic programming dictates. A tiger does not have the ability to make decisions of right or wrong. Human beings were given that ability, yet we continually desire to abdicate that responsibility. Remember Flip Wilson, that great comedian, who in his skits would cry out, "The devil made me do it!"? Flip Wilson was merely echoing the modern church that teaches that "God" will change our lives. Before I proceed further, let me make one thing very clear. As I stated earlier, the devil cannot make us *do* anything. Satan has been defeated, yet he still has power; but that power can only be effective as *WE* give him power through our own actions and desires.

To those who refuse to read the Bible, there is a seeming dichotomy in the next step that must take place. If someone uses his God-given will to make the decision to change his life, he must recognize that he cannot accomplish the task by himself. The saying, "a leopard cannot change its spots," is so true, and it is true in our lives as well because we cannot, in our own strength, change our own faults. When you read the Bible you will recognize that even Jesus could not do miracles through His own abilities. Even the Son of God had to rely on the Father to give Him the strength and the ability to change the world forever. So how does that relate to us? Changing our own lives is an earthshaking accomplishment. No matter how "good" someone is or no matter how "bad" someone is, they have not been given the strength or even the ability to change their life.

Every one of us must make the willful *decision* to change our lives, and then we must make the *effort* to do so, recognizing that our strength is not enough. Where most Christians fail is in the *effort* part. We fail because we refuse to realize that our *effort* must be continual and ongoing and that we will never reach our goal by expecting God to do the work. God's job is to give us the strength *when we make the effort.* God will give us that strength only when we refuse to yield, and when we refuse to place ourselves in a situation which could lead to temptation and failure. As we use God's Holy Spirit and His strength, will we repeatedly fail? Yes, and that is not only acceptable, but it is part of God's plan for our lives for us to evaluate that failure and learn from it.

Every person on this earth has the opportunity to choose how they will live their lives. We all have the opportunity to recognize that God exists, we all have the opportunity to accept the existence of the Son of God, and we all have the opportunity to accept that Son's message and forgiveness. The problem from a Christian viewpoint is that too many of us stop right there. We say we accept Jesus Christ but we never change our lifestyle, which in reality means that we have not accepted Jesus Christ, because to accept Him is to do more than just recognize His existence and leave it at that. Remember that at the end of the Sermon on the Mount, Jesus said that whoever *follows* (meaning obeys) these words of mine will be like the man who built his house upon the rock. Why is the world such a difficult place, and why is it so difficult to be like the example that Jesus gave? Because, as I said before, this life is a test and God wants to see who will choose to truly follow Him, not with just their lips, but with their lives. I am reminded of another e-mail I received about an old Cherokee Indian, and I would like to share it with you.

An elder Cherokee Native American was teaching his grandchildren about life.

He said to them, "A fight is going on inside me, it is a terrible fight and it is between two wolves.

One wolf represents fear, anger, envy, sorrow, regret, greed, arrogance, self-pity, guilt, resentment, inferiority, lies, pride, competition, superiority, and ego.

The other wolf stands for joy, peace, love, hope, sharing, serenity, humility, kindness, benevolence, friendship, empathy, generosity, truth, compassion, and faith.

The same fight is going on inside you, and inside every other person too.

They thought about it for a minute and then one child asked his grandfather, "Which wolf will win?"

The elderly Cherokee paused, then replied quietly……………… "The one you feed."

For the first fifty-one years of my life, I fed the wolf of anger, fear, frustration, envy, and greed. I wasn't happy and I was in a constant state of frustration, because no matter how hard I worked or how hard I tried, I was a failure. My marriage failed and I had no job, and it wasn't until I reached the bottom of the valley that I decided to ask God for help. Stop reading this book right now, and ask yourself which wolf you are feeding. Are you angry or frustrated? Do you hate anyone or anything? Do you spend your time trying to change the world? Do you feel that no one understands? Do you spend your time worrying about what other people do? I have the answer for you and it isn't taught in any church of which I am aware.

The answer, if you truly want to please God, the answer, if you truly want to work for God, is this: STOP. Listen carefully now. Stop trying to change the world and everybody else and *change yourself.* Is there any Christian in existence today that recognizes that God is still in charge of the world? What was it that Jesus said? Did He say to stop trying to get the splinter out of everyone else's eye and get the log out of your own eye? What was He talking about? Didn't He mean that our first priority should be to prepare ourselves? How can we prepare ourselves when we are too lazy to even read the Bible and too mean to look in a mirror at our own life.

The reason that we Christians feel that it is our collective job to change the world is that the church teaches us that once we have accepted God and Jesus Christ, our job now becomes that of convincing everyone else. It is called "witness," but no program exists to provide a foundation (a "rock" if you will) that will provide a basis for making that "witness" effective. The church teaches that "witness" should be done with our mouths, when, in fact, nothing could be further from the truth. The **only** *witness* that could be in any way considered effective is the daily witness given by our lives, our actions, our thoughts and even our reason for existence. Look in the mirror for just a minute. What are your personal concerns? What do you think about? What do you talk about? When you meet with your friends, what is your conversation about? But even more importantly, what is the tone of that conversation? As I write this, I am sitting in a restaurant at 5 a.m., eating breakfast. The waitresses are cleaning up and refilling the salt shakers, and all those other little things that most of us don't even think about, and as I stop for a moment, I realize that in their conversation, they are quoting Bible passages to one another and they are having a good time. These ladies are happy and their love for God is so obvious.

Why are the rest of us Christians so unhappy? Do we have the weight of the world on our shoulders, or do we *think* that we have the weight of the world on our shoulders? Somehow I don't think we do because that is God's job and He really doesn't need our help, even though most of us seem to question His abilities these days. I have a question that I would like to have answered, and it is this. Why do we, as soon as we become Christians, feel that we have been given the responsibility to alter the course of the world? Have we suddenly been anointed as God?

The topic (in case you forgot) is preparing ourselves to serve God. Do we really have to *prepare* ourselves to serve God? The answer is yes, but the church fails to recognize that requirement. Oh, I forgot, the church provides Sunday school classes taught by a well-meaning but biblically illiterate teacher who has his or her own worldly agenda. One who has never read the Bible except to study for the next week's lesson and who could care less about anyone but themselves.

O.K., I admit it. I have vented for almost fifteen pages and I have repeated myself, but now it is time to actually begin the step-by-step process of preparing ourselves to serve this wonderful God of ours. First of all, don't worry about having to become a missionary to some country whose name you can't even pronounce. While the job of missionary is a great and selfless service, for ninety-nine percent of the rest of us Christians, God has a job right here at home. I made this same mistake when I first became a Christian, and I had to learn what God wanted for me the hard way.

Whether you have been a Christian for fifty years or whether you became a Christian yesterday, the same steps apply in preparing to serve God. To be honest, if you have been a Christian for a long time, it is going to be more difficult to prepare yourself to serve God, because you are going to have to "unlearn" all those untruths and dogmas that plague the Christian church, no matter to which denomination you belong. The first step that *everyone* must take, that is if he truly "believes" in the existence of God and His Son, is to read the New Testament of the Bible. When I say "read," I am not talking about the few selected passages that most churches constantly reread; I am talking about starting at Matthew and reading every word, while letting the Holy Spirit teach you what God has to say to you specifically. Read only for short periods, because the Bible is much too complex to be digested except in small bites. Before you begin reading, ask the Holy Spirit to help you understand, and don't be afraid to use a highlighter or some other type of marker that will help you return to passages that seemed to jump out at you at a particular time.

I know the question will arise: "Why should *I* read the Bible? After all, I attend church every Sunday and we study the Bible in Sunday school, and, gee, it is so difficult to read?" The answer is this: God has a message and a job for each of us and we must discover our job individually, just as Paul did during his time alone in the desert. Am I against organized religion? Absolutely not. Organized religion dates from the Book of Acts, and Jesus gave Peter the job of founding His church. The problem is the fact that organized religion has lost its way.

As I began reading the New Testament for the first time, I had no idea that the four Gospels told the same story. I was fascinated by the Book of Acts, but when I came to Romans, I became so confused that I couldn't continue and I had to stop. I recognize now that was God's way of telling me to stop and digest what I had already read. Later, I started over, and I was able to continue without hesitation or confusion. No, of course I didn't understand everything that I read, but I had started down the path to learning about a very personal God and His relationship to me individually. During the time of my (very deep) depression, all I had to do was pick up the New Testament and start reading and my depression was gone. What a wonderful experience, and I would like to see some psychologist or psychoanalyst perform a study of the effect of reading the New Testament on depressed patients.

I am just going to say one more word about reading the Bible, and it is a word of warning. First of all, don't join some Bible study. Listen to what I say here – NO ONE CAN TEACH **YOU** THE BIBLE except the Holy Spirit. The reason for that is that just as we were created individually, God has an individual message and job for each of us. Second, don't read the New Testament for the first time and think that you have discovered a message for the world. Any message you might receive is for you, not everyone else. Last, as you start reading, ask the Holy Spirit to guide and teach you. Keep in mind that the Holy Spirit is the only one who can teach you God's word, not some preacher who hasn't read the entire Bible for even himself.

All right, the first step in preparing yourself to work for God is to read the New Testament. Are you willing to make the effort? I promise that you will never regret it, and I would love to hear from anyone who reads the New Testament at least three times. So what is the second step? Well, I am going to warn you right now that the second step is difficult. As a matter of fact, it might be the most difficult thing that you have ever done in your life, because you are going to have to change your entire paradigm.

The second step in preparing yourself to work for God is to begin ignoring the world. SAY WHAT? I can hear the howls of protest and the thousands of questions, and I can even hear those who think that I have lost my mind (as if I ever had one), but pay attention here. Jesus told us that no man (or woman) can serve two masters, and He was right. Who do you want to serve, God or the world? If you want to serve God, stop worrying about, or even paying attention to, what is going on in the world; believe me when I tell you that God has it under control. Are you concerned about which candidate will be elected? Don't worry. God will appoint the one that **HE** wants to be in office, and it won't necessarily be the candidate that you want to elect. Are you concerned about your retirement and whether Social Security will still be in existence? Don't even bother. God has it under control, and there is nothing you can do about it anyway, so why worry.

Here is the most wonderful part about working for God. If you work for God, He will take care of your retirement. Worry about Social Security? How useless. God can and will take care of you just as He takes care of me. Let me give you an example. This weekend, my little company may have the biggest weekend in our history and there are a thousand things to be done. What am I doing? Right now, as I sit here at my computer, I am working for God. That is my first priority and that is what I am going to do. Does that mean that I am to ignore what needs to be done to prepare for this weekend (beginning tomorrow)? Again, the answer is *no*, because after I have finished working for God today, He will provide the time and the help to prepare my business.

Will I have the time and energy to do both? I am reminded of a story told by the surgeon who removed the cataracts from both my dad's eyes. He had spent a full day in surgery, over twelve hours, and was just sitting down to dinner at home when the phone rang and the hospital needed him immediately for an emergency operation to save a child's eyes. Taking his wife with him, he started the drive back to the hospital when they came to a stop sign. As the car came to a stop, the surgeon looked over at his wife and said, "Honey, I just can't go on. I am totally exhausted." His wife, a very wise woman said to him, "All right, you have reached your limit, so we are just going to have to depend on God's strength to get you through this. Let's just stay right here and pray for His help."

After sitting at the stop sign in prayer (don't try this at home), he drove to the hospital and began scrubbing for the operation. As he walked into the operating room, he felt like it was a brand new day and he had just gotten eight hours of sleep. He was wide awake, relaxed, the operation was a success and he has never forgotten that incident where God performed a miracle. The point of my story is that if you work for God, He will work for you, and He will take care of you even better than you could take care of yourself even in your wildest dreams.

The Bible tells us that while we are *in* the world, we are not to be *of* the world, but most Christians refuse to believe it, or else they don't understand what that means. Every one of us, whether we are Christian or not, exists on the surface of this planet, and that is the definition of being *in* this world. Prior to our decision to take God seriously and our decision to accept Jesus Christ as our Savior, we were all *of* this world. That means that we were affected by the happenings that take place in the world, we were concerned with the problems that take place in the world and we worried about what might happen to us. Once we decide to let God take over our lives, we should no longer be concerned with anything other than serving God, however every modern Christian continues to be concerned with problems such as the election of our leaders, the strength of our military, our personal and/or business tax burden, the price of gasoline, whether our children will be able to attend college, our job security, our health and on and on.

So why does the church advocate worrying about the world? The answer is very simple; the church is locked in a struggle with God Himself for control of this world. Other than singing continual praises to a God which they know nothing about, the church is attempting to return to the dark ages wherein the church controlled every aspect of the lives of the very people they professed to serve. Go back in history and look at the

Israelites before the coming of Christ. The Temple controlled all aspects of life for every Jew, but was God pleased? No, because He had the temple destroyed and the Jews scattered throughout the world. Fast-forward to the Dark Ages when the Catholic Church controlled everything, including the very lives of the common people, and the inquisition tortured anyone who could be suspected of anything. God brought a man named Martin Luther, yet the church still has not learned the first and most elementary lesson about God. He is in control.

If we have made the decision that God does indeed exist and that He is that all-powerful, awesome God that we sing and talk about, why can't we recognize that fact that He is still awake and in control of this world. Is it because we don't like the way that He is running things? Sadly, the answer is yes, but I have a message for you: **GET USED TO IT!** The Bible states that God's ways are not our ways, and our ways are not God's ways; yet I have never heard even one "pastor" talk about what that means or, even more appropriately, speak about what that means within the context of our own personal lives. So here it is. Put this into your mind and review it every hour: God is alive and He (not anyone else including our President) is running this world. So why does He allow earthquakes, floods and terrorists to kill millions? Because that is His plan and nothing more needs to be said about it. I told you before that this life is just a test. So why worry; let God do the heavy work. The church has again failed to tell us that this all-powerful God or ours not only created "good," He, in His own omnipotent wisdom, created evil. SAY WHAT? Yes, it's in the Old Testament, but I'm not going to tell you where because I want you to find it for yourself.

There will always be problems in this world, and there will always be practices in this world of which we don't approve. Gambling, drunkenness, abortion, greed, murder, you name it will always be present, but it is not our job to change the world. Recognize that, acknowledge that, reconcile yourself to that, and, lastly, don't fret about that, because God has it under control. Once you have accomplished the above, only then are you ready to serve God. If you are worried or even concerned about what is going on in the world, you lose the ability to hear God's direction for your life. You might think that this will be the most difficult thing that you will ever have to do, but the benefits are tremendous. You will lose that anger, that frustration, that feeling of helplessness that has plagued you (read me) all of your life. I used to tell my wife, "You know, all I want from this world is *peace.*" It wasn't until I gave all the troubles of the world to God that I found the peace that I had been seeking all my life, and you will too.

I know so many Christians today who walk around in a state of continuous anger. Why? The answer is that they are concerned about all the things that are happening in this world. I also see many Christians worried about money or sickness or some other matter. Give it to God, and when you do, He will take care of you and *all* of your needs. This one simple matter is where so many Christians fail, yet it is the first step that all of us must take if we are to be able to truly call ourselves "Christians

If step one in our preparation to be able to serve God is to stop being concerned about what is taking place in this world, then step two is very similar, but listen closely and don't take the next sentence out of context. The second step that each of us must take on the journey toward serving God is to stop being concerned about (the lifestyle of) others and begin being concerned about our own lifestyles. You see, the church has taught us, if only by implication, that once we are saved, we now must go out and either save everyone else or change the world so that no one else can be allowed to do anything *bad.*

Of course, reaching and teaching everyone about Jesus Christ is a wonderful goal; the problem is the fact that not one of us has prepared ourselves to be the teacher that Christ wants us to be. How many of us could walk into a university and teach even the most basic course on engineering? The answer is that no one can teach anyone anything without extensive preparation, and an engineering course is infinitely less complicated than even the most basic course on Christianity. So why does the church teach us that once we are saved, we are now qualified to teach the world? Here in the heart of the Bible belt, one cannot even walk down a sidewalk on Main Street without having a Christian "tract" shoved into their hand. Are we supposed to save the world by handing out tracts? Sorry, but that day is over. It might have worked once, but the Christian that just handed you the tract is the one that will abuse you or steal from you the first chance they get. So what are we to do in order to prepare ourselves to serve God?

Since most Christians are either too lazy or too arrogant to read even the New Testament of the Bible, I am going to give them a shortcut. If you have never read the Bible, read just the three chapters of Matthew that contain what we know as the Sermon on the Mount. In the entire world, there is no better instruction on how to become a Christian, yet never, in all the years I have attended many churches, have I heard this sermon preached as a guide to the lifestyle of every Christian *today*.

FAILURE!

Even if you have read the entire Bible numerous times, turn to Matthew, Chapter 5, and read through to Chapter 8. Only this time recognize the fact that Christ is talking to *you* (and to me) individually. If not one other word of what we know as our guidebook (the Bible) existed, these three chapters would be totally adequate as our guide toward true Christianity; yet the church today ignores the application of these words to our lives. Why? Because it isn't easy, and the church is afraid that if it isn't easy, then some of us might get discouraged and turn away, when in fact, most Christians have already turned away.

We have turned away through our refusal to continue our journey down the narrow path. If someone believes, yet does not exemplify that belief through a change of their own life and actions, then that belief is less than worthless. A Christian cannot profess belief in Jesus Christ then ignore His teachings and continue to desire worldly things and desire worldly pleasures.

The second step in preparing to serve God is to change our own lifestyle into a lifestyle that is acceptable to God. Do you tell fibs, cheat on your taxes, cheat on your wife; are you trapped by homosexuality, gossip; are you continually angry at the injustices of this world; are you frustrated; or are you just angry at your fellow man. Your job is, through the strength of the Holy Spirit is to get those problems out of your life. I personally picture this step as taking a shower after working in the garden. Every time I work in the garden (go into the world), I get dirty (make mistakes), but after I make a mistake I do two things. I must recognize my mistake, and then I must ask the Holy Spirit for His help so that I will get better at not repeating those same mistakes. Please remember what I stated earlier; not one of us can change our life without the help and work of the Holy Spirit. Neither the Catholic Church nor the Baptist Church nor any other denomination can change your life. Changing your life is like changing the spots on a leopard. It can be accomplished only through the power of God Himself (listen closely here) as *WE* work both with ourselves and through God.

Does that sound complicated? It really isn't. What I am trying to explain is that God has no intention of changing us into perfect Christians with a snap of His fingers or some almighty magic bullet. God does want us to change our lives and become living examples of the life of Jesus Christ, but He wants us to work at it and use His power to accomplish that change. We have to take the first step, and I am not referring to taking Christ as our Savior. I am talking about taking steps beyond that initial acceptance of salvation, and again this is where the church has failed because in most denominations, acceptance of Christ has become the end in and of itself and God is expected to do the rest of the work.

FAILURE!

Will I ever become perfect? No, God doesn't expect that, but I can improve, and through God's help, I will improve to the point where God can use me as His servant. We Christians usually fail to recognize that until we begin cleaning the dirt (our worldly hang-ups) out of our lives, God cannot and usually will not use us in His service. Notice that I said "usually," because God can, contrary to the belief of some Christians, make His own decisions. Here is what I believe about how our relationship with God works. After we have decided to accept that God exists and take Him seriously, we must demonstrate by changing our lives that we are serious and not just giving Him lip service.

When I asked the question of whether *I* will ever become perfect, I did it for a reason. It took twelve years of preparation before I could begin the work which God had planned for me, and during that time I had many failures and I had much to learn. Let me be very clear. I am not even close to being a good Christian even now, yet when I look back upon my life as it was before I put God in charge, I can see a change that is nothing short of miraculous. Is my work done, and can I sit back and rest on my accomplishments? Absolutely not. My work must continue for as long as I live, and my dependence upon the Holy Spirit's help must never end. When God created human beings like you and me, He never intended them to be perfect. His intent was to give us the reasoning power that would enable us to make our own decision of whether to allow Him into our lives. His intent was also to determine whether we would pass the test of taking Him seriously.

So what should be the goal of every Christian? Let's go back to the verse at the beginning of the chapter. ***Jesus saw Nathaneal coming to Him, and He said of him, "Behold an Israelite indeed, in whom is no guile!"*** I know that I have talked about this before, but this one statement is so important because it exemplifies one of the few times that Jesus seemed to be amazed at finding a man who had no deceit or cunning, or as we would say in modern times, this man didn't have either an agenda or an axe to grind.

The other time that Jesus was amazed occurred when Jesus was asked to heal the servant of a Roman centurion. This man, not even a Jew, had such great faith in the power of the Son of God that he knew that Jesus had only to give the order and his servant would be healed. Jesus marveled at his faith and said, ***"Truly I say to you, I have not found such great faith with anyone in Israel."***

So, do you want to impress God, or better yet do you want to work for God? If the answer is yes, then you must do two things: Get all *guile*, i.e. deceitfulness, cunning, self-enrichment, politics, and worldly agendas out of your life, and replace them with a life and a faith that is real and not just lip service.

9

WORKING FOR GOD

Do not work for the food which perishes, but for the food which endures to eternal life, which the Son of Man shall give to you, for on Him the Father, even God has set His seal.

Do nothing from selfishness or empty conceit, but with humility of mind let each of you regard one another as more important than himself;

Do not merely look out for your own personal interests, but also the interests of others.

A revelation came to me today: **I am to take care of God, and He will take care of everything else.** This seems so obvious, yet it can be both the truest test of a Christian, and it can be the existential leap of faith that will forever free the true Christian from the bonds, cares, worries and the sicknesses of this world.

What does it mean that I am to take care of God? Good question. First let me explain how this thought came about, then what it will mean to you. It was morning of the usual day of the week that I have set aside to write this book, yet I had not sat down at the computer because I didn't feel the thoughts flowing. Even though I had been thinking about the book and about God within my life, I was, in retrospect, concerned about my business, and I as I finally did sit down at the computer, I was planning to write a letter to my webmaster about some actions that I wanted taken regarding the web site. As I hit the "on button" God seemed to hit my "on button." The thought came to me that it was my choice whether to work for God (the book) or be concerned about my business. Which path would I take? You, the reader, might want to take a minute to review my chapter on

Calvinism here, because as I stated, the Calvinists believe that we don't have choices, yet God gives us choices every day. The problem is that most of us make the wrong choice instead of the choice that God desires.

Our choices can be as simple as deciding whether to spend fifteen minutes reading the Bible or to spend that time reading some pseudo-Christian novel or watching television. Another simple choice could be whether to put some of that hard earned money to work for God or to use it to purchase that new CD or a new sweater or something else that you think will make your life more complete. The overriding question that repeatedly comes to my mind is this: Why do Christians continually make the wrong choices? I believe that there are several reasons, and the first reason is that the church tries to lead us to believe that in order to be a "good" Christian; we must *always* be **holy** every second of our lives. What the church doesn't teach is that even Christians cannot be "holy" all of the time. After all, we were created as human and even though we may have had our lives transformed through the power of the Holy Spirit, we are still human. God doesn't expect us to be "holy" all of the time. After all, God created this world. Why wouldn't He want us to enjoy it? I'm willing to bet that even the Pope and Billy Graham watch a secular movie to relax once in a while. Why shouldn't we be able to do the same? Christians leave the church primarily because they just give up on trying to be perfect all the time, and they are taught by the church that if they can't be perfect all the time, they are "sinning."

Another reason that Christians continually make the wrong choices is that the Church teaches a confusing message about God. For instance, the church teaches us that God created this earth, but in the next breath the church leaders are trying to make sure that we all vote for the "correct" political candidate (the one approved by the church). Gee, has God died? Isn't He in control anymore, and does He not appoint our leaders (politicians) as the Bible states? To make things even more confusing, the church tells us that we must be concerned about laws of which the church doesn't approve, concerning things such as lotteries or gay marriage, being passed. Has God become so aged and infirm that He can't even control Congress? Heck, anybody can control Congress if they have money. Are you trying to tell me that God needs our help? Maybe we should all write God a check for $20 so He can lobby the nearest Senator. Ah, well, maybe not; after all, these days $20 will buy two Senators.

As long as the Church pursues a double path about God, there will be no hope of educating those people who pursue Christianity, and education is a must because not one of us can hope to intimately know that very real, very powerful, very intimate and very much in control God of ours without the teaching of the Holy Spirit. Will someone send a memo to Pat Robertson, the Pope and the leaders of the Baptist Convention to the effect that God is still in control and we are not to be concerned about the world? Maybe it would help if we sent them a copy of the Bible, because none of them seem to have read it.

Let me return to the decision that I talked about before, that of trying to decide whether to spend fifteen minutes reading the Bible or reading that new novel. Notice that I talked about reading the Bible for only fifteen minutes. Listen closely, because this is important, and it is the reason that a lot of Christians fail. It is all right to only spend fifteen or twenty minutes reading the Bible. Why? Because within that short period of reading the most important book ever written, the Holy Spirit will have a message for you. You may not even recognize that message until days later, but He will bring it back to you. When we try to read too much of the Bible in too short a period of time, the Holy Spirit does not have a chance to speak, for the simple reason that our human intellect is severely limited. After all, as I keep repeating, we are only human and that is the way that we were created. Come on church and you fellow Christians, lighten up! Some of you who have read the Bible will remember that Christ, when He was talking to the Jews about new converts, said something to the effect that once a new convert is brought into the fold, the church makes that new convert "twice as much a servant of hell as before."

I really think that verse is applicable today, because the Christian church is doing exactly the same thing by attempting to force the rest of the world to conform to its wishes. Have you ever heard the saying, Do as I say, not as I do!"? How can the secular world accept Christ when every day "Christian" leaders are caught in sin?

To return to my original thought, that of discovering why Christians make wrong decisions, I have come to the conclusion that it is due primarily to the fact that none of us really and truly believes that God exists. Oh, yes, we sing that **OUR GOD IS AN AWESOME GOD,** but who among us really believes it, especially around election time when all the "Christians" run around trying to get out the vote for *God's* candidate. Think about this for a second. Doesn't trying to get *our* candidate elected and a government acceptable to *our* beliefs, sound just like the Muslims? Isn't that exactly what they are trying to accomplish, the establishment of a Muslim government? Most Christians will be the first to rail about the interference of government in the affairs of the church, when the Nativity scene or the Ten Commandments is involved, yet those same so-called "Christians" are the first to attempt to get the church (or their version of it) to interfere with the affairs of our Government when they want a law passed. Let me say it again, the modern Christian church, from the Pope to the smallest country church, has become exactly like the Muslims in that it wants a government created in the image of its beliefs.

Who among us really believes that God will take care of every aspect of our life, including our business (if we are smart enough to give it to Him) and, yes, even this great country of ours? Most Christians refuse to recognize that the Bible states that **God** appoints our political leaders. Why? Simply because: 1. they haven't read the Bible and 2. The church refuses to teach any aspect of the Bible that does not suit their agenda, and to be perfectly honest, I can reach no other conclusion but that the church's agenda is political. Remember Pat Robertson? There is an example of a man who is falsely using the name of God to lift himself into a position of power. Does Pastor (using that term awfully loosely) Robertson really believe that he can change the world? I don't think so. Even he isn't that gullible. In my opinion, Pat Robertson and those other perennial "Christian" presidential candidates such as Al Sharpton and Jesse Jackson just want financial gain.

Let me tell you about my business. It has been twelve years since I gave my life to God because I couldn't run it (my life) myself, and it has been ten years since I began taking my Christianity seriously. The first years were rough, and there were times that I really wondered whether God was really in my life, but I see now that He was training me and leading me down the exact path that He wanted so that I would arrive prepared to do the job that He had given me, that of serving His people. As I have learned to follow God's directions, God has not hesitated to take care of every other aspect of my life, including my business. As I write this, in June of 2003, the world of business is in turmoil, the stock market continues to bounce around with no one sure of the future. Large corporations continue to go bankrupt, and small businesses are closing daily, yet my business which is in the recreation industry, is thriving. We are in our sixth year in a row of setting new sales records, and it just keeps growing. Why? Let me assure you it has nothing to do with my leadership. It is nothing more than the fact that my very personal God has it firmly in hand. Yes, I hear someone out there saying that the recreation industry as a whole is growing, so what! Well then, let me ask you this: Why have thirty-eight of my local direct competitors gone out of business and I am thriving? Some of them lasted less than a year. Why? The answer is very simple, I work for God, and (pay attention here) God (in return) works for me.

Am I being disrespectful to our omnipotent God? Not at all, and again here is where the church has once more failed because it refuses to teach what our God is all about. So what is this invisible but all powerful God all about? The first thing that I will tell you is that our God is a very personal God. We all know (but refuse to recognize) that our God is within each of us in the form of the Holy Spirit. If He wasn't a very personal God who is intimately interested in every moment of each of our lives, why would He have given Himself to each of us? Think about it. That is exactly what God has done. He has put Himself into every person who is born. Those people who refuse to believe in God call Him "our conscience" or "that inner voice," yet that is nothing less than that "still small voice" described in the Bible as one of the prophets asks to **see** God. Can we **see** God? Yes, we can *see* through hearing Him talk to us every day, if we will just be still and listen. Of course, the problem here is that most Christians can't **hear** God speaking because they are too busy trying to tell everyone else what to do and how to do it.

The apostle Paul, an educated and extremely intelligent man, had to spend three years alone in the desert before he would even consider spreading the word. Personally, I had to spend almost ten years in my "desert" before God began telling me what job He had for me. Some Christians will spend their entire lives in their own personal deserts because they refuse to listen to anyone except some egotistical preacher who doesn't have the faintest idea of what God is all about.

I want to tell you that our God is a very personally involved God. He wants to be, and I promise you that He is, involved in every aspect of your life. So why does He allow us to be poor or sick or lose a loved one? There is a very simple answer to this question. As a matter of fact, the answer is so simple that very few people will believe what I am going to say. Our God, in His relationship with us, is a very straightforward and uncomplicated God. We are told that He wants only that which is right and good for us; yet if that is true, why do we have to suffer so much? Just for a moment, picture a young two-year-old child with its mother in a grocery store. You remember those "terrible twos" don't you, mothers and fathers? This young child wants everything and anything that captures its attention, yet the parent firmly refuses to purchase that snack or candy or toy because she knows that giving a child everything that it wants is not in the child's best interest, and that parent, just like God, wants only those things which are right and good for their child. What happens next? The child throws a tantrum, blowing the importance of the item and of the moment totally out of proportion. Does that sound like us? Of course, it does, because, just like that child throwing a tantrum, most of us Christians are stuck in our own personal "terrible twos" and we steadfastly refuse to grow despite the coaching of the Holy Spirit.

Listen closely to what I am going to say next. If we who call ourselves "Christians" have put God in charge of our lives, and we are dedicated to serving Him, we will **never** have to suffer. Did you see the word "never"? I mean it. NEVER! Am I saying that bad things will never come into our lives, or that we will never be sick or depressed? No, sorry, we still live in this world. What I am saying, and this is really hard to grasp, is that even though death, sickness and disappointments will touch our lives, we won't have to suffer. And get this; we won't even have to worry about it, because we will be able to recognize everything as God's plan. Let me give a couple of examples of the highest order. The husband of a very loving and dedicated Christian couple died last year. This man was the epitome of a loving husband and a dedicated worker for the church and for God Himself, and a year later his wife is still mourning. My question is, "Why?" Of course she loved him and misses him, but why can't Christians realize that instead of mourning a loved one, we should be happy that they have passed the "test" of life on this earth and are now with God in heaven? I don't understand why churches insist upon having funerals. A life that served God on this earth and has passed the test should be celebrated, not mourned. Didn't Jesus say that we must love God even more than we love our own mother or father, or even our own life? Again, the church has failed to teach this fact and allowed Christians to be concerned about the problems of this life, not the plans of God. Our life here upon this earth is nothing more than a test. It is a test of whether we will make the correct choices, and I will be saying more about that later.

I lost my own mother when I was fourteen and I was totally lost. I can look back now and see God's hand forcing me to grow, to find my own way, and to learn to be independent in this life. I am going to tell you something now that is going to sound very cruel and callous. As a member of that race called human beings, most, if not all, of us only grow when we are forced to by some hardship or adversity. If you don't believe that, how many children of wealthy parents do you know that are "achievers"? How many people do you know who had everything as children, grew up to be useful and productive members of society? Oh, yes, they do exist, and I can think of one, but as a general rule, most of the people of today that we recognize as achievers grew up under difficult circumstances.

Perhaps the most outstanding example of this human trait of fighting to overcome seemingly insurmountable obstacles is a man named Stephen Hawking. This man, when he finally became confined to a wheelchair and lost almost all of his physical abilities, decided to grow beyond the bounds of himself to become the foremost theoretical mathematician that the world has ever known, surpassing even the great Albert Einstein. He has trained his mind to think light years beyond the comprehension of most of the smartest people in the world. Even the best educated mathematicians and scientists of this day have trouble understanding his most basic books. Mr. Hawking, who is agnostic, has only one problem, and it is common to many Christians today. In his anger at being deprived of his physical self, Mr. Hawking refuses to recognize that a God does exist, when in fact, he should be grateful that he has been given the opportunity to become the world's greatest mathematician **only through his adversities.**

Think about two things for just a second. First, Mr. Hawking fails to recognize that he became the word's greatest mathematician only through the fact of his adversities, and second, he was given that opportunity only through the planning of a great and wonderful God who knew that Mr. Hawking would be able to reach beyond himself. I seriously doubt that, if he thought about it, Mr. Hawking would return to a life without physical handicaps but with ordinary mathematical skills. What do you think? While there probably are many people in this world who would aspire to become a great mathematician, I am willing to bet that not one of them would be willing to pay the price that Stephen Hawking has through the suffering brought about by Lou Gehrig's disease.

Wait a minute; am I saying that God purposefully allowed Stephen Hawking to become physically crippled through the acquisition of Lou Gehrig's disease? Yes, I am, and He allowed it because He (God) has a plan that involves every person in this world. God wants every one of us to recognize Him, and if you happen to be one of those to whom God attaches great importance because God has something that He wants done, be prepared to go through your own personal hell until you get the big picture and begin working for God. While Mr. Hawking has achieved greatness within the mathematical world, he still doesn't believe in God and that is so sad.

If we return to our thinking on the subject of Calvinism for just a moment and review the question of whether God gives us freedom of choice, we have to acknowledge that God gave Stephen Hawking freedom to choose whether he would allow his physical handicap to rule his life and wallow in self-pity, or overcome this very difficult disability. I have to be the first to admit that I would not be nearly strong enough to do what Mr. Hawking has done in just overcoming his physical limitations, and I certainly don't have the mind to become a great (or even mediocre) mathematician, in spite of my engineering degree. Remember, God gives each of us only the adversities that we *can* overcome, and each of us has different levels of strength and ability (through God).

It is important to remember that when God allows adversity of any kind into our lives, He will either give us the strength and ability to overcome that adversity, or He will (if we let him) pick us up by our bootstraps when we are at our lowest point. Remember, as I said earlier, God brought me through when I had no job and no hope and considered suicide as my only option. Look around you as you drive down the street or walk through a shopping center or store. What do you see? You see overwhelming anger, disappointment, frustration, poverty, sickness and misery. Road rage has reached epidemic proportions. There are over 800,000 homeless people in the United States right now. Of those 800,000 homeless people, 200,000 are children. I ask you, whose fault is this? Is it the fault of the government? Is it the fault of these families themselves because they are too lazy to work? No. The United States is *supposedly* a nation "under God" and therefore a nation by default "Christian."

The blame for the sad state of affairs in this nation rests squarely on the shoulders of every Christian man and woman (and especially church) in this country today. Now, I recognize that is a pretty strong statement, and I am prepared to give justification for it. First of all, this is a nation supposedly founded "under God." According to repeated government census figures, over eighty percent of the population of this United States is "Christian," and at the time of this writing, even our President is a "born again" Christian; yet who among all of us "Christians" is concerned about the "working poor" or even the 800,000 homeless people who have nowhere to sleep but under some highway bridge. Oh, sure, almost every church has a food drive at some time of the year. Christmas is usually the best excuse to give a few cans of food, and our conscience is salved for another year.

You will remember a few chapters back I talked about my own Baptist church spending ninety percent of their budget on their building fund and ten percent on missions. I wonder what the results would be if we compared the entire budget to the amount given specifically to help the people of our area who are either out of work, homeless, losing their job or in some situation where they have no hope. Want to bet that the figure would be close to one tenth of one percent? Well, just for fun (no not really, it was more like shame), I went to my church, First Baptist Mauldin, interviewed the financial secretary and found out exactly how much money was given specifically to help families in difficult circumstances. What was the answer? Less than one percent of the budget of the largest church in Mauldin, South Carolina, is used to help families in need. What a shame, and what a travesty to the memory of the life of Jesus Christ.

To put this figure in context, here is a church in an area that is losing its largest employer. Thousands of employees have already been laid off, and the plant is moving almost its entire operation to the Far East while the members of my own church continue to build an ever larger monument to their own greed. Here is a church whose own members are affected by the nation's economy, and, sadly, they have no plans or even desire to help even their own members. If they won't help even their own members, how can they be expected to help someone from another area? Oh, I forgot. They will send some teenagers to repair houses for a week.

At this point, it would be valid and acceptable to ask me why I am so concerned about helping people and seemingly unconcerned about "witnessing," so let's look at the Bible and the words of Christ Himself. I am, of course, referring to the only specific commandment that Jesus Christ Himself ever gave us: *"A new commandment I give to you, that you love one another, even as I have loved you, that you also love one another."*

John emphasizes this commandment in a most succinct and concise way when he says, "If someone says, 'I love God' and hates his brother, he is a liar; for the one who does not love his brother whom he has seen, cannot love God whom he has not seen." And then John places his own emphasis upon this idea by referring to the words of Jesus as he, in his next verse says, "And this commandment we have from Him, that the one who loves God should love his brother also." You see, even John himself recognizes the words of Jesus as a specific Commandment (and so identifies them as such), while the Christian church of today refuses to recognize or even teach this commandment, or even the very ideal that it encompasses.

Of course, every Christian reading this book will immediately jump up and with great offense scream, "But I *DO* love everyone!" At this point, I say to them, "O.K. just exactly what have you done to **show your love***?* The answer in most cases has to be "nothing" and you might want to review the Book of James. In the second chapter of James, this statement is found: *"What use is it my brethren, if a man says he has faith, but he has no works?* Oh, sure, those Christians might have given a few dollars to the church, but remember that ninety percent of *that* money went toward the building fund. How many people who call themselves "Christian" actually took some individual action of any kind, which helped someone in "need?" Here is an even more important question. How many of you have taken some action to help **anyone,** whether the person was in need or not?

Whenever, I think of "helping" someone, I think of my neighbor. Here is a guy who is just a plain working man, totally unpretentious, yet when someone needs help of any kind, he is there in a heartbeat. Tree in the road after an ice storm? Don't even bother calling him, he's already there. Get stuck in the mud? Call him. This guy doesn't attend church (as a matter of fact, he refuses to attend a church), yet he is the personification of what *should be* the Christian ethic and the Christian presence. Come to think of it, it is probably a good thing that he doesn't attend church, because he would have learned that his actions are not acceptable to most "Christians" and are certainly not taught in the so-called "Christian" church.

The subject of this chapter is working for God. I think that we can safely say that when Jesus Christ came into this world, his purpose was to work for God. As a matter of fact Jesus repeatedly stated that His sole purpose was to do the will of The Father. Most Christian churches teach that Jesus Christ's main purpose during His time on earth was as our "Savior" and to provide a means of forgiveness for the sins of the world and hence the rise of "Me Me Me" Christianity

While it is without a doubt true that Jesus Christ and His death upon a cross provide the means of salvation for the human race, that particular act was not the primary purpose of His life. After all, God in His supreme wisdom could have forgiven our sins through **any** means that He wished. God's (and His Son's) primary purpose was to provide a model by which we individually are to live and, by our lives, become the "sons of God" ourselves. Think about the word that you would have to use if you were to describe His life or, to put it in modern terms, the "job description" of Jesus Christ. There is really only one word which is appropriate to use to describe the life and the works of Jesus Christ, and that word is one that most Christians would not like to use as a self-description. As a matter of fact, most Christians today desire exactly the opposite treatment, and that sad fact is again the fault of the Christian church.

Whether you have read the Bible or not, a few moments reviewing the life of Jesus Christ and the impact of that life upon the community of the time will make it obvious what I am proposing. Let's take a minute and review some highlights. The Gospel of Matthew contains what has become known as the "Sermon on the Mount." Jesus taught a crowd of people the most important series of lessons in the entire Bible. This particular sermon was so important and so relevant that it could serve as the entire Bible, even if nothing else about the life of Jesus Christ was preserved, yet most of that sermon is ignored by the present-day church. This gets a little complicated, but stick with me and I think that your entire paradigm will be changed if you will just let it.

The words of Jesus were the explicit lesson of how we are to live; yet it is after His sermon that Jesus teaches us Christians an even more salient lesson of how we are to explicitly treat our fellow man. What did Jesus do after His teaching? He recognized that the people who had come so far to hear Him were hungry – **and He fed them.** Most churches teach only the superficial meaning of this act, i.e. God can do miracles. The true meaning of the act of feeding this mass of people is that Jesus Christ was the ultimate servant of all of the people. Did you catch that? The only word that is appropriate to describe the entire ministry of Jesus Christ, the only word that could possibly be used as his job description, is the word **SERVANT!**

The modern church, again, does not follow through in passing along the entire lesson that Jesus was trying to teach. We hear, from the pulpit some of the words that Jesus taught, but the final and most important lesson of feeding our fellow man is ignored. I can't help but wonder if anyone in our churches and in those divinity schools has ever read the Bible. Not only are Jesus' words misinterpreted, they are ignored. I know that I have stated it before but it is worth repeating that Jesus called his *words* the "solid rock," but the church in its infinite ignorance misread the statement and calls **Jesus** the "solid rock" and ignores both His words and His intent in stating them.

Take a moment to think about every interaction that Jesus had with the people of the day (other than the church leaders whom He repeatedly insulted for their ignorance). In every case Jesus acted as a servant to every person whom He met. Without exception, Jesus Christ placed Himself as a servant to everyone. When the lowliest of "street people," a group of blind beggars, asked to be cured of leprosy, He took the time to heal them; yet the church passes this off as nothing more than Jesus proving that He was "God" by performing a miracle, and again the church has missed the entire point of Jesus' ministry. First of all, Jesus did not and would not take credit for performing any of His miracles. He stated explicitly that He had no power and that everything He did was through the power of God the Father. Second, the point of the exercise was *not* to prove that He was God; the point was to demonstrate His (and the Father's) first priority, that of taking care of God's greatest creation, people. Can we do any less and still call ourselves followers of Jesus Christ? The answer is a resounding NO! I cannot help but wonder at what Jesus would think about the self-serving church leaders of today as they run for political office.

    I am not going to pretend that I know the reason why the church throughout two thousand years has failed to recognize the true reason for Christ's existence, but that failure can no longer be ignored and must be dissected and corrected. The very first church in the immediate time after Christ's death was concerned primarily with helping their brothers. We read in the Book of Acts that people sold their worldly goods and brought that money to the church for the good of all. Listen closely. Right here is the very first failure of the Christian church. When the leaders of the church stopped using the money given to the church to help people and began using those gifts to build buildings, the church began to fail. Does the Christian Church (of any denomination) really believe that building ever larger monuments to their own greed and egotism will convince people to believe in Jesus Christ? The Christian church in America today has become exactly like the Jews of old, building ever larger "temples" in which to worship God while people who are struggling are ignored.

    I find it unbelievably strange that the secular world has, in many instances, taken the lead in following the example of that man we call our Savior, namely Jesus Christ. As I told earlier, I found one of those examples right here in Spartanburg, S.C., at the Headquarters of the National Beta Club. I was on my way home one afternoon and God gave me a message that I couldn't ignore. There, right in front of me was a billboard of the National Beta Club with their motto in big letters; **LET US LEAD BY SERVING OTHERS.**

I had already started work on this chapter and there it was, right in front of me, exactly what I had been trying to communicate, the fact that serving others is the highest and most genuine form of leadership. It is also the exact form of leadership that God Himself wants us to perform in our own lives when we truly desire to pattern our own life after that of Jesus.

For just a moment, let's compare that small but succinct motto directly to the life of Jesus Christ and let's also compare it to some of the "Christians" who are trying to lead us today. To start, I would ask the question: Can Jesus can still be considered a "leader" given the context of 2000 years of history and our ability to rationally look back at what He accomplished? Of course, the answer has to be a resounding YES, given the fact that even after two thousand years, this one man is still the most followed, most quoted and most admired man who ever lived. Even the Muslims, who despise the Christian religion, recognize this same Man as a great prophet to the point that they include the same four Gospels of our Bible in their worship.

All right, we have established the fact that Jesus was and is the greatest leader who ever lived, so let's see just exactly how He did, in fact, lead. It might be easier to first examine what Jesus **did not** do in order to lead, and the first point to examine is the fact that Jesus never ran for office or tried to be a political or church leader. Are you listening, Pat Robertson or Al Sharpton or Jesse Jackson? Remember, in those times the church (the Temple) held all the political power, and there is another lesson for today's church leaders, because look at where all that (political) power got them. The second thing that Jesus **did not** do as a leader was tell everyone what to do or how to live. The third thing that Jesus did not do is hang around with only the "good" people of the time.

The very first attribute that Jesus demonstrated in His life and actions was that fact that He "listened." Listening is a skill at which the entire human race fails at one time or another, but Christians have the worst listening habits of all because they seem to feel that they already know everything. Of course, we are aware that God had given His Son unique listening skills, which included the ability to search the very mind of everyone He met, but we, as Christians, must not let His unique abilities be used as an excuse. God has given each of us who follow Him the ability to "learn" about others if we will just keep our mouths shut and our ears open. As followers of our Lord, it must be our first order of business to develop a sincere relationship with those people with whom God has brought us into contact. Forget about *chance* or *luck* meetings, because God is indeed in control of everything, and if you meet someone, it is because God planned it and desired it. We Christians keep mouthing that "Almighty God" stuff but seemingly few of us really believe it.

I have stated this before, but now is the time to put the following statement into context regarding our own purpose in life and "working for God." Everyone in this world who doesn't know, understand and have a working relationship with God is hurting. Yes, I mean everybody, and that is where we come in, because our job in what I call "working for God" is to befriend, help and be a model for those people who have been put into our life.

How do I know that everybody is hurting? Look around you. What do you see? On the highway you see anger, frustration, road rage, selfish driving practices and "me first" attitude. In the workplace you see people trying to climb the corporate ladder by trying to knock everybody else off. Selfishness, greed and lying are so commonplace that everyone begins to think of them as acceptable. Sam Waxhall, Leona Helmsly, Martha Stewart and dozens of other corporate "leaders" have become household names as they await trial, sentencing, jail, fines or whatever, for corporate theft, lying and other forms of greed.

On the home front, personal bankruptcies are at record highs because couples think that possessions will make them happy. America has become the highest debtor nation in the world and the divorce rate became well over fifty percent years ago. Is everybody hurting? You bet, and most of them don't even recognize the degree of hurt which they are experiencing until suicide or homicide begins to look like an option.

I want the reader to stop right here and go back and read the last four paragraphs, beginning with the words, "As followers...." Did you go back? OK, I had previously described God as a very personal and very active God, and then I stated that no meeting was due to luck or chance. God demonstrated the truth of those words just an hour ago.

After finishing the paragraph ending with the word "option," I turned off the computer and went up to see a friend of mine who runs a tire store. As I walked into the store, my friend was changing the tires on another man's automobile, so that man and I began to talk as we were waiting. After a few minutes, our conversation turned to the Bible and it turned out that this gentleman had read the Bible from cover to cover five times, just as I had done. We both laughed about that, and my new friend put forth a challenge by saying that I could start any verse in the entire Bible and he would finish it.

Since I love challenges, I quoted the first part of a verse that most people miss, and sure enough he recognized it right away and finished it properly. I was impressed, to say the least, and I knew that I had found a potential new friend.

As our conversation continued, my new friend seemed fascinated with my seeming peace and contentment and just plain happiness, and I began to sense something missing in his life but I didn't pry; I let God do the work. When all of the work on his car and my truck had been completed, he asked me to join him for a cup of coffee at a nearby restaurant so that we could talk some more. To be honest, I didn't have the time, because I had scheduled a meeting with one of my suppliers who was making a special trip for me, but I recognized that here was God calling me to help one of His people and I gave no indication that I was reluctant to go with this new friend. Do you see the decision point? Here was God giving me an opportunity to serve Him, but I had to put the cares of the world aside. What would your decision have been? Would you have served God or yourself?

When we had settled in at the restaurant, he (I will call him Joe), began asking me about my business and why I was so successful. I made the point of assuring him that my business and my business acumen were totally irrelevant. The only fact that was of any importance was that my primary interest was working for God, and as long as I took care of the jobs that God gave me, God would assure that my earthly business was successful.

Now, that statement will sound like total hooey to ninety-nine percent of the population of the earth, but to a dedicated Christian it makes sense. Why? Well, let me ask you this, which is more important, my feeble earthly business or the business that is important to God? The answer, of course, is obvious; what God wants and needs done is infinitely more important than the entire business world, but very few people recognize that fact, including most Christians.

God may allow a business to fail from time to time to suit His purpose, but if you are dedicated to working for Him, you can bet that He will open another door to your success. Most Christians refuse to recognize that the key to their earthly success is giving God the day to day cares of this world and putting all of our effort into serving Him. How? By serving His people.

To continue with my story, it turns out that because Joe's businesses had not been successful, his wife had taken a job, and Joe's pride had been damaged. Did I tell him that? Not on your life. It isn't my job to tell someone else what is wrong with their life, and besides, I'm just not intelligent enough to even figure it out. My job is just to talk to him, be a friend, and let the Holy Spirit do the work. Do you get the picture? Most of us, when we see someone having problems, jump in with both feet and start telling them what to do, when in reality we don't have a clue. God knows the answer, so why won't we just back off and let them lead themselves to where God wants them.

Let's take a minute and analyze my story. First, God led me to drive downtown for *a reason*. Did you get that? God really is alive. God is in control, and He really wants you working for Him. I can't say it strongly enough – forget politics, forget the problems of the world, God has that all under control. Our job is to help God's people – nothing more and nothing less. I will get to "why" later.

Second, when I arrived where God wanted me to be, there was someone whom I had never met but with whom God wanted me to talk. Are you open to strangers? What is your personal visual image? Are you happy, self assured, at peace with yourself and the world, or are you like most Christians, worried, unhappy and closed to someone who might not look or think like you, or, gee, might be below your station in life? Remember how this stranger seemed drawn to talk to me by my obvious happiness and contentment? No one willingly goes where there is anger, worry or distraction.

Let me say it again: if you don't have your life in order and you haven't gotten yourself *ready* to work for God, you can't do it and He can't use you. Isn't it obvious to anyone that if you are worried or even concerned about something, that worry and concern will blind you to any opportunities that God might place in your path? Even worse, your worries and concerns will lead you to endless diversions from God's real purpose for you. Come on, all you somnambulant pastors and churches – get your people ready to work. Only then will all that praise and worship be meaningful to Him.

All right, we are ready to get to the important part of my little story (if you have prepared yourself for God). A stranger and I were having a conversation and what was I doing? I was listening. Did you get that? I will repeat myself because it is so important. I was listening, and I was listening *intently*. This man was my entire focus and my entire world for a few minutes, because (listen closely) I didn't have any other concerns to distract me. Are you beginning to see why preparation and having your life in order is so important? This may be the most important thing that I say in this entire book, so pay attention. If it were my choice, I would tell every church and every so-called Christian to immediately stop that drivel they call "witnessing" and begin to prepare, through the program I have previously described, to "work" for God. Listen up, church.

I have one more thing to say on this immediate subject concerning our opening conversation, and it is this, because most Christians will have ignored the implication. While I was listening, I was not (get this) talking. When your mouth is open, you can't listen. That is a fact. Learn it.

The next aspect of my little story is also important, and it concerns the fact that I had to make a decision, a decision I really didn't want to make. I had to neglect my earthly business – the source of my income. Look again at that last sentence. Do you see how incorrect it is? My business is **not** the source of my income – God is! God is the one who is behind my success. God is the one who provides. If I had an appointment with my largest customer, I would have ignored it (I hope) to serve God by serving one of His children. What would your decision have been? Be careful what you say, because I guarantee that He will test you on this. Keep in mind that I told you earlier about the time that I failed this test, and I will never forget it.

Let's return to my story, and if you will remember, we are at the restaurant having coffee and talking. Keep in mind that Joe has read the Bible from cover to cover five times and he is a serious Christian, but he is troubled because God seems to be ignoring him. Does that sound like anyone reading this book, because if it does sound familiar, there is something that God wants you to learn? Here is a fine and gentle man who has been a Christian for twenty-five years, reads the Bible, attends church regularly and has a good marriage. What could be wrong?

Well, there may be nothing wrong! God may just be just trying to get your attention, and He also wants you to grow. Is that all right? Of course, we must never stop growing, just as we must never stop learning. Why does God sometimes have to put us through difficulties? The reason is that we aren't paying attention to Him (and I have to tell you that He doesn't like that), and He may be trying to take us to the next level. Let me tell you what I do when difficulties arise in my life. First of all, I recognize that God is trying to speak. You see, I really do believe that He is sovereign, and I really do believe that He will protect and take care of me as He has promised. If I can know that, I now can recognize that any problems that I may encounter, are through Him.

Is our relationship with God really that simple? Am I being naive? The answer is YES to the first question and NO to the second, and that is what is so wonderful about our God. Those of us who are known as His creation need to recognize that we aren't very wise. Oh, yes, we are intelligent – we just aren't very wise about using that intelligence, and sometimes God has to get the attention of those of us who aren't used to listening (back to the preparing thing). Anyway, when problems arise in my life, I just sit down and quietly ask the Holy Spirit to show me what He wants. Does He show me? Always and without fail. What more could we ask of God?

We had been in the restaurant less than five minutes and had just started sipping our coffee and I already knew Joe's problem. Did I interrupt him and tell him what to do? No, I just let him keep talking for two reasons, and the first reason is very, very important. Not one human being on this planet, including Oprah or Dr. Phil or Dear Abby is wise enough to figure out what the real problem is in someone's life. They may be able to identify the symptoms and they may hear what the person is saying, but they don't have the ability to go into that person's life, and certainly not into their thoughts.

So, I have known this gentleman for approximately one-half hour and I think that I know his problem, so what do I do? Well, first of all, unlike most Christians, I don't blow him out of the water with some pronouncement about how to get his life back on track, because most people resent advice, no matter how true or well-meaning. The second reason is that I am usually wrong, because all I can see is the tip of the iceberg. What to do? I let him keep talking, and I let God start working, by keeping him on track and asking a few simple questions with the objective of letting him solve his own problem through the input of the Holy Spirit.

It is not my intention to write a textbook on how to help people; someone who has much more wisdom than I, can do that and I hope that someone will. The problem is not getting a textbook written, because they already exist. The problem is getting the organized church to recognize the fact that the only way to serve God is through serving His people and to accept the fact that the church must change if it is to be successful in doing what God wants.

Individual churches must reverse their inward pursuit of becoming ever larger and begin to train their members to clean up their own lives so that they can finally begin to love, accept, befriend and help the millions of people who don't know about or have rejected God.

Let's take a close look at the statement above because I am advocating three separate and seemingly unrelated changes that, when taken together, can forever change the face of organized Christianity. The first change concerns the fact that most churches consider themselves successful when they win the numbers game by collecting the most members. Then they can justify the next step of building one or several new buildings to house, seat and entertain their collection of people. Serving Jesus

Christ isn't about collecting anything, including people – serving Jesus Christ is about *serving* His people.

The second change concerns training Christians to clean up their own lives. I'm sorry, but walking up to the altar and mouthing a commitment without making the required changes in your own life is like expecting a fish to function out of water; yet every church of which I am aware accepts new Christians by their word alone and makes no effort to train those new Christians.

The last change is the most difficult of all, learning to care about other people. All of us need to allow the Holy Spirit to lead us to those people who need our care or our support or even just our friendship. We may be in the greatest rush, but when the need arises, we will be given the opportunity to make a choice. What will your decision be? Will you work for God or will you work for yourself.

And the King will answer and say to them, "Truly I say to you, to the extent that you served one of these brothers of mine, even the least of them, you served Me." (My paraphrase)

We Christians need to start worshiping God with our lives, not just with our mouths. Only then can we say that we are "working for" and truly worshipping God.

10

A MESSAGE FOR SINGLES

One who is unmarried is concerned about the things of the Lord, how he [or she] may please the Lord; but one who is married is concerned about the things of the world, how he [or she] may please his wife [or husband].

I was married for 24 years. I don't regret any part of that marriage, and I wouldn't change the fact of that marriage for anything; but in the fourteen years since my divorce, I have realized that having another person in my life cannot bring happiness, simply because that other person is also a human being with problems, needs and wants, just like me.

The divorce rate in the United States surpassed fifty percent years ago, and the divorce rate for second marriages exceeds sixty percent, yet ninety-nine percent of these very people involved in multiple marriages are just looking for happiness, and they think that they will find it in another mate or partner that God has waiting "just around the corner." I will be the first to admit that after my divorce, I went looking for a new mate so that I could be "happy" again, but it didn't take God long to show me that was not what He wanted. God wanted **me,** and He wanted my full attention **right now.**

I've stated this before, but let me say it again because it is so important. If you are a believer, yet you are having problems, sickness or whatever troubles in your life, **God is trying to get your attention (and your commitment)!** When I look back at what God put me through—sickness, depression, poverty—I am amazed at the commitment that God made to me that He would put so much work into bringing me to Him, and I am so grateful. Anything that I suffered in those five years when He was putting me through the fire, was nothing (and I would suffer it again) in order to achieve the peace, happiness and completeness that I have today through serving Him directly. I want to add one more statement here, and that is this: If you are a non-believer and you are having problems in your life, God is the only one who can solve them. Try Him. I promise you that He is real. I also promise that He will require something from you; however, whatever it is that He wants from you will bring you happiness and fulfillment unlike anything you have ever imagined.

In this chapter, I have a message for single people, but first, since the subject of the book is the failure of the Christian church, I have to address another point where the (Protestant) church has again ignored the Bible and the very words of Jesus Christ. Almost every Protestant denomination of which I am aware allows and even endorses remarriage after divorce, despite the specific instructions of the supposed leader of that same church.

Whoever divorces his wife and marries another woman commits adultery against her; and if she herself divorces her husband and marries another man, she is committing adultery.

Has the church forgotten that one of the original Ten Commandments stated: ***Do not commit adultery***?

Here, in the Gospel of Mark, Jesus is plainly stating that anyone that remarries is committing adultery, and the sin of adultery is specifically one of the original Ten Commandments. What is the church thinking? In my opinion, they are thinking that they would rather subvert the teachings of Jesus Christ than lose the income from even one member. Pandering to the power of money? You judge.

In fairness, it must be noted that Jesus' same statement, as recorded in the Gospel of Matthew, does contain one caveat with which I do not disagree. In Matthew, Jesus words are recorded with the addition of the phrase, "...whoever divorces his wife, except for immorality, and marries another woman commits adultery." (My underline) Even the disciples were taken aback by Jesus' statement, as they said, *"If the relationship of the man with his wife is like this, it is better not to marry."*

Jesus gives all of us, but especially in my opinion, singles, another option in the long statement of Matthew 19:12 where He talks about eunuchs. In the last phrase of a long sentence, Jesus states, *"... and there are also eunuchs who made themselves eunuchs for the sake of the kingdom of heaven."*

When He talks about the "kingdom of heaven" in this statement, He is not concerned with our reward at the end of our life. In my opinion, He is talking about our individual service to God and the *opportunity* we have to serve Him (listen closely now) with our *whole* life. Go back and reread the passage at the beginning of the chapter and you will begin to see that the state of "singleness" is a God-given opportunity to serve Him as no person who is married could ever hope to imagine.

For those of you who have been married, take a moment and think about the things that frustrated you most during your married life. Isn't it true that you had to spend most of your time thinking about what your spouse needed or wanted and/or how to keep your spouse happy? Well, if you were a proper wife or husband, that is what you did, right? If you are spending your time figuring out how to serve your mate, you don't have that much time left to think about serving God. Which is better? It's your choice.

Please don't misunderstand what I am saying here. The state of matrimony was originated and ordained by God Himself from the time of Adam, so it certainly is not bad; but I want the "single-again" readers to understand that their very "singleness" is an opportunity which, if they care about God at all, should be considered with the greatest care.

In my case, it was as if God was repeatedly saying to me, "You had your time to be married; now it is time to serve Me." Even though I know that the failure of my marriage was mostly my fault, I never once felt that God was chastising me or punishing me. The thoughts that the Holy Spirit brought into my mind went something like this: "All right, you had a pretty good marriage in those twenty-four years, and now I want you to take what you learned in that marriage, plus what I am going to show you, because I now have a specific task which I want you to accomplish for Me, and that task cannot be accomplished if your loyalty is divided.

You see, I had a choice. I could try to serve myself by finding another wife, or I could serve God by making myself a "eunuch" for His sake and for His service. For most of you, that will not be an easy or even an obvious choice, because there will be other singles that will want you in their lives and the temptation will be great to repeat the mistakes of the past. We humans don't want to change, and even if we desperately wanted to change ourselves, it is, as I have said before, impossible to change ourselves without the help of the Holy Spirit.

It may sound strange, but I think that the "luckiest" (I put the word "luckiest" in quotation marks because there is no such thing as luck) people are those of us whom God puts through a living hell in order for Him to get our attention and our service. These are the people for whom God has a special place of service and a special job, and He will do *anything* to get them to recognize and submit to His will. Don't misunderstand or underestimate my use of the word "anything." I am quite serious about the fact that our loving God can and most definitely will go to any length required to serve His plan. He will without hesitation take us to the very precipice of life itself in both a figurative and very literal sense, but what we decide when we reach that point will either open entirely new pathways or end our lives.

I am talking now to those people who have reached the literal end of their rope. It is a dark and scary place to be and there is no way out. Let me repeat that, THERE IS NO WAY OUT. Only the few of us who have been there can recognize the end of a blind tunnel and know what it means. There is no way to proceed, because the rock walls stop our very movement; there is nothing at our disposal or within our abilities that will enable us to break through, and within the one dimensional time line of our lives, we can't go back. Scary? You bet.

Why does a God, whom we think of as loving, allow such terrible things to happen in our lives? Why would a loving God allow a divorce, sickness or the death of a loved one, a son or daughter, a mate or lover, a friend or even a beloved pet? Listen closely, because I am going to tell you the answer, and you won't find it taught in any church within my sphere of knowledge.

Every living thing within this present world of ours must die. It is difficult to understand and it is even more difficult to accept, especially when that death touches our own lives, but it is a fact ordained by a God who has a plan for this world and the worlds beyond. Death is something that a person who chooses to recognize our omnipotent God must not only accept, they must even more importantly learn that they are not given or allowed control over it.

Here is what is important but so difficult for us to understand. Whenever a hardship or a death touches our lives, we are being touched by God Himself, and most importantly, we are being given an opportunity to make a decision. The fact of death or hardship is not what is important. The only thing that is important at that point in time is the fact that God is giving us the opportunity to make a decision, and that decision will be the most important of our entire lives because depending upon the decision that we make, we will or will not proceed to the next phase of where God wants us to be.

Believe me when I tell you that every one of us has been given a purpose within this life. The decision of whether to accept and submit to that purpose is totally up to us and requires each of us to make that existential leap of faith that takes us out of our own control and gives the control and power over our lives to God for His use and purpose and ultimate plan.

I can look back at my own life and see the (several) decision points, that I was given, and as I look back, I can easily recognize that the decisions that I made to follow God's lead were so powerful and had an impact that was so positive that I am totally humbled by His wisdom. There are times that I wish God had brought those decisions to me sooner so that I could have avoided so many mistakes and frustrations, but I also have to recognize that He brought me to my decision points only as I was ready for them. He will bring those decision points into your life also, but only as you have made yourself ready for them and you have worked to acquire the wisdom to make the correct decision.

I want to repeat myself so as to emphasize the two main points that I want everyone to understand. First of all, I mentioned that each of us will come to several points within our lives when we will have to make a very important decision. God is, has or will call every one of us to serve Him at some time in our lives. Notice that I didn't say "worship" Him! He has enough of that, and I talked in an earlier chapter about the fact that God is tired of our worship when nothing else accompanies that worship. What you the reader must understand, is that God wants nothing less than your entire attention, and if He doesn't get it in your lifetime, He is going to be disappointed, and you will be the one facing that disappointment at the end of your life on this earth. Just remember that He gives you the choice and that choice is yours to make (contrary to the teachings of the church).

My second point concerns the fact that we must make the effort to prepare ourselves and be ready to take the next step that God will offer us. Let me explain that statement with this example. No company of which I am aware would hire an architect to design a skyscraper if that architect had not been to college and received a degree in architecture and had some previous experience in smaller projects. I am not belittling God when I state that He is just like any earthly employer in that He wants people who are committed enough to prepare themselves and dedicated enough to perform the job. Unlike any earthly employer, God can and will use anyone and everyone who has the commitment and is willing to make the preparation.

I don't care who you are, or what your intelligence or abilities, God has a job for you if you are willing to take it. Did you notice that I didn't say anything about sacrifice? God doesn't want sacrifice. God wants dedication. Why do we forget that Jesus came to give us life to the fullest. I made the same mistake when I was a new Christian. I thought that God would want me to become a missionary to some third world country, and because of that, I was afraid to commit to His will (again false church teaching). It was only when I finally gave up everything in my possession and gave in to His will that I found that the job that He had for me was the greatest opportunity of my life, and the reward was beyond measure.

Whether you are going through a divorce or already single again, you have been given an opportunity. The choice is yours to make. Do you want a fleeting and superficial happiness through another mate, or do you want purpose, fulfillment and peace in your life as you work for the Great Creator? Not many of us make the correct choice, and sadly because of our reluctance to really and wholly trust that great God of ours, few of us obtain the peace, happiness and reward that God has waiting.

This is a short chapter because the premise is very simple, but I need to address one issue so that there is absolutely no misunderstanding of the fact that I do not advocate divorce under any situation. Yes, I am divorced, but I don't think that divorce was God's choice or intent, and it was only after the fact of my finalized divorce that I was given the choice of accepting God's will for my life. If anyone reading this is married, then I have only two words for you—STAY MARRIED—for two reasons. First, you will be doing God's will as you love and serve your family, and second, service to God can be made only by serving others, whether you are married or single.

11

ARE YOU WILLING

(to be like Jesus)

The first thing that you had better understand is that being "like Jesus" is not a glory job. It was difficult, physically and mentally tiring and frustrating work for Jesus Christ, and it will be that and more for you. Jesus Christ was cursed, beaten, disbelieved, hated and finally killed by those He came to serve. Are we to expect the same treatment? Thanks be to God, for most of us, the answer is NO; however, we had better be prepared to face frustration and rejection. Jesus Christ's job while here on this earth was to be the servant after whom we are to pattern ourselves; however, in order to be our Savior, He had to suffer and be killed. He accomplished His mission so that we would not have to suffer the same fate. Keep in mind where Jesus Christ is now, seated on the right hand of God. Wouldn't it be great to be seated with Him? Actually, the more proper question should be *won't* it be great to be seated with Him, because if you are willing to make the effort, that is where you will be seated.

The most wonderful thing about wanting to be like Jesus Christ, is the fact that we can be. The Church teaches that while Jesus Christ was on this earth He was wholly God and wholly man, but I disagree, because while He was on this earth, even though He was born of God, He was wholly and *only* a man. Am I belittling His ministry? Absolutely not! Am I trying to make Him appear as anything less than the Son Of God? Absolutely not! He got tired. He got frustrated. He got angry. He became sarcastic. He needed some space. Doesn't that sound like us? It sure sounds like me, and I hope that it sounds like you, because then you can call yourself human. Our humanity and its accompanying frailty is a wondrous gift from God Himself because (this is important, so listen closely) it allows us, and it even forces us, to *depend upon God the Father,* just as Jesus Himself did.

What I am going to say next will be considered nothing less than heresy to some Christians who have never read the Bible. Jesus Christ never healed anyone. What? Yes, Jesus never healed anyone – Every miracle that Jesus ever performed was accomplished by God the Father – and Jesus said so. Repeatedly.

When we become Christians, and even more importantly, when we attempt to become like Jesus Christ, we must first achieve an understanding of just how God works, and how Jesus Himself worked during His time with us. What I have shared with you so far and what I am about to tell you is going to sound very strange to those of you who have never read the Bible, or even the New Testament, from cover to cover, but here it is. Jesus repeatedly stated that He never, repeat never, did anything except through the Father. Jesus repeatedly made the point that He had no power. As Christians, this is our first and most important lesson in how God works. God did not give even His own Son the power to accomplish miracles. You see, God reserves all extraordinary powers for Himself. Why? Because only God Himself has the wisdom to use those powers. Take the time to read about the time that an entire town rejected Jesus' teachings; the disciples wanted to call down fire from heaven upon the town and destroy it, but Jesus would not let them. My point here is that if God were to give us HIS power, we would not have the wisdom to use it wisely. How many of you have wanted to hurt someone or even get rid of them because of something that they did wrong? Do you see the danger? God wisely reserves all of his extraordinary powers for Himself exclusively. Only God the Father can create life. Only God the Father can heal the blind, make the lame walk, the dumb speak and, the greatest miracle of all, raise the dead. What this reserving of power means is that there is a "safety net" for us and our decisions so that God will never let happen those things which would compromise His plan for this world.

Does this mean that we will never be tempted or make mistakes? Of course not, facing temptations and mistakes are some of the ways that we learn and grow in God's favor. What is important is how we handle those temptations and mistakes. Did we give in to temptation? Did we look back on a mistake and recognize it for what it was – something not to repeat? That is how we grow. For most of us, giving in to a temptation happens every day of our lives. It is only when we either do not recognize what we are allowing to happen to ourselves or when we do not grow in God's strength so that we are able to resist the next time that the temptation comes knocking, that we are failing ourselves and therefore God Himself. The next time that you make a mistake or are going through temptation, remember that here is another opportunity for you to grow in God's favor. If you remember, I discussed this at length in my chapter on Calvinist doctrine.

I want to repeat something that I said earlier, because I know that a lot of people are going to be bothered by my statements that Jesus Christ did not have the miraculous powers of God during His earthly ministry and that He did not have the power to perform miracles. That power came from His Father. These statements in no way take away from the importance of Jesus' life and ministry. Why then am I making a seemingly miniscule point that really doesn't mean anything, because we certainly recognize Jesus as part of what we call the Trinity and, therefore, God now that He is in Heaven? After all, the healings really did take place; they are fully and objectively documented. The people of His time were in awe, wonder and even fear. As a matter of fact, I find it strange that when Jesus performed some wondrous miracles the people of the time either begged Him to leave them or they began to look for ways to kill Him. Almost sounds like the people of today, doesn't it?

The so very important point that I must get across to you, the reader, is that because Jesus was fully human, we can be just like Him. Do you get tired? So did Jesus. Do you get angry? So did Jesus. Have you ever been sarcastic? So was Jesus. Pay attention here. Getting angry and being sarcastic are SINS. If you don't believe me, try it with your pastor. Get angry. Be sarcastic. He will tell you that you are sinning. God doesn't sin. Not now and not ever. God doesn't die, but Jesus did. God, by His own power, performs miracles. Jesus couldn't, except through the power of God.

There are two more reasons in my inventory of arguments. I believe that God sent Jesus to earth only as a man so that He could experience firsthand what it is like to be human. Jesus had to experience firsthand the frailties, the heartaches, the frustrations, the disappointments that we as humans experience every day. The second reason is this, and it is the most wondrous of all. Even though He was only a mortal man, he overcame temptations along with all the other negatives that all of us face every day. *He overcame them, and so can we.* Isn't that wonderful news for us?

Jesus Christ led the way and He overcame. He was totally mortal and He overcame. But if He was totally mortal, how did He, how could He, overcome? He overcame all of the trials that each of us face the same way, AND THE ONLY WAY that is possible for us humans; (listen closely) He depended solely upon God, The Father. Not once did Jesus rely upon His own strength. Read about Jesus' temptations after forty days in the desert. As the devil offers temptations, Jesus does not reject them out of His own strength; He rejects the devil's temptations by quoting the Word of His Father. Do you see now why it is so important to read the Bible from cover to cover? If we do not know the words of our Father, we cannot resist Satan.

I don't know about you, but I spent years fighting sin and temptation, and I always lost every battle, because my weapons were my own strength. It was not until I began reading the Bible and discovering that only God's strength was sufficient to overcome my challenges that I began to be successful. Paul discovered the same secret. You see, Paul and I are using the same technique that Jesus Himself used, leaning upon the wisdom and strength of the Father to win the battle that we face every day. Is it belittling Jesus' ministry to accept the fact that even the Son of God had to rely upon the almighty power of the Father Himself? No way! There is only one God and that is God the Father; at no time did Jesus ever call Himself "God" during His earthly ministry.

Why is it that the church fails to teach us how to win in everyday life? Is it because the church is afraid that if it teaches that Jesus was a mortal man during His time upon earth, we won't be able to accept Him as God as He resides at the side of the Father in Heaven? I don't have the answer, but I do know that because of that lack of teaching in the church, it took me a long time to understand how to live my life. As I would try to apply Jesus' actions to the everyday problems of my own life, I would always have doubts about my own ability to "be like Jesus," because in the back of my mind the fact of Jesus' godliness got in the way.

The question of how I could realistically follow in His footsteps when He had abilities far beyond mine became the "limiting factor" in my life. Of course He could resist the temptations of Satan, because He had the strength of God. Wrong. Of course He could make the wind stop blowing, because He had the powers of God. Wrong. I want to tell you a story, but I hesitate to do so because there are those reading this who will think that I am making it up. As a matter of fact, I would have a difficult time believing what I am about to tell you except for the fact that it happened twice.

I logged off seventy acres of timber on my farm in 1995, and the next year as I was preparing to replant trees, I had to burn several large piles of brush. Now, I am extremely careful about burning in or near my woods, but the conditions were right and I lit the fire on a large pile of brush. Several minutes went by and the fire caught rapidly. As I was watching the fire, the wind suddenly appeared, blowing the tops of some tall trees about a hundred yards away. This sudden wind appeared quite strong, and needless to say I panicked. My first (and human) reaction was to try to put out the fire, but that was impossible; and so lacking any means to put out the fire and avoid a forest conflagration, I prayed. Knowing that within five seconds this sudden wind would be ripping sparks from my fire and throwing them into the woods, I asked the Holy Spirit to stop the wind. To my total amazement, the wind stopped immediately, and not so much as a breeze stirred the flames. I watched in humble awe for the next several hours as the fire burned down with the wind totally absent. What happened here? Did I stop the wind? Absolutely not. I, like Jesus, depended upon the power of God to accomplish that which I needed.

I am ashamed to make the admission that I doubted that God performed this act for me. Oh, I knew in my heart that God can do anything, *but stopping the wind just because I asked Him?* I try to be a pretty humble guy (notice I said "I try"), and I just couldn't picture God performing a miracle for me, just as He did for Jesus Christ when He and the Disciples were in the storm on the Sea of Galilee, that is until it happened a second time. I was burning trash in the evening even though a light breeze was blowing. I had been monitoring the breeze for about a half hour to make sure that burning would be relatively safe, and again I lit the fire and watched over it. Less than a minute after the fire had been lit, a real wind appeared; but this time I knew what to do. I immediately prayed to the Holy Spirit, and again the wind immediately stopped. After this example, I knew that God was showing me that He can still perform miracles, and He will when it suits His purpose, but let's now look at God from the standpoint of when He chooses not to perform a miracle. What do we do then?

As a child, I had rheumatic fever which left me with a slight arrhythmia (irregular heartbeat – the same problem that

George H. W. Bush has). This did not noticeably affect me in my younger days, but as I have gotten older it has become a problem that seriously affects my stamina, and I have to take medicine to keep my heart beating regularly. Not long ago, my heart went into arrhythmia, and my medicine would no longer bring it back into sinus rhythm. I prayed that God would correct this problem, in effect asking for a miracle, but it did not happen. Why? The answer is very simple; God is using this "problem" to accomplish something that He wants to happen. Am I happy about it? The answer has to be *no*, but that is the great thing about being close to God. I can accept those hardships that He has allowed into my life, knowing that in the end, He will take care of me. Perhaps His way is for me to get a pacemaker, and that is OK.

You see, I don't have to worry or even be concerned; God is always with me. The Bible states that God allows everything to happen to us *for our good.* In other words, if you have given your life to God, He will continuously watch over you. How can this be when we lose a loved one? How can this be when we get sick or have an accident? How can this be when God allows my heart to continue to beat irregularly, thereby endangering my very life?

If you learn nothing else from this book, pay attention to this very paragraph, because I am going to teach you how God works. First and foremost memorize this statement. God loves every one of us human creatures, EVERY ONE. Next, recognize that because He loves us, He wants to get our attention so that: 1. we will pay attention to Him, or 2. we will learn something that He needs us to learn. I had to learn this most important of all lessons in my own life but it wasn't easy. God had to end a professional career and obliterate my finances, all because He wanted my full attention. Before you say just how terrible that is, consider this. If I had listened to God when He first called me instead of being so stubborn, none of that would have had to happen. Do you feel a faint call from God? I suggest that you had better start listening, because God will do whatever it takes to get what He wants. If He wants you, believe me He is going to get you. Of course, you can refuse, and that is what most Christians do, and then they wonder why their life is such a Hell. God does give us the total freedom to choose, and that one thing is what makes Him such an awesome God.

I almost forgot. There is just one *more* thing that makes Him an awesome God. When we do choose to serve Him, He blesses our lives in the most wonderful ways. If you choose to serve God, you will know a peace that you (read me) have only dreamed of. You will have a happiness that will be so great that you cannot even imagine it. Every time that I think of the happiness that I have now, I think of Ted Turner or Madonna or Donald Trump. Each one of these people is a mega-millionaire or even billionaire, yet not one of them is happy. If you don't believe that, ask them how many divorces they have had. How can I be so happy and at peace with myself for the first time in my life? It is simply because I finally have a job serving someone who needs me.

You see, in this world, I never worked for someone who really needed me. God evidently needs me because He continually blesses me beyond all measure. Oh, I can hear someone out there saying, "Look at that poor fool; he doesn't have a penny to his name and he is trying to tell me that he is happy." Well, I sure hate to disappoint that person, but I am a multi-millionaire. In ten years of serving God, He has taken me from being dead broke, without a job (or even the hope of one), $60,000 in debt, sick, depressed to the point of suicide, to total happiness, overwhelming peace, a real job (serving Him) and a net worth of over $3 million. No, serving God is not about money as Jim Bakker would have you believe; serving God is about having *meaning* in your life, and let's talk more about that.

If you remember, the title of this chapter is *Are You Willing To Be Like Jesus?*, and that title is appropriate because Jesus came to earth to serve God. He didn't come to earth to serve Himself. He didn't come to earth to be glorified, although that is what some misguided churches are doing. Listen to me closely. Jesus Christ did not come to earth to usurp the throne of God the Father. There is still only one GOD which we should be worshiping and that is none other than God the Father (and HIM only). Jesus didn't come to earth to make a name for Himself; He came to earth for one reason only, and that reason was to serve God the Father. So how did He do it? How exactly did Jesus serve God? It's an excellent question because how can anyone serve God? After all, what does God need? Isn't that what serving is all about; providing a service that is needed or supplying a particular item that the recipient needs or requires? What in the world does God need (answer nothing) or what would He like to have (here is the key)? If Jesus can be described as the perfect servant as the Bible states, then let us investigate just how He warranted that title.

The most appropriate place to start our investigation is the Gospel of John. Early in the Gospel of John something takes place at a wedding feast in Cana that is thought to be the first "miracle" that Jesus performed. The host of the wedding feast did not purchase enough wine for the guests and ran out of wine. Think about it. For the host this is a calamity of the highest order. His and his families' name is about to be ruined. This social faux pas will be gossiped about forever (when you think about it times really haven't changed) unless more wine can be found but the 7-11 is closed. Jesus, at His mother's urging, steps up to the plate and, in short, creates wine from water. Why did Jesus waste His valuable time creating wine and forever frustrate Southern Baptists? We stated that Jesus served God. Did God need more wine? Somehow I don't think so. But then who was Jesus serving? Himself? God? The host? The answer to this question will forever answer the question of how we (you and I) can ourselves serve a God who has everything.

Listen closely because the answer to this question is so simple that it can be confusing. As a matter of fact, this answer has eluded the entire Christian Church for two thousand years, because as a Christian for fifty-one years and a dedicated

Christian for the last twelve years, I have NEVER heard this taught in any church that I have attended. Here it is. In creating wine so that the wedding feast would not be a failure, Jesus was serving the host of the wedding feast. Now hold onto your chair, because in serving the host of the wedding feast, Jesus was actually serving God. Whew.

    An appropriate question that could be asked at this juncture is this, "How can serving people be construed as serving God?" We have already established the fact that God doesn't *need* anything. God has it all. As a matter of fact, God *OWNS* it all. Since He created this entire universe and our world within it, He can legitimately lay claim to owning it all. Therefore, how can we as mere mortal humans, ourselves creations of The Almighty God, kid ourselves into thinking that we can somehow *SERVE* God. There is nothing that we can give Him that He hasn't already created. There is nothing that we can make with our hands that He cannot make better. No choir exists that can serenade Him better than the choir of Heavenly angels. Who are we trying to kid when we say that our tithe is serving God, or our election as Deacon is serving God, or singing in the choir is serving God? There is only one way that we can serve God, and Jesus showed us how to do it every hour of every day of His ministry while He was with us.

    Jesus Christ repeatedly said that He was serving God and He demonstrated to us that service every day as He served His fellow human beings. I'm not just talking about the miracles that He performed, although they were the highest forms of service. Jesus spent every day of His ministry walking, talking, teaching, working and *serving* people. What kind of people? Sinners. Here is just one more example of where the so-called Christian Church has failed. The modern Christian church teaches its members to *AVOID* sinners. It's almost as if they are telling us to keep away from sinners at all cost. My question is why? Is sinning (or sinners themselves) some kind of disease that might be caught if we get too close? Is sin contagious? If it is, then Jesus must have taken anti(sin)otics because the only people that Jesus avoided like the plague (an appropriate term, don't you think) were the leaders of the church. Do you know what I think? If Jesus Christ returned today, the people that He would avoid most today would be the leaders of our modern church, because they have become just exactly like the Scribes, Sadducees and Pharisees of the Temple. Think about it, we Christians are doing and teaching exactly the same lessons taught by the Jews of Jesus' day. *Stay away from them! We are better than them! Witness with your mouth but cheat them every chance that you get! Separate yourself from everyone who doesn't think exactly like us! Make and pass laws so that no one can sin!* And on and on.

Why in the world would the Christian church want its members to stay away from sinners? Yet that is what we are taught. I find it strange that we are told to "be like Jesus" but yet we are not to do as Jesus did (help the lost). Why do church members drive 500 miles to build houses for the poor and ignore the poor of their own city? As I stated in the opening chapter, I think the reason is that Christians are afraid to initiate an ongoing relationship; and what a shame it is that we Christians are so afraid to give of ourselves and of our precious time to help someone in need.

The question is this, "How can I serve God?" The answer is that we can serve God in only ONE WAY, and that is by serving the one thing that He loves most, HIS PEOPLE. The question is, "How can I be like Jesus?" The answer is, by doing exactly what Jesus did, loving and serving the most precious possession of God Himself, His people. What people? The people who are unloved. The people who are in trouble. The people who are looking for some way to get through each day. The prostitute who takes cocaine to help her forget. The homosexual who just wants to be loved but who doesn't even know what love is. The vagrant who has lost it all and wants a chance to start over. The mentally ill person who needs loving guidance and a lot of patience. The rich man who cheats everyone in order to accumulate more money because money is his God. Perhaps the person who needs help most of all is the people who think that they are Christians, but who have not read even the New Testament from cover to cover. You see, they are committing the sin of arrogance, because they believe with all their hearts that they know everything about being a Christian, when in fact they and others like them are the primary reason for the failure of the church. God has given us an instruction book, but very few Christians have read it. Do they think that this pleases God?

We have spent a lot of time together discussing who and what Jesus was, who He served and how. You may not agree with everything that I have said, and that is all right, because we can agree to disagree, but we both want to serve God, so let's now proceed to the next step where we learn to be "like Jesus."

What should be our first step in our attempt to be just like Jesus? I think that we should take the same actions that He did as a child (i.e. study God's word). Now, don't let that verb "study" throw you because what I am suggesting is that you just sit down and read the New Testament beginning with Matthew. If you don't like to read, go to the nearest bookstore and purchase a set of tapes or a CD. Think of all the time that you waste while driving to work in the morning and returning in the evening. What are you doing during that time behind the wheel? Listening to the radio or talking on the cell phone probably, but why not put that time to good use.

As you open your book or load your new CD, take just a second and ask the Holy Spirit to open your heart to an understanding of God's word. This is really important, so listen closely; there is a message *just for you* in the scripture almost every day, and all you have to do is make the effort and ask the Holy Spirit to show you. I guarantee you that He will. What does studying the Scriptures have to do with being like Jesus? As a child, Jesus studied the Scriptures so intently that at age twelve, He confounded the learned teachers of the temple with His wisdom, knowledge and, above all, His understanding.

Again let me refer to the time of His temptation by Satan, when He was able to reject all of Satan's offers, NOT BY HIS OWN STRENGTH, but by His knowledge of the Scriptures. Are there temptations in your life? Of course there are. There are temptations in everyone's life, but how many of us are able to resist them? You will be able if you will just read the New Testament. What could be easier? Do you have problems in your life? The answers are waiting for you if you will just make the effort to find them.

If you are a Christian, and you recognize that Jesus Christ is the one and only Son of God the Father and you accept the fact that He died for your sins, wouldn't it be the absolute highest calling to attempt to be like Him? Here again the Church has failed by stopping short of allowing members to reach their full potential and be *just like Jesus.* Yes, the church has made a step in the right direction through the initiation of the WWJD (What Would Jesus Do) program, but again they have stopped short of the goal. It is almost as though the church leaders feel that it would be blasphemous to lead us to believe that we, the common man, could be like the Son of God. Doesn't the Bible state that we were created in His image? It certainly does. Didn't Jesus live, suffer and die just like an ordinary man? Yes, He did. Is it blasphemy to want to emulate the Son of God? I think not. Rather, I think that doing all in our power to emulate the very Son of the God that we love and worship is the highest calling to which any human being can aspire. It's just too bad that the church refuses to believe that it can be done.

Where do we start? We start by recognizing that we are children, and we begin doing what children all over the world do every day. We go to school. No, we don't have to climb on a bus and take a class. Our schoolroom can be right in our hand, in a book called the Bible. As I said earlier, the Bible is the most complex book ever written; however, God has given us a teacher in the form of His own Holy Spirit, and the Holy Spirit *and only the Holy Spirit,* can teach us exactly what God wants us to know.

Since we (supposedly) are Christians, the most appropriate place to start reading the Bible would naturally be at the beginning of the New Testament. Those first four books, MATTHEW, MARK, LUKE and JOHN, called the Gospels, are the story of our Savior's life and work. What better way to learn to be like Jesus than to read about His life. You know, I challenge you, whether you are a Christian or not, to read the four gospels, because when you do, you will have learned how to be an ideal human being and a true servant of the entire human race. Want to know something? I have seen a lot of people who refuse to believe in Jesus Christ who more closely resemble Jesus than ninety-nine percent of the Christians that I have come across. I would be willing to bet that if those same people were to take the time to read the Gospels, they would immediately understand what Jesus was about a whole lot better than most Christians seem to.

Why is it that so many people who refuse to believe in God, love and try to help their fellow man and so many "Christians," whom I suppose DO believe in God, are arrogant, selfish and self-indulgent, caring less about their fellow man? If anyone figures that one out, will you call me? By the way, I have a question for all the politically involved "Christians" out there. Who was the most famous and the greatest bleeding-heart liberal of all-time? Come on, all you "Christian" conservatives, give me an answer. Well, in case you don't know, His name was Jesus Christ, and if you don't believe that then read His story. Actually, that may be the reason why so-called "conservative Christians" refuse to read the Bible; they might find out that Jesus was a liberal.

I have to tell a funny but slightly embarrassing story about myself when I first started reading the New Testament. I had finished Matthew, and as I started reading Mark, I got this feeling of, like Yogi Berra said, "Déjà vu all over again." Of course, I didn't realize that the four Gospels are all the same story, just told by different people. Anyway, I continued on and as I got halfway through Luke, the third Gospel, I knew that I had been down this road before. It was not until I had read through the Gospels for the second time; that I began to see the awesome beauty of the story of one man's life as seen through four different pairs of eyes. I am aware of the fact that some people have a real problem with the differences found in the four Gospels, attributing the differences to either fabrications or nonexistent happenings, but I want you to perform a small experiment that will immediately explain the differences as documented by the authors of the Gospels.

If you teach Sunday school, this is an excellent teaching tool, no matter what the age of your class. Pick four class members at random and take them outside to the front of the church. When you get to a specific location, tell them that you want them to watch what is happening for exactly one minute. Take no questions and allow no talking among them. When the minute has expired, hand each person a writing tablet and a pen and tell them to describe in detail what they just saw without comparing notes. Do you think that everybody will have seen the same thing? Will they describe it the same way? Will they even be close to each other's description? The answer to all three questions is, "probably not." My point is that if four people did not agree on what they saw for one minute, how could their descriptions agree over what they witnessed for a period of three years?

All right, the subject is preparing ourselves to become like Jesus and the first step is to read the New Testament of the Bible; utilizing the Holy Spirit as our guide. Difficult? No, but like anything else that is worth doing, it takes commitment and some precious time that could be used elsewhere, like watching TV or reading a magazine or straightening up the living room for the fourth time. Let me address my fellow guys for just a minute. We guys need to work at keeping our priorities in order, and I just wanted to make sure that we are all aware that football and NASCAR absolutely do take precedence over God. After all, isn't that why God created football? Also, never, ever allow your children to see you reading the Bible. They might think that you were a wimp, and what kind of an example would that set?

In what I call the preparation sequence, there exists a step that very few Christians even think about, much less act upon, and that is the primary reason why ninety-nine percent of Christians fail in their personal walk with God and continue to suffer failure in most other aspects of their lives. The common paradigm of the church today, and especially the Baptist Church, encourages people to make a decision to "believe" in Jesus Christ and to accept Him as their Savior, but that "decision" becomes the end in an of itself. Nothing could be further from the truth, because believing in and accepting Jesus must be followed by an even more deliberate and even more difficult decision. For most people, the decision to bring Christ into their life is made with their "hearts," but the next and more difficult decision must be made with their "heads." Gee, maybe that is why so few people are able to make it. By that I mean that the next decision must be made on a cognitive, conscious and intellectual level. Let me walk you through the reasoning process involved in making this decision, but first we must identify exactly what this decision is and what it involves.

This step involves making the decision once and for all that God really does exist. I am quite aware that the above sounds terribly silly, but I can assure you that it isn't, because most Christians and most Christian Churches have not reached the point of recognizing that this decision must be made. The point that I am trying to make is this. Deciding that God really does exist is the ultimate "existential leap" and like every "leap" that a person takes, it is difficult, it is breathtaking, it is scary, but it is above all, the most rewarding decision that you will ever make, and it will change your life forever.

That decision certainly changed my life, and I would never go back. Allow me to explain. If you approach any Christian and ask them whether they think that God really does exist, they will look at you as though you have just lost your mind, and they will probably reply something like this: "Of course I believe that God exists. I also believe in Jesus Christ and the Holy Spirit. That is why I call myself a Christian." The problem here is that every Christian will *say* that they believe in God, but that exact point is where belief ends and concern with the world resumes. Let me give you a true example of a Christian who might not be typical, but his thinking is typical, and his lack of belief in the everyday existence of our God is oh-so-typical and oh-so-sad. This man (I will call him Bob) swears up and down that he believes in and serves God every day of his life, yet he carries a concealed weapon everywhere he goes. The question that I have is this: "O.K., you say that you believe in God, yet exactly *what* do you believe about this God of yours? Obviously you don't believe that your God can protect you or you wouldn't be carrying a gun. Or perhaps you don't believe that your God wants to protect you, and what kind of a sorry God is that who will not or, even worse, cannot, protect His people?

Let me tell you a true story about Bob. Last fall, Bob was walking to his automobile, through the parking lot of a major discount chain, when he was assaulted, beaten and robbed in the blink of an eye, and get this, it all happened before he could even think about drawing his pistol. There are several lessons to be learned from this example, but the most important by far is this: Bob, while he professed to believe in God, was not depending upon God for protection in his daily life. Bob was depending upon his pistol, and I believe, without a doubt, that God allowed that little incident to happen to prove to Bob that nothing *in this world* can protect him from the forces of evil. My question to you is this: What are you depending upon? Are you depending upon yourself in conjunction with the things of this world for your protection, or perhaps your success, or are you depending upon the *ALMIGHTY* forces of our God, who can protect you in all circumstances and from all forces of evil. To continue with the story of my friend Bob, as is typical with most Christians who *refuse* to read the Bible, Bob learned nothing from the experience that God allowed to happen. He just went out and bought a new holster that would allow him to draw his gun faster. So what did Bob just prove? He just proved beyond all doubt that he doesn't believe in God. Does this sound familiar?

Let me give you another example of where we need God's protection. Do you drive a car? Of course you do, so let's do some simple mathematics involving combined velocities. Let's suppose that you are driving on a two lane rural road at the speed limit of fifty-five miles per hour, and suppose that another car is coming toward you, again, at the posted speed limit of fifty-five miles per hour. The approach speed of the two vehicles is 110 miles per hour. Let's suppose that one of them has a blowout at the wrong time. Do you think that given your own reflexes, driving skills and vehicular limitations that you could avoid a collision? I somehow don't think so, and I used this as an example because of the recent spate of accidents involving a well-known tire manufacturer. Again, my point here is to make you understand that you can never hope to protect yourself from the daily evils that are in this world, but *if you depend upon God for protection, you can and will be safe.* I am an example of His protection. As an engineering consultant, I have driven all over the country for the last ten years without receiving a scratch. Did I ever have an accident? Yes, two small one's where no one was hurt, and the reason for those was that I wasn't paying attention, but for now, let me get back to our subject. Have YOU taken the leap of truly believing in God?

Why is it so difficult for people to believe that God really does exist and that He is truly in control of this world? That is an easy question, and there are three primary reasons. First, we, as humans have nothing to relate to, that even comes close to God, what He is and the totally awesome presence and power that He possesses. Second, we look around at the world every day, and we see terrible things happening. We see earthquakes that kill schoolchildren, we see floods that kill thousands and, yes, we see the twin towers collapse, killing and injuring good people. The third reason is the saddest of all. The church has failed, and its leaders do not have a clue as to what is happening, because they haven't read the Bible or, at the very least, they don't understand it. When the church leaders do not understand God, how can they expect their flock to understand God?

Let me now prove to you beyond all doubt that some of the people reading this book have not *truly* decided that God really does exist. That God *really* is in control of this world. That God really will control your life *if you will just ask and allow Him to do it.*

If you really believe that you have decided that God does, without a doubt, exist, then why?

1. Why haven't you done the first thing that He wants you to do – read the Bible from cover to cover (more than once)?
2. Why haven't you changed your lifestyle by eliminating the aspects of your life that God doesn't want in your life (through His power)?
3. Why haven't you quit worrying about the world, i.e. finances, promotions, politics, wars, taxes, Saddam Hussein, etc. By the way, whenever I think about Saddam Hussein, I get great joy in knowing that God has a terrible punishment in store for him, and both you and I will see that punishment meted out.
4. Why haven't you quit worrying about everyone else's lifestyle and begun focusing on your own imperfections? This particular question is perhaps the greatest failure of Christianity over the last two thousand years.
5. Why are you still concerned about politics?

The point that I am trying to make is this: if you truly believe in God, your focus will be entirely upon God, not upon this world. Why? God created the world, didn't He? If we can believe that He has the capability to create the world, why can't we believe that He *still* has the capability to run it on a daily basis? Why do we believe that we have to help this awesome

God of ours run the world? Even the Pope has proven that he does not believe in God. I don't say that as an insult to either the Pope or the Catholic Church, because the Pope is just like every Baptist preacher that I know. They don't believe in God either. The reason that I state that the Pope doesn't believe in God (or the Sovereignty of God) is that recently he was reported to be railing against the entry of Poland into the European Union. As the head of the Catholic Church, why should he care? As the head of the Catholic Church, he should only be concerned with the work of God, not the work of politicians. Believe me, God is appointing and controlling the politicians – WE DON'T HAVE TO.

God specifically tells us in the Bible that we are not to be concerned with the problems of this world, and we are not to be *of* this world. Read that again – closely. You see, we have a choice: God or the world. What is your choice? To be honest, my choice for fifty-one years was the world, even though I thought of myself as a Christian, and I have to tell you, I paid dearly for making that choice. The good news is this, since I made the correct choice, that of forgetting the world and making God the center and focus of my life, I have been rewarded beyond measure. WOW.

Let me take this thought into the context of our job (because almost everybody has one or wants one). How can I state so emphatically that we should not be concerned about getting a promotion or a raise, and does that translate to the next logical step whereby we are not to be concerned about work itself? Absolutely not. If you, as a Christian, have a job or run a business, your only goal should be to perform that job or run that business to the best of your ability in a totally honest manner. Listen closely. You are not to be concerned or worried about your reward, whether it is monetary or promotional or whether you will even keep that job. If you are a person believing in, and devoted to, our Almighty God, then you can bet that your reward should and, I promise you, will come from that same God. By the way, I will warn you now, expect to be tested on this by God Himself.

Let me tell you two stories that will illustrate my point. The first story concerns a lady whom I will call Molly. Molly was a Human Resources Manager for a medium size company with several locations, and she had been with this same company for several years and took pride in her work. As the company grew, new HR managers were hired for each of the different plants which Molly had previously covered, and a new general manager was hired. To make a long story short, business became scarce in the early 90s and a reduction in force took place which also entrapped Molly. Molly was heartbroken, and as she drove home after picking up her last check, she was crying and asking God why this tragedy had to happen to her after she had worked so very hard. She was driving on Interstate 85 toward Greenville, S.C., crying her heart out, when suddenly an audible voice, as though someone was in the car with her said, *"Because your job for me there was finished."* Molly felt an immediate peace envelope her. As she described it to me later, she said that it felt as though someone had thrown a warm blanket around her and her worries and tears were wiped away. To prove that God can work for us, Molly had a new and better job within three weeks, at a higher salary AND (this is important, so listen closely) when her latest company was sold and she lost that job she didn't worry or fret one bit. As she told me, "God got me that job, and I know that He will get me another." HE DID.

All right, let me stop for just a second and summarize where we are in our process of becoming like Jesus. We have identified three steps, and let me reiterate them. The first step was to read the New Testament of the Bible. Notice that I didn't say to *begin* reading the New Testament, I said to *read it,* because only after you have finished, can you have the knowledge to cognitively take the second step. Do you remember the second step? Now that you have read the New Testament, are you ready to make that existential leap? Are you ready to believe, with all your heart, with all your being, with all your cognitive knowledge that God not only exists, but that He really does run this world with all of its attendant problems? That He really is in control despite the fact that wars, famines, disease, accidents, floods and terrorists also exist?

Can you accept the fact that our God really is in control? Can you accept the fact that our God (if He really does exist and is in control) doesn't need our help to run the world, because at this point, right here, is where the Church stops believing in God. The Church would have us believe that our God needs our help. The Church, where we sing about "an awesome God," where we learn in Sunday school about an "Omnipotent" God, also teaches us that we must vote to abolish abortion, vote to end gambling in the form of education lotteries, and vote to reduce taxes. Does anyone see the conflict of ideas, or are we all too involved in our own selfish agendas. Most self-proclaimed "Christians'" agenda's are really and truly concerned with this world and whatever world problem is pushing their button at the moment, when, in fact, their attention needs to be focused on what God wants.

This one single step in the Christian faith is so important that it could warrant a book entirely by itself, and it is the step by which every faith that has propounded to follow God the Father and Creator has failed. Take the time to read just the Book of Exodus in the Old Testament, and you will see that in spite of the fact that God led the Jews *daily* through the desert, they still weren't willing to believe. After you finish Exodus, read 1st Samuel and you will see again where the Jews rejected God as their King and demanded a human king like all the other nations. Take a moment and ask yourself the question: "Isn't this exactly what we Christians are doing today when we trust in our politicians instead of our God?" When will we learn that God is indeed in control? Is the Christian Church doomed to the same failure as the Jews of the Old Testament? I warn you now, as the voice of one crying in the wilderness, God will, in time, remove us from His favor, just as He did the Israelites who worshipped other Gods. The Gods that we worship are the politicians, and that is very insulting to God.

Well, then, what is your decision? If you can accept that God is in control, then you are ready for the third step, and I'm sorry to say that it will be the most difficult so far. This step will require changing the entire paradigm of your life. It will require time, concentration, prayer, renewal and, above all, help from the Holy Spirit. On the positive side, taking this step will give you the reward of a sense of peace that you will never before have known. You see, as you step ever deeper into God's program, the work becomes more difficult, but the rewards, yes, the rewards, become ever more magnificent.

The third step sounds very simple but in reality, for most people, it is very difficult, and so I have concocted a little ditty to help you remember. The ditty goes like this: "Remove your focus, and redefine your locus." What does it mean, you say? Well, it means to "Remove your focus (from the world) and redefine your locus (upon God)." If you are not familiar with the word locus, it concerns the center of great activity or intense concentration. Come to think of it, if we are calling ourselves Christian, shouldn't the center of our activity and concentration be upon God? Christ said that we are in the world but we are not to be *of* the world. He also said that we are not to be concerned with the things of this world, yet the things of this world have become the primary focus of most Christians today, from the Pope to the preacher of the smallest Baptist country church, to the newest member of any congregation. What is so insidious about this misplaced focus is that it is done in complete innocence and in an attempt to "help" God change the world for the better. Since when does God need our help? Since when has God (The Creator) relinquished control to us humans (His Creation). IS THERE NO ONE IN THIS WORLD WHO CAN SEE THAT WE HAVE BEGUN TO FIGHT GOD?

I regret that the answer to that question is *no*. There doesn't seem to be anyone that recognizes the fact that we are not living up to what Christ asked us to do. To put it simply, the Church has put the cart before the horse. This really is not an oversimplification, so please bear with me. Allow me to make an analogy here; I talked about putting the cart before the horse, and in my analogy, the cart will be the world, while the horse will represent God's people. As I have said before, the Church is concerned with making the world a better place, and this is no less than a noble endeavor, but totally futile. First of all, I will grant you that the world needs a lot of improvement; one can surmise that fact just by watching the nightly news. Murder, rape, kidnappings, child molestation, terrorism, wars, disease, robbery, the list goes on and on. The question begs to be asked, "What can anyone do about it?" A better question to ask would be this: "What can *I* do about it?" Again, I have to admit that when they reach this point of asking, "What can *I* do about the problems of the world?" most Christians have copped out and either given up or begun looking for the easy way out. For most Christians, the easy way out is to become affiliated with a political party or join a street protest against some particularly heinous practice such as abortion. The reasoning here seems to be that if enough of "us" get together, then "we" can make a difference. What is not elucidated is that by joining a group, "we" are hoping that someone else will do all the work, and that is one of the primary reasons for failure.

The second reason for failure, and without a doubt the most important reason of all is the simple fact of human nature called "resistance." Here is what I mean by resistance, and allow me to use smoking as my example, because I am an ex-smoker. Back when I smoked, I became very irritated when someone told me that I should quit smoking or when someone forced me to go somewhere else to light my cigar. Oh yes, I knew without a doubt that smoking was bad for me, but boy-oh-boy, no one was going to tell me how to run my life. Not then – not now – NOT NO HOW!

Do you see the pattern? When anyone tries to force their will upon someone else, "resistance" is the immediate result.

Resistance changes to resentment and resentment builds to the point where a stone wall is erected and nothing positive can be accomplished. It is just human nature, and it is for that very reason that God gives us the total freedom to choose. Listen closely. Here is one of the primary reasons why I am being led to write this book. If God, in His infinite wisdom, gives every person on this earth the total freedom to choose their own way of life, why don't we allow the same thing? When are Christians going to start realizing that it is not God's will that they be in control? Only God can be and is in control. It is our job to show people the benefits and the happiness that result from following God's will and allowing Him (and only Him to be in control). In other words, our only job is to bring people to God through our demonstration of what has happened in our own lives by letting God be in control.

Since I talked about smoking earlier, I would like to tell you the story of the most wonderful and awe inspiring thing that has ever taken place in my life. This story took place in 1970, long before I cared about God or even wanted Him in my life. I had graduated from college only two years before, and I had been married and starting a family for only four years, so I was in effect just starting out with my life. Even though this story took place over thirty years ago, I can recall it as though it happened yesterday. That is how real and how powerful this story has been in my life.

I was having a dream, and that dream was so real that it was truly frightening. I was sitting in a doctor's office reading a magazine, when a door on the opposite wall opened and the doctor walked across the room and up to my chair, followed by a nurse. I looked up from my magazine, and the doctor said just one sentence to me, but that sentence changed my life forever. He said, "Mr. Smith, I'm sorry but I'm afraid that it is terminal." That is all that he said but that is all that needed to be said. I knew immediately what he was talking about because I had been trying to quit smoking for the past year, totally without success, and I knew that the doctor was telling me that I had terminal lung cancer. It seemed that every time that I tried to quit smoking, I ended up smoking more. I was up to three packs a day, I hated even the taste of cigarettes, but I was hopelessly hooked, and there was nothing more that I could do (on my own).

Remember now, God had not been invited into my life, and frankly I didn't even care whether He existed or not. At no time did I ask God to help me quit smoking, but He in His infinite love and kindness came to my aid. Back to my dream. The doctor has just told me that I have terminal lung cancer, and in response I begin a litany of reasons why I could not (or should not) die. I can remember telling the doctor that I had just graduated from college, I didn't have any life insurance, I had a young baby girl, my house wasn't paid for and on and on. The next thing I remember, my wife has me by the arm and is shaking me for all she is worth. I am sitting up in bed and the bed is absolutely soaked from my sweat (you would be sweating too).

My wife said to me, "What is the matter, you were screaming?" In my exhausted state I could only mumble, "Somebody is trying to tell me something!" Even as I said that, I knew without a doubt that God had just given me a message – even though I had totally ignored God. I fell back onto my pillow and went immediately to sleep. The next morning, I awoke totally rested, jumped out of bed, took a brand new carton of cigarettes and threw them into the wastebasket. I next found the pack that I had opened the evening before and threw them away also; and I am proud to say that I haven't smoked since. The most wonderful part of the story is that there was absolutely no withdrawal.

Throughout the intervening years, I have wondered repeatedly why God would choose to warn me about smoking and leave others to die. Or did He warn them also? I don't know, but I have felt that there was something that He wanted me to accomplish. What is it? I don't know that either. I just try to go where He seems to lead.

To return to the subject of this chapter, I was talking about the fact that we Christians try to force other people to live by our rules, and those actions always lead to resistance and resentment. We try to "change the world" by enacting new laws and *forcing* everyone to fit our mold. Do those methods work? Well, remember back to my first chapter in which I proved that the Church has failed. Why haven't we learned our lesson? I will tell you why. Every Christian wants to change the world, but no one single Christian is willing to take the responsibility for changing just one person. We are all working under the "let someone else (or the government) do it syndrome." Meanwhile, the church has adopted the "Change the laws and the world will change, paradigm."

All right, let me say it once more and then I am going to move on to the next subject. There is no law that we can pass and there is no law that we can change that will bring people to Christ. Isn't that the objective? In talking to most Christians, it seems that we have forgotten that fact. There is nothing that we can do in this world to make things better. So why not forget about the world? Why not disregard the problems of the world, because I promise you, God has it under control, and why not start doing what God wants us to do. Taking care of His people one on one. Do you know of someone who is unhappy, in poverty, sick, in despair? I promise that you do, whether you realize it or not. I have told you the most powerful story of my life. Now let me tell you the saddest.

Twelve years ago when I was going through my divorce, God had allowed me to be put in the valley to the point that I just thought I couldn't take any more and I was considering suicide. I went to church that Sunday morning and I had decided to take my life sometime the next week. As I left my Sunday school class, I told my teacher goodbye, and I came right out and told him that I was at the end of my rope. He suggested that we pray together, which we did, and then he said goodbye and walked off.

As I drove home, I wondered whether he would call later and check on me or whether he would even remember. As it turned out, he either didn't care or he just forgot, because he never called. Yes, God did come to my aid, and I didn't take my life, but I have never forgotten that there was not even one so-called Christian Sunday school teacher who cared enough to make a phone call. What would you do? Look around you. The action isn't in the political arena; it is right next door. It is staring you in the face, but you aren't looking. What is your decision? Are you going to get out the vote in the next election, or are you going to get out of your self-imposed shell and help the person(s) to whom God is leading you? Are you willing to make a lasting commitment for Jesus, or are you a typical self-serving Christian who wants to get home to dinner.

Let me make one last comment regarding the story about the Sunday school teacher. The entire thrust of this book is to identify the failure(s) of the Christian church. The fact that this person, who had been placed in a position of serious responsibility and trust either did not care about someone who was contemplating suicide or had not been sufficiently trained in what to do should someone consider suicide again points to the fact that our churches are failing and have failed the people who depend upon them for help and leadership.

Ask yourself, does your church require that anyone desiring or serving in a position of authority have read at least the New Testament and has had sufficient training to identify people who may need help? If it doesn't, then even your church is ignoring the Bible, which says *"...but everyone, after he has been fully trained, will be like his teacher."* Isn't that each Christian's objective, to be like Jesus Christ? Well, we can't do it until we submit to the training of the Holy Spirit, and the only way that we can submit to the training of the Holy Spirit is to read (and reread) the Bible.

We have covered the first three steps in redefining ourselves to emulate Jesus Christ. Now how many of you can remember them?

> Step one: Read ALL of the New Testament.
> Step two: BELIEVE that God exists and is in control.
> Step three: Remove your focus and redefine your locus.

Now we proceed with step four. Do you remember that I told you that the steps will become more difficult as we proceed toward the goal of being like Jesus? Well, I have both good news and bad news for you; the next step is going to be the most difficult of all for a lot of people. The good news is that if you have made it this far, God is definitely helping you (because what I am trying to convince you to do is just not natural human nature), and the next steps will be as natural as walking. Of course, you had better remember that we had to *learn* to walk, just as we are going to have to *learn* to be like Jesus.

In the New Testament, there were only two everyday people just like you and me that just totally astounded Jesus when He met them. I mean Jesus was totally astounded by these two people and that can be easily discerned in the tone of His remarks when He talked about them. One of these people was the Roman officer who wanted Jesus to heal his servant, and Jesus was "blown away" by this man's faith. The second person, and the one that I want to spend some time with, is Nathanael. Now Nathanael was the disciple found by Philip, and Philip invited him to "Come and see (Jesus)." "Jesus saw Nathanael coming to Him, and said of him, "Behold an Israelite indeed, in whom is no guile...."

Notice not only what Jesus said, notice how it was said: "...an Israelite *indeed*...." It was as though Jesus could not believe His senses, and I believe that He (Jesus) was awed. If we were to place that statement within the context of today, Jesus would have said, "Look at this, a Christian without an agenda to control the world, unbelievable!"

Let me ask you a question. Why was Jesus so excited to meet a person without guile? Know what? I think Jesus would be even more excited to meet someone without guile today because there just aren't very many of them around, and to find someone without "guile" is like finding a diamond – a rare gem indeed. So what does the word "guile" mean? My dictionary defines "guile" as "treacherous, cunning, skillful deceit," but, of course, I don't know anyone like that, and I'm sure that you don't either. I just can't believe that every Israelite of those times could be described as treacherous or cunning or deceitful; remember these folks were God's chosen people.

The word "guile" also has some much more subtle meanings and I think that if we explore those subtleties, we will find out why Jesus was so excited. "Guile" could be described as something as simple as "self-serving," or how about "manipulative." Are we getting closer to home (?), because I know a lot of people like that. For the purpose of this text, I would like to submit that a person with "guile" is one who has a self-serving agenda and who is willing to use various "tricks" to get their way. Conversely, people "without guile" would be those who **are not** trying to enrich *themselves* in every way that they can find. Did you catch the "themselves"? In my opinion, a person's life should enrich everyone. I'm not talking just about money when I use the word "enrich." I'm talking about love and giving and helping and maybe just being a friend. Therefore, a person "without guile" would in our everyday society be described as "innocent" or even "naïve." How many of us are willing to be described as either one of those definitions? Not many of us, I think, and therein lies the reason for the pleasant surprise that Jesus found in meeting Nathanael. Here was a man who did not have an agenda of self-fulfillment. Here was a man who did not "use" people to gain something for himself. Here was a man who was probably as honest, as open, as innocent, as any person that Jesus met, and Jesus was pleased and surprised.

Let me tell you a story that happened to me the other day when I was at the Post Office just before Christmas with my neighbor whom I will call Jack. Jack and I were on our way to have lunch and he had to stop at the Post Office to mail a letter "priority" mail. The priority pack cost $3.85 and Jack handed the lady a twenty dollar bill. Now, I don't know why I was watching every move so closely, but I watched the lady hand Jack his change and she gave him a ten, a five, and five one's, and eighty five cents. I'm not usually a very sharp guy, but I think that God wanted to show me something and He had me totally focused on what was happening. Jack looked at his change, and without a moment's hesitation said in his slow Carolina drawl, "I think that you gave me too much change."

This took place during the Christmas rush. The clerk looked up and blushed. And I could tell that she was having a rough day and was so grateful. I could tell that Jack had made her day. Think about what had just happened for a second. Jack had just mailed a priority letter and made money on the deal. Would his choice be to enrich himself or to make the world just a little better place in which to live? Would he make his day, or would he make someone else's day? Perhaps this story is the best example of our definition of the word "guile." The Bible, in using the word "guile," was not talking about treachery or deceit. I think the word means nothing more than being open, above board and honest, and Jesus was surprised.

Wouldn't it be great if each one of us were to "surprise" Jesus Christ? To be honest, I don't think that He gets many pleasant surprises these days, especially from the Christian community. After all, we are too busy trying to change the world. Listen closely. Here is the total reason for this book. WE *CAN* CHANGE THE WORLD! We *can* change the world, but we have to do it a little at a time, and we can't do it through someone else. We have to do it ourselves, and we have to work at it every day.

Step four – living without guile. As you work at your job, are you concerned with yourself, or are you willing to make someone else's life a little better? Are you worried about that promotion, or are you mentoring someone else? In short, are you working for yourself or are you working for the company and your fellow workers? Remember me? I spent fifty-one years of my life working for my own interests and I failed miserably. I have spent the last ten years of my life learning how to work for God, and I am a success beyond my wildest dreams. Do I ignore the world? Of course not. The world is where God wants me to work for HIM. Here is the secret that the church doesn't tell us. When we are genuinely working for God, He will make sure that we get paid.

Here is the next secret that the church doesn't tell us. Question – How do we work for God? Answer – By working for His people. Notice carefully that I didn't say that we work for God by working for the church. Every modern Christian seems to think that working for the church is all that they need to do and the church will work for God. That isn't how it works. I haven't attended a church in over a year but I feel closer to God than ever. I refuse to attend an organization that is only concerned with building a bigger clubhouse. I refuse to tithe to an organization that gives ten times more money to the building fund that it gives to missions. Do I tithe? Absolutely! Well, if I don't give to a church, where does my money go? It goes to a university scholarship. It goes to a family with a sick child and no insurance. It goes to an overseas missionary. It goes to someone who didn't have a car. In short, it goes to where God and only God tells me to send it. Listen up. Here is the key. Do I use the resources that God has given me for myself, or am I willing to make someone else's life a little better? No, you don't have to impoverish yourself. God doesn't want that, He just wants you to use your tithe, your time, your energy, your smile, your wisdom, your skills, WITHOUT GUILE!

Did I just tell you to witness for God? Yes, I did, but not with your mouth. Most Christians today think that witnessing is telling someone else how to live their life. Witness with your life! Gee, I wonder why the church doesn't tell us that? Is it just me, or does it seem to you that there are more non-Christians than Christians who are doing God's will?

Did you notice that I said that I send my money to where God tells me? How do I know where He wants it sent? How do I know what He wants me to do? Should I go out and search the world to learn His will? No. The answer is this, just be quiet and listen and He will tell you exactly what to do. This leads me to the next step.

Step five – being receptive. Let me explain it this way. When you drive down the road, are you listening to the radio, are you talking on your cell phone (I have a terrible story about that subject), are you worried about your job, your next paycheck, etc. or are you just thinking about God? The radio in my car broke four years ago and I'm not going to have it fixed. God gives me so much to think about that I have to carry a recorder with me wherever I go, so I won't forget what He is telling me. Does this mean that I *shouldn't* listen to a radio? The answer is *no*, but make some silent time to listen to God. God talks to us in many ways, and yesterday morning He used an interview on the *Today* show to enable me to finish this chapter after I had been stuck for two weeks. Do I think about God every moment of the day? No, I enjoy music, but the silence in my life has become so rewarding because that is when God is able to talk to me one to one.

I feel so sorry for the people who have to have some sound entering their brains at all times. Teenagers listen to the radio, women talk on their cell phones, men listen to a game or a talk show. Everyone is so busy being entertained that they don't have a chance to think. Worst of all, they don't give God a chance to talk. Do you remember my statement that most Christians *really* don't believe in God? It's true. If those Christians really believed in God, they would be listening to Him. Of course, a lot of "dedicated" Christians listen to their favorite Christian radio station, and they believe that is what God wants for them, but is it really? Please don't think that I am knocking "Christian radio," because I certainly am not, but how much time are you dedicating *solely* to God for one on one conversation? I certainly hope that it is more time than you spend reading the Bible.

Would you like to know for sure exactly how to have a conversation with our wonderful God? It works like this; tell God that you want to start listening to what He has to say about your life. Start reading the New Testament from cover to cover, and stop talking or listening to someone or something else. As you read the New Testament, some statement will in some way stand out, and then during your silent "listening" times, God will begin talking to you about that particular part that you read. I do have one word of warning for anyone beginning this process, and that is to be careful about what it is that you think that God wants. I can tell you from experience that The Holy Spirit has a very soft voice and it may be your own mind talking and not Him.

It takes a lot of patience and a lot of practice to discern God's voice from your own desires. I am probably a much slower learner than most people, and I had to read the New Testament four times before I began to understand what it was that God wanted of me. One more word of wisdom, if you are going through some difficult times, I promise you that it is for a purpose. Stop and ask God what He is trying to teach you. In my own journey, whenever I have felt that God has abandoned me, I just stopped and asked Him what it was that He was trying to teach me, and the answer was given almost immediately. It usually turned out that I had strayed from where He wanted me to be. If you remember, a while back I mentioned that I was having heart problems. Is this happening because I have sinned or have done something wrong? The answer is *no*. This is just another challenge that will strengthen me as I put my trust in His hands. Even though this is happening to me, I am so grateful to our God for calling me that there are times that I have to yell out and tell Him how much I love Him and how grateful I am. You too can have that overwhelming happiness and an overwhelming sense of gratitude – but it does take time and work on your part.

I warned you that it wouldn't be easy, and if you have been a Christian for a while, you are going to have to change some paradigms, but we have arrived at the last step. WHEW. Before I identify what this last step is, I want to ask you a question, or maybe several questions. The question is this: *What do you want out of life?* Wealth, power, prestige, health, a mate, a home, a job, a great car, whatever: Those answers are all wrong. No matter which one or all of them you had, your life would still be incomplete. Just so you know, I can testify to that fact because at one time I had it all, and I was still unhappy. The *real* answer, and the only answer, to the question to what you want out of life is one word, and that word is the same for everybody *FULFILLMENT.* Fulfillment is the only "thing" that will truly make anyone's life complete. It isn't money. It isn't power (except for Donald Trump). It isn't anything except happiness, and let me add another word here, *peace,* but they are both, and for all practical purposes the same.

HOW DO WE ACHIEVE HAPPINESS??? (And don't forget peace). Listen up Donald, Madonna, Ted, Bill and you too, all of you high powered executives who just got caught with your hands in the piggy bank of some corporation. Happiness is not acquired through grabbing all that you can get. You know, I really wonder if that $6,000 shower curtain brought Dennis Kozlowski happiness. I would really like to ask him. True happiness can be achieved only through "service." Does that mean that I should give all my money away? Not hardly. Money has nothing to do with it. I am talking about a one on one type of service. A service in which you help just one individual make a better life for themselves. A service in which you become the only Jesus Christ that person will ever see. Finding a person who is willing to help another human being without pay, and probably without even thanks, is a miracle in itself. Very few human beings can be a Mother Teresa, and that is O.K. One of the first mistakes that I made as a new dedicated Christian was to assume that if I wanted to truly serve God, then I had to give up every worldly possession and every worldly pleasure. That is not what God wants or demands.

I have defined six steps that must be taken in order to become like Jesus Christ. Are there or can there be more than six? The answer is *yes*, but the six which I have identified are key to achieving that goal. If you are like me, you cannot remember all of the six steps, so allow me to briefly repeat them, along with some comments below:

1. READ – Read the New Testament (more than once). A strange thing happened to me after I read it for the first time; I couldn't wait to read it again. Wow, what a book. It sure beats fiction – even so-called "Christian" fiction.

2. BELIEVE – I promise you, God is not dead. He is not asleep. He created this universe and all that is in it, so why are you worried about it. Jesus said to not be concerned with the world, so why are you trying to elect the politician of the day? The word "belief" also encompasses the word "trust," so why don't you trust that God does have a plan and it's a whole lot better than yours.

3. ALIGN – Line up the focus of your words, your thoughts, your goals, your marriage, your very life with the meaning and the love of our God. Does this mean that we are not to enjoy life and have fun? Of course not, Jesus came that we might have an even richer life. Whatever you do, ignore any pompous parody of a preacher who tells you that you are not to enjoy the life that God gave you – just put Him *in* your life.

4. GUILELESSNESS - What is the purpose of your life – to look out for number 1? Is the thrust of your thinking and your energy directed toward enriching yourself? Yes, you can be rich here on earth, but what excuse do you make to God when you face Him at the final judgment and He asks you what good works you did.

5. RECEPTIVE – Be receptive to the will of God the Father through the Holy Spirit. Even Jesus constantly listened to His Father: *"I do the will of Him who sent Me."*

No person can learn the will of the Father if he is constantly bombarded with external stimulation in the form of radio, TV, cell phones, etc. Even one's own thoughts and wishes, and especially anger and frustration, can get in the way.

6. SERVE – Get this straight. There is no way that you can serve God, because He already owns everything. The only way that we can serve God is by doing what pleases Him, serving our fellow man. The human race is God's pride and joy, His crowning achievement, and to not respect and honor that achievement is nothing less than a sin. Make up your mind. Are you going to serve God or are you going to serve yourself (just like most Christians)?

As I started this chapter, I told you that being like Jesus would be difficult. As my Daddy used to say, "If it's easy, it ain't worth doin." It has taken me ten years and I'm still not there, but I have to tell you that the journey is amazing and the rewards are phenomenal.

12

SO YOU WANT TO BE A CHRISTIAN?

Therefore bring forth fruits in keeping with repentance...

That small sentence from the Bible, *"Therefore bring forth fruits in keeping with repentance...,"* seems to be one sentence that causes the most confusion and therefore failure among Christians, and especially new Christians. Every new Christian, upon reading that statement, interprets the word "fruits" as meaning new converts, when in fact the word "fruits" has a much deeper meaning that is usually entirely overlooked. Looking within the context of Jesus' teaching and throughout all of His teachings, it can be readily seen that Jesus is not only talking **to us,** He is talking **about us.**

The "fruit" that Jesus Christ is talking about is the most important of all the works that we are to do or can ever do for Him, the work (fruit) of changing our own life. When Jesus uses the phrase "bring forth fruit," He is ordering each of us to change our lives. This life change includes our physical self as well as our outlook, our desires, our style of life and our interaction with others. In short, we must change and/or eliminate every less than Godly facet of our old lives that was present within us before we accepted Him as our Savior. Ask yourself this question: "How can I hope to change someone else's life if I cannot even change my own?" The dichotomy of an unchanged life attempting to change the life of someone else is obvious to everyone, yet Christians never seem to consider the fact that an unchanged life is an unrepentant life. That fact shows in our lifestyles, our actions, in our anger and belligerence to the world around us and most important of all it identifies us to all as "unbelievers."

Does anyone remember the line from a song that was popular back in the Sixties that went something like this: "**You can't run your own life, and I'll be d----- if you'll run mine**"? That line is so true so let's put it into a Christian context as someone tries to witness to a person who refuses to recognize God. The line of the song would go something like this: **You can't change your own life, and I'll be d----- if you'll change mine!** Do you understand that your own life, and by that I mean *everything* about your life, is a more powerful witness than anything that you can say?

How many times have you seen self-professed Christians going blithely through daily life without a care or concern for anyone but themselves? These very Christians are the ones giving "witness" *against* God and His Son every day through the actions found within their own lives.

Let's start our change into the Christian life with something as simple as our appearance. No, I'm not talking about clothes. I'm talking about how we appear to others as we walk, talk, drive or even enter a room. Everyone knows that the instant they look at someone they have formed a first impression. You need to understand the impression that you give to total strangers, because that initial impression is going to determine your effectiveness as a Christian. So let me tell you a little story.

I was on vacation up in Pennsylvania last week and as I walked into the hotel dining room for breakfast, there sat an older gentlemen, dressed in a business suit, who seemed to be staring intently at me with an obviously questioning look on his face. As soon as I saw him looking at me, I smiled, nodded and said, "Good morning" in a quiet voice so as not to disturb the other patrons.

The impact my simple greeting and obvious friendliness had on this gentleman was surprising even to me. His face lit up, and it appeared to me that my simple act had made his day for whatever reason and his reaction made me feel good in turn. The point of my story is that each one of us who strives to follow Jesus Christ must make the effort to go through life giving everyone the feeling of being blessed for being around us for even a moment. Is this difficult to do? The answer is yes, but only initially. As we discover what Jesus is all about, liking people and wanting to make their lives better begins to come naturally. If you remember, I told the story of the saddest statement that I have ever heard within the confines of a church, and the statement was this: "I have to love people but I don't have to like them." That statement is so sad because all of us have to learn to "like" people (accept them including all their foibles) before we can ever hope to love them or else all of our efforts will be a sham.

Is there anyone reading this book who is feeling down? Want to feel better? It's as simple as this. Go out and find someone else who needs help – serve them in whatever way that they need and God will take care of you. Is this some pie-in-the-sky theory? Not on your life, because I have proven it many times. When we work for God, He will look after us with ten times the care and love that we could imagine. As you become a Christian, always keep this fact in mind. There is nothing that God needs, period. After all, He is God and He can create anything. There is no way that we can serve Him. He already has it all. So what does He want from us? He wants us to serve our fellow man.

Whether it's a smile, a handshake, a listening ear, a hug, a gift, a moment of your time or driving fifty miles out of your way as a gentleman did for me when I was in the Army, the act of serving your fellow man is doing no less than serving God Himself.

I will warn you now that your attempts to change your appearance not only to your fellow man, but to yourself as well, will be difficult and take continuous effort. Why? Because neither our parents nor the church teaches us to do it from childhood, and that is a failure that can no longer be tolerated.

One of the greatest fallacies of the church today, and possibly the single greatest illusion taught by the "born again" denominations, is that in order to solve the problems of the world, all we have to do is to tell everybody about "Jesus" or hand them a tract or a pamphlet. Believe me, that thinking became invalid in the 1970s with the accessibility to everyone of radio and television. "Witness" as practiced by the majority of Christians today is like pouring water over the proverbial duck's back. One would be hard pressed to find anyone not in the third world who has not heard of or does not know just who Jesus Christ is, and the problem comes out of the fact that the nonbeliever sees so many of us spouting the name of "Jesus" but continuing to live the same selfish, greedy, self-involved, domineering lifestyle.

FAILURE!

"Witness," in order to be effective, must replace the running of our mouths that makes us feel good, with a silence that "listens" to other people with the objective of helping *them* feel good. Did you get that? Our job as Christians is not to make ourselves feel better. Our job is to help and serve others, and most of the time, the most effective way to accomplish that is for us to keep our mouths shut and listen. That statement brings me to our next step.

Go down to the nearest supermarket; stand unobtrusively to the side of the entrance where you won't be noticed and count twenty-five people that enter or leave (excluding children). Of the twenty-five people you counted, how many of them did you think had problems and needed help? The sad fact is that probably all of them needed help in one form or another, and that fact should have become obvious to you as you watched them walk into the store. Sadly, the church teaches us that all we have to do is walk up and mouth the name of Jesus and their problems will be solved, when nothing could be further from the truth.

A good question to ask here would be, "How can I tell whether someone needs help?" The answer is easy. All you have to do is look at two things: the expression on their faces and how they walk. Look especially at their eyes. The Bible states that the eye is the window on the soul, and when you look people in the eye, you can see their true state of being. This is the reason that people who have a genuine interest in other people make such good Christians – they study people and they have learned over time what to look for, and best of all – they care.

The other facet that I told you to look for is how the person walks. Even a person with a limp (like me) will have a spring in his step if he is happy. Let me give you an example. Turn on the TV and watch the series, *The Apprentice*; then toward the end of the show, watch Donald Trump walk into the boardroom. Seriously, have you ever seen an unhappier person? The Donald looks like he has lost his best friend, or else his underpants are waaaaaaay too tight.

So let's turn this idea around. How do you look as you make your way through society? Are your undies too tight, or are you right with the world and especially "right" with God? When are most Christians going to realize, and when is the church going to begin teaching, that in order for any one of us to be happy, complete and fulfilled within the context of this temporary life here on earth, we must not only accept God and His Son, we must also take the responsibility (and make the effort) to change our own lives? (**FIRST,** before we try to change everybody else.)

The church tells us that we are always to have problems, and that is correct. The unidentified "problem" that plagued the Apostle Paul is a great example, but the church fails to finish the lesson, that when we correct our own failings, God will take care of all the rest of any other problems that show up. My own life is a prime example, in that I have problems, I just don't have worries. Did you get that? I have a bunch of things going on in my life that could be described as "problems." The great thing about having a true relationship with God is the fact that He will (and does) take care of everything so that I don't even have to worry.

Get this, because here is the important part. If I don't have to worry about whatever is happening in my life, then I don't have any problems. Is this so hard to grasp? If I am doing the job God has given me, He will take care of *anything* that gets in my way. Yes, I have an arthritic hip, but He gets me through the day. Yes, I have a cardiac arrhythmia, but He led me to a doctor that found a medicine that keeps it well under control. Why worry? This life can be so simple if we just let it. I take care of the job which God has given me and He takes care of everything else, including politics and the entire world.

One last caveat is necessary as we finish talking about getting our lives in order prior to becoming real Christians and attempting to serve God. We will *never finish* the job of remaking ourselves in God's image, because for us mortals, to be like God is impossible; yet the answer to this conundrum is very simple, because all that God expects is for us to begin the walk and He will support us in our trials. In other words, if you are an alcoholic stop drinking, if you are a homosexual stop sexual activity with others of the same sex, if you are angry control your temper.

I know of a local pastor whose temper is so out of control that he regularly throws furniture around his house. His son is a drug addict and has "learned" to have the same problems with his own temper. This man calls himself a "man of God" and has a PhD, yet he refuses to change his own life. Is it any wonder that the Christian church is failing? I guess that he is, like most Christians, waiting for God to do the work.

This particular pastor ought to spend some time reading the Bible, because if he did, he would be aware that Paul addressed this very issue at length: *"you therefore who teach another, do you not teach yourself? You who preach that one should not steal, do you steal?"* In this pastor's case, Paul would have told him to put a hold on his temper before he stands in the pulpit. Please understand, Paul is telling us to change our own lives before we try to change someone else's life, and his words are so appropriate to Christians today.

All right, we are making serious changes in our lives and if we have stopped wantonly sinning and being concerned about the world, the next step is to change our appearance. But in order to accomplish that, we must change our *attitudes*.

Take a moment and seriously reflect on your own personal attitude. You might even want to put some (a lot) of prayer into this effort, because God will always tell you what you really don't want to hear or recognize. Think about your day to day interactions. Do you get angry or frustrated when you have to wait for someone else or wait in line? Does traffic drive you crazy? Do you see your fellow workers as lazy or stupid (at least compared to you)? If you answer *yes* to any of these questions (or you can think of more scenarios), you are suffering from the "me first" syndrome.

I suggested that every Christian spend a lot of time and prayer on the subject of changing his own attitude, and I want to take a moment to quote A.W. Tozer on the subject of prayer: "God has not placed Himself under obligation to honor the requests of worldly, carnal, or disobedient Christians. He hears and answers the prayers only of those who walk in His way."

Now this may seem like a "Catch 22" situation to most new Christians who may be trying to change their own lives or attitudes. After all, we know that we can't change our lives by ourselves, and if God won't answer our prayers until our life is changed, what are we to do? Again, here is why our God is so wonderful; He will answer our prayers as long as we are making a serious *effort* to change. If someone is a confirmed liar, he must make a serious and continuous effort to stop lying. If someone is a thief, he must begin a serious effort and a specific program to stop stealing. God knows exactly how weak we all are because, after all, He is the One who created us, and that is why He is willing and able to help, but we must make the serious effort.

I have discussed "attitude" before and to best explain my meaning, let's return to the description of Jesus' first meeting with Nathanael in which Jesus exclaims, *"Behold, an Israelite indeed, in whom is no guile!"* This is so simple that no great, lengthy explanation is needed; Jesus has recognized a man who is not selfishly concerned with his own well being. Nathanael, very simply described, is a man at peace with himself and with the world, and he doesn't need to worry about the cares of the day (and in those days there were many).

How many Christian business people in the world today can be said to be without guile? In my own personal experience, there aren't many. I have told before about the fact that any business person identifying himself as Christian raises a red flag, even to the point where I won't do business with that person because I know that I will probably be cheated or worse. That kind of business person is guile personified.

Listen to what I am going to say because this is important. Any business person who is a *true* Christian does not have to lie, cheat, steal or resort to the slightest subterfuge in order to be successful, because if he is truly serving this great God of ours, He will take care not only of their lives and their businesses, but their families and every other aspect of their lives as well. Of course, if you were to tell this to church attending Christians, they would nod their heads and say, "Amen," but they wouldn't believe it in their heart.

Why do all of us modern Christians worry about everything? We worry about our business, we worry about money and taxes, we worry about everybody else's moral values and we worry about the world. The latest "worry of the day" for modern Christians is making sure that the Ten Commandments are everywhere in public view. I just can't figure out why, but the evidence repeatedly points to the fact that we just refuse to believe in God. If the poorest or the sickest Christians really believed in the existence of and the supreme power of that entity that we supposedly worship every Sunday and worked to serve Him, their worries would be over.

In case I have lost you, I am talking about attitude, and so far I have covered being at peace with everything in your life, which should include God, your family, your business and, most of all, your fellow man. Something that most people refuse to recognize is the fact that if they aren't being honest, even in business, they will never achieve peace. Think about this question: why are most politicians and clergy very insecure people? I'll let you figure out the answer, but the question brings to mind one of Jesus' teachings from the Sermon on the Mount: *"Therefore do not be anxious for tomorrow; for tomorrow will care for itself."*

I have one last lesson concerning attitude, and it concerns "humility," i.e. the state of being humble. Humility, to most present day Christians, seems to be a terminal disease that must be avoided at all costs. I guess that when the average Christian recognizes God, and His Son, he thinks that he has been given equality with his God and any trace of what might have been ignorance is replaced with what can only be described as arrogance.

I hinted at "humility" in an earlier paragraph when I talked about keeping silent instead of spouting your own opinion about changing another person's life. It is very easy to discern an arrogant person from a humble person; an arrogant person does not listen to someone else. Whether listening to an opinion or a problem, an arrogant person always has a ready solution or opinion, whereas a truly humble person will recognize the fact that he probably doesn't know even one-tenth of the problem at hand.

Everyone, at one time or another, has had a conversation with an arrogant person. As you talk with another person, watch closely and see the person's mind at work. An arrogant person, "pretending" to listen, is actually concentrating on his own reply before you have even had time to present your own view. The sad fact is that the arrogant person could care less about your own views; his only goal is to glorify himself. Heaven forbid that he might begin to understand. Do you remember my story about the man that I got out of jail? Here is a guy that is so intelligent, but his own arrogance assures that he will always be a failure in life. God is still working in this guy's life, but he hasn't been able to overcome the hurdles which the man himself creates through his own arrogance.

The subject is becoming a Christian, and I want to review the subjects that we have covered. First of all, make sure that you recognize, as I had to, that the fact of taking Jesus Christ as your personal Savior is only the beginning, a first baby step, if you will. The mere intellectual recognition of the need for a Savior becomes a snare for most Christians, because they cannot or will not make the next step, that of changing their own life, usually because they expect God to do it for them. The church reinforces this fallacy through the poison of Calvinism, which distorts the teachings of Jesus and allows everyone to think that merely "believing" provides salvation for all time and without caveat.

Any person who refuses to change his life through the elimination of unacceptable practices, who refuses to change his attitude and appearance, who continues to be concerned about whatever is happening in this world and who has not learned to humble himself, has not really accepted the existence of God.

Face it, when any one of us really begins to understand this great God of ours, we have no choice but to become humble before His greatness, because when we compare ourselves to Him, there can be nothing on this earth that could be more humbling or even more humiliating as we look back at our previous life.

This is a short chapter and there is a good reason for that fact. *Being* a Christian is easy, because as Christ stated, "My burden is light," but be aware that *becoming* a Christian is much more difficult and can be compared to "entering through the narrow door."

For just a moment, picture an overweight person trying to slide sideways through a narrow opening. Can you visualize it? The picture isn't meant to be funny, because it is the picture of every one of us as we struggle to go through an opening that is impossible for us to enter until we lose the excess weight brought about by our worldly lifestyles. If it took Paul three years of direct tutelage from Jesus Himself, why do we have the audacity to think that we have instantly become "Christian" and now have been commissioned to tell everyone else how to live?

Allow me to repeat the following story just one more time because it is what being a Christian is all about, and let me encourage all parents out there to read and discuss this story with their own children. Maybe if we can teach the children, they can assure the success of what we call the "Christian" church.

My compliments to the author of this story.

One day, when I was a freshman in high school, I saw a kid from my class walking home from school. His name was Kyle. It looked like he was carrying all of his books. I thought to myself, "Why would anyone bring home all his books on a Friday? He must really be a nerd." I had quite a weekend planned (parties and a football game with my friends' tomorrow afternoon), so I shrugged my shoulders and went on.

As I was walking, I saw a bunch of kids running toward him. They ran at him, knocking all his books out of his arms and tripping him so he landed in the dirt. His glasses went flying, and

I saw them land in the grass about ten feet from him. He looked up and I saw this terrible sadness in his eyes.

My heart went out to him. So, I jogged over to him and as he crawled around looking for his glasses, I saw a tear in his eye.

As I handed him his glasses, I said, "Those guys are jerks. They really need to get a life!" He looked at me and said, "Hey, thanks!" There was a big smile on his face. It was one of those smiles that showed real gratitude.

I helped him pick up his books, and asked him where he lived. As it turned out, he lived near me, so I asked him why I had never seen him before. He said he had gone to a private school before now.

I never would have hung out with a private school kid before. We talked all the way home, and I carried some of his books. He turned out to be a pretty cool kid. I asked him if he wanted to play a little football with my friends. He said yes. We hung out all weekend, and the more I got to know Kyle, the more I liked him, and my friends thought the same of him.

Monday morning came, and there was Kyle with the huge stack of books again. I stopped him and said, "Boy, you are gonna really build some serious muscles with this pile of books every day!" He just laughed and handed me half the books.

Over the next four years, Kyle and I became best friends. When we were seniors, we began to think about college. Kyle decided on Georgetown, and I was going to Duke. I knew that we would always be friends, that the miles would never be a problem. He was going to be a doctor, and I was going for business on a football scholarship.

Kyle was valedictorian of our class. I teased him all the time about being a nerd. He had to prepare a speech for graduation. I was so glad it wasn't me having to get up there and speak. Graduation day, I saw Kyle. He looked great. He was one of those guys that really found himself during high school. He filled out and actually looked good in glasses. He had more dates than I had and all the girls loved him. Boy, sometimes I was jealous.

Today was one of those days. I could see that he was nervous about his speech. So, I smacked him on the back, and said, "Hey, big guy, you'll be great!" He looked at me with one of those looks (the really grateful one) and smiled. "Thanks", he said.

As he started his speech, he cleared his throat and began. "Graduation is a time to thank those who helped you make it through those tough years. Your parents, your teachers, your siblings, maybe a coach...but mostly your friends. I am here to tell all of you that being a friend to someone is the best gift you can give them. I am going to tell you a story..."

I just looked at my friend with disbelief as he told the story of the first day we met. He had planned to kill himself over the weekend. He talked of how he had cleaned out his locker so his mom wouldn't have to do it later and was carrying his stuff home. He looked hard at me and gave me a little smile. "Thankfully, I was saved. My friend saved me from doing the unspeakable."

I heard the gasp go through the crowd as this handsome, popular boy told us all about his most desperate moment. I saw his mom and dad looking at me and smiling that same grateful smile. Not until that moment did I realize its depth. Never underestimate the power of your actions. With one small gesture, you can change a person's life, for better or for worse.

God puts us all in each other's lives to impact one another in some way.

"Christians tell me that they would never deny their Savior, Jesus Christ, yet they deny Him every day as they reject His people!"

G. Vaughn Smith **2005**

THERE IS ONLY ONE WAY TO **PLEASE** GOD

and

THERE IS ONLY ONE WAY TO **SERVE** GOD